Garden of EVIL

The Granny Killer's Reign of Terror

IRONBARK PRESS

Garden of EVIL

The Granny Killer's Reign of Terror

BY LARRY WRITER
WITH STEVE BARRETT & SIMON BOUDA

IRONBARK PRESS

Published in 1992 by IRONBARK PRESS
Level 1, 175 Alison Road, Randwick, NSW.
© Larry Writer

National Library of Australia
Cataloguing-in-Publication

    Writer, Larry, Garden of Evil: The Granny Killer's Reign of Terror.

    ISBN 1 875471 12 X.

        1. Glover, John Wayne. 2. Serial murders — New South Wales — Sydney —
Case studies. 3. Murderers — New South Wales — Sydney — Case studies. I. Title.

    364.1523

Editor: Dean Boyce
Cover design: John Collins
Interior design and finished art: Kylie Prats
Tape transcription: Jenny Bouda
Printed by: Globe Press

HOW THIS BOOK WAS WRITTEN

Garden Of Evil is very much a team effort. It was written by Sydney-based author, editor and journalist Larry Writer in the months of January, February, March and April, 1992, after senior crime reporters Steve Barrett of Channel 9 News, Sydney, and Simon Bouda, formerly of *The Daily Mirror* and now crime reporter for Channel 9's *Sydney Extra*, convinced Ironbark Press that the story of the hunt for John Glover was one that had to be told.

Steve Barrett and Simon Bouda, who covered the North Shore Murders Investigation with distinction and accuracy from its beginning to its tragic end, had developed a close rapport with key members of the task force and, with total access to all police files on the case, were uniquely placed to provide much of the information that would lead to the true, definitive telling of this amazing and horrifying episode in Australian criminal history.

Barrett, Bouda and Writer, recorded hundreds of hours of interviews over 18 months with the key participants in the story of the hunt for the north shore serial killer. These interviews, along with information gleaned from literally thousands of pages of previously unobtainable documents and records of the case comprise the source material for *Garden Of Evil*. Larry Writer sifted and shaped this mass of information and used it as a foundation to write the narrative that follows.

Nothing in this book has been recreated. Conversations and events are recounted and corroborated according to witnesses' memory or sworn testimony. Events have been substantiated by those who were there. Every possible step has been taken to ensure the accuracy of this book.

Included among the interviewees are members of the North Shore Murders Task Force — commanders, homicide investigators, computer experts, surveillance police, physical evidence, scientific and forensic investigators, general medical officers and experts in protecting the aged. Also interviewed were community leaders, relatives and friends of the victims, nursing home and retirement village staff, and other members of the public. John Wayne Glover was interviewed in Long Bay Gaol.

The publishers would like to thank all those who co-operated to help us tell this story, those who spoke to us on the record and those who preferred to remain anonymous. However, extra special thanks must go to the following: NSW Commissioner of Police Tony Lauer, Detective Superintendent Mike Hagan, Detective Sgt Dennis (Miles) O'Toole, Detective Sen Sgt Geoff Wright, Detective Sen Sgt Ron Smith, Detective Sen Const Paul Mayger, Detective Sen Const Murray Byrnes, Detective Sen Const Paul Jacob, Detective Sen Sgt Gordon Green, Detective Sen Sgt Bob Myers, Detective Sen Const Dave Forbes, Detective Sen Sgt Dennis (Doodles) O'Toole, Detective Sen Sgt John May, Detective Sen Sgt Kim McGee, Detective Sen Sgt Kerry Larsen, Police Elderly Liaison Co-ordinator Brien Gately, Dr Rod Milton, Dom Lopez, Barry O'Keefe, Dr Johan Duflou, Joe Sands, Stan Bennett, William Cleveland, Merle Cleveland, Elaine Avis, Maggie Hughes, Nelune Rajapakse, Jim Keddie, Stephen Shepherd, Russell McPhedran, and the executives of the Channel 9, Sydney, newsroom for their support.

ABOUT THE AUTHOR

Larry Writer is the author of the critically-acclaimed *Winning — Face To Face With Australian Sporting Legends, Australia — The Moments That Mattered, Five Star Brandy — Greg Alexander And The Rise Of The Penrith Panthers* and *Rex Mossop — The Moose That Roared.*

He is also the editor of *Someone Else's Daughter — The Life And Death Of Anita Cobby, Local Hero — The Wayne Pearce Story, The Story Of Australian Rugby League, A Magnificent Obsession — 200 Years Of Australian Sport, The Kangaroos — The Saga Of Rugby League's Great Tours, Sterlo! Story Of A Champion, Backpage Of Sport, Backpage Of Cricket, Border's Heroes, Ron Casey — Confessions Of A Larrikin, Big Mal — The Mal Meninga Story* and *March Of The Dragons — The Story Of St George RLFC.*

Before forming Ironbark Press with Deborah Wood and Ian Heads, he was a senior writer and editor with Australian Consolidated Press and for some years was that company's European Editor and London Bureau Chief.

Contents

Foreword
by A. R. Lauer APM
Commissioner of Police

The inner workings of a police task force — the laborious hunt for clues, the long hours and the build-up of friction between colleagues in the absence of a breakthrough — hardly ever come to the notice of the public.

Such issues are usually well hidden.

But headlines and television footage are constantly in the public's consciousness, amplifying hysteria and honing in on the fear of crime that exists within us all.

The media treatment of crime, while no doubt well-intentioned, often has the unwanted outcome of paralysing a community. It also raises the pressure on police, in no small way, to get a result — and in very quick time.

No recent investigation illustrates this series of points more than that chartered by the 70-member North Shore Murders Task Force.

Established in frightful circumstances in November, 1989 — immediately after the slaying of two elderly women within 24 hours of each other — the task force was, in the blink of an eye, catapulted into public prominence. Immediately, so much was expected of it.

At this invidious time in Australian police history I was NSW Deputy Commissioner (State Commander). Although I was far removed from the detailed legwork carried out by task force members, it was my ultimate responsibility to assess the nature of the killings and to assign the appropriate resources. Over the painful 12 months that followed I was kept informed of case developments.

The burdensome role of commanding the task force was undertaken by the then-Detective Insp Michael Hagan, an experienced and resourceful investigator. The exemplary way he handled the case flowed on to all his officers and we have much for which to thank Hagan and his team.

From the outset, the task force confronted a strange concoction of problems. Firstly, serial murders of this type were a new phenomenon and thus required new criminal investigation techniques.

Secondly, the crimes were linked to a particularly vulnerable group in society — elderly women.

In essence, the crimes had an effect on every Australian, they reached every home and every living room. The serial killings changed the way we lived our lives and in suburbs such as Mosman altered drastically the way people conducted their personal affairs. As a result, there were many more victims than those attacked physically by John Wayne Glover.

While the frightened community sweated on updates on the investigation, police desperately worked at bringing the offender to justice. The task force's work load took on voluminous proportions: 740 suspects were investigated, the FBI lent expert assistance, and a mass of other enquiries — many necessarily covert — were made.

The kind donation of computer equipment from Rank Xerox and Olivetti — to digest the detailed information of the investigation — was evidence of the palpable community support that existed during this period. In many ways, this is a case in point of how police and the public can join forces against a common evil.

This book chronicles one of the most disturbing and serious crimes in recent New South Wales history — indeed it was the most extensive inquiry of its type in Australian police annals. But perhaps even of greater significance, it examines closely the feelings of investigators on the case; the strains on relationships and the like — and this, in my view, is the lasting quality of the text.

I hope *Garden Of Evil — The Granny Killer's Reign Of Terror* will stand as a tribute to every police officer and member of the public who contributed to the collective effort which resulted in the capture of this dangerous felon.

Prologue

The glorious old Sydney harbourside garden suburb of Mosman is an unlikely setting for evil. The people of Mosman are proud of their suburb and with good reason. Drive around Mosman Bay, Balmoral, Clifton Gardens and Beauty Point today and you'll not fail to be impressed by the spectacular bays and inlets, the sweeping water views. Walk down the proud, wide streets dappled by expansive, long-established trees that stand sentinel over well-tended, dark brick and red tile Federation homes and see the homeowners working in their gardens or playing with children and pets and you'll know at once that this is a nice suburb, a decent suburb.

Yet had you, a stranger, strolled down these streets during a 12-month period in the very recent past, these same homeowners would have returned your friendly greeting with a hostile and suspicious gaze, possibly scurried inside to chart your progress from behind the bars of a security door. They may even have reported you to the police.

Although the newly-monied high fliers of business, the lively arts, academe and the media have moved in, Mosman remains at heart a conservative, old-wealth, ageing suburb. During your drive you'll be struck by the large number of elderly women making their way around the glitzy shopping centres of Military Road and Spit Junction and the sedate roadways that feed on to them.

These elderly women, most of whom live alone now, cling to Mosman because it is close to the city, has good public transport, strong community groups and excellent services and facilities. Though some continue to live with just their memories for company in their family home, loneliness or encroaching infirmity lead many to sell up and move into the growing number of home unit blocks, retirement villages and nursing homes that have sprung up all over Mosman.

The elderly women of Mosman — women who dress in the gracious floral fashions of earlier, more genteel, eras and whose names are Gwendoline, Winfreda, Doris, Euphemia, Daisy and Phyllis — are as much a feature of the suburb as the handsome houses and streets, the military reserves, the traffic jams around Mediterranean-like Balmoral on a summer Sunday, the bellows and shrieks of the beasts of Taronga Park Zoo that carry across the shiny waters of Little Sirius

Cove. Yet during that 12-month period in the very recent past — March 1, 1989, to March 19, 1990, to be exact — every elderly woman in Mosman, and as it turned out the entire north shore of Sydney, was the potential prey of a serial murderer, a killer so unremarkable in appearance as to blend chameleon-like into the fabric of the community, so daring as to strike in broad daylight, and as voracious as a tiger turned loose in a deer park.

* * *

Were you to amble down a fairly typical Mosman street, say Wyong Road up towards Quakers Hat Bay, in the late afternoon of a summer's day in 1989, you might have noticed, even smiled and nodded to, a neat, stocky, grey-haired man in his late 50s mowing the front lawn of his home, No.18. The home, once of two storeys but with a third level tacked on fairly recently, is solid and unprepossessing, just like its owner. No.18 blends effortlessly into the streetscape. No reason why you'd want to, but if you'd stayed to watch, you would have seen this seemingly average suburban man, clearly houseproud and fastidious, sweep the grass cuttings off his gently sloping lawn and garden plots before packing his gardening tools away in a shed and walking back up the brick-paved path to the front door and disappearing inside.

Inside and out of view, he showers, then in his bedroom on the second level pulls on a light-coloured short-sleeved shirt over his thickening yet still powerful torso — on his upper left arm is tattooed an eagle and a shield. His trousers are grey and he chooses a pair of brown brogues from his wardrobe. Now he combs his neat, longish white-grey hair, undoubtedly the most memorable of his features. His face, once handsome in a vulpine way, is growing pudgy with age but this ruddy jowliness has lent the man a trustworthy, an avuncular, air. Should you be lost in a strange suburb you'd not think twice about approaching him for directions or, if you were old and frail, asking if he could kindly help you carry your parcels to the front door.

Dressed, he kisses his wife goodbye, calls farewell to his two teenage daughters, leaves the house and, once in his two-car, street-level garage, climbs into his blue Ford Falcon station wagon, still shiny from its regular weekend wash and polish. He then drives the three kilometres to the Mosman RSL Club in Military Road. A member who can be found there six days out of seven, he strides into the bar area where he buys a glass of white wine and takes his place at a poker machine. He stands before it, eyes fixed on the assorted pineapples, cherries and jokers spinning and settling before his steely-blue glare. Though he engages in superficial pleasantries and small talk, he encourages no one to linger for a longer chat. He is a loner amid the good-natured hubbub, quietly sipping his wine and mindlessly pushing the button of his machine.

After an hour or so, during which time his payouts have been, as usual, meagre, the man inserts a last coin, presses the button, then with a resigned air slips out of the club. Nobody notices him leave. Although with daylight saving there are a few more hours of sunshine left, the air temperature is cooling down. The grey-haired man strolls south down Military Road towards the Raglan Street intersection where there is a concentration of shops. The Dolphin fish shop, Arena's fruiterers, a french pastry shop, a bookstore, a newsagent, a dry cleaner, a bank or two. The man is consumed by the throng of shoppers.

From out of the ruck of activity shuffles a woman aged in her 80s, possibly 90s. She wears a floral dress and a jaunty hat. Though painfully frail, she carries in one hand two plastic shopping bags laden with fruit and groceries and a handbag, and in the other a walking stick. She rests for a moment at the Raglan Street traffic lights while she waits for the green walk signal. Her home is just minutes away.

The man watches her intently. Watches her cross at the lights and teeter at a snail's pace down Raglan Street. He follows her. If you'd ended up there that afternoon, shopping in Military Road, and noticed the man disappearing around the corner after the old woman, you might have thought how fortunate we are that there are still good samaritans left in this world, gentlemen willing to lend an old lady a hand with her parcels.

CHAPTER 1

Into The Maelstrom

It was November 2, 1989, and Detective Sgt Dennis O'Toole was worried. Doris Cox, an elderly resident of the Garrison Retirement Village at Mosman, had survived this savage bashing, but the manner of the attack left him in little doubt that the bastard who'd rammed the defenceless 86-year-old's head into a brick wall and left her for dead was the same bastard who had viciously murdered Gwendoline Mitchelhill and Lady Winfreda Ashton in Mosman earlier in the year.

Dennis O'Toole — a man of prodigious energy nicknamed "Miles" because of the distance he covers pacing up and down a room while on the telephone — was back at the Garrison yet again this day investigating the Cox attack of a fortnight before when the phone rang. It was Detective Sen Sgt Geoff Wright of the Regional Crime Squad, Chatswood, on the line. "Better get up here, mate. An old lady dead in a laneway leading from Longueville Road to Austin Street, Lane Cove."

By the time the homicide detective arrived at the laneway, the battered body of 85-year-old Madge Pahud had been taken away by ambulancemen. Although well-meaning residents had hosed the scene clean of blood, footprints, and any other clues as well, enough blood residue remained to convince police that, contrary to the advice of one doctor who attended the victim, the cause of Madge Pahud's death was definitely not a heart attack.

Madge Pahud was still alive when discovered at 3.30pm, sprawled face down in a large pool of blood in the lane, by a nine-year-old girl who at first thought she had stumbled upon a pile of rags. The child ran to fetch her mother and neighbours who raised the alarm and tried to assist the stricken woman. Two local doctors arrived to find Madge Pahud breathing but unconscious. Her glasses were broken, the frames resting under her chin. An earring lay nearby. Two grocery bags stood upright and intact near her feet. Her legs were splayed apart. A soft leather carry bag and a blue plastic bag containing a carton of milk, a bunch of bananas and ther groceries were strewn nearby. There was no sign of a handbag. By the time the ambulance arrived shortly afterward, Madge Pahud was dead.

A police team comprising investigators from the Regional Crime Squad North at Chatswood, Chatswood detectives, and members of the Physical Evidence and Fingerprint Section raked the area but came up with little except the realisation that the murderer of Gwen Mitchelhill and Lady Ashton, the attacker of Doris Cox and God knew how many others, for he was surely the same man, had ventured away from his home turf of Mosman to strike in Lane Cove, a middle north shore suburb about 10 kilometres away.

O'Toole noted one thing. Doris Cox had lived at the Garrison Retirement Village, and Madge Pahud resided in a home unit within a complex at the rear of the Kamilaroi Retirement Home. Perhaps there was a retirement home connection.

A post mortem conducted that night at the City Morgue by Dr Sylvia Hollinger confirmed the worst. Detective Sen Const Murray Byrnes attended the post mortem and straight after rang O'Toole to report that, like Lady Ashton and Gwen Mitchelhill, the victim had suffered heavy blows to the back of the head with a blunt instrument. The blows had fractured the skull. There were lacerations to the victim's face and head. Miles O'Toole and Detective Sen Const Paul Mayger were assigned by Mike Hagan, chief inspector of the Regional Crime Squad, to take charge of the Pahud murder investigation and immediately set themselves up in Lane Cove police station. Inspector Bert Oosterhoff vacated his office to accommodate O'Toole and Mayger and their team and extra typewriters and telephones and a computer were crammed into the tiny office.

Miles O'Toole had been in Homicide only since April, having joined five weeks after the Mitchelhill murder on March 1. He worked on that case until the Lady Ashton killing on May 9 when he was seconded to that investigation. The Cox assault on October 18 added to his workload, and now this...

The immediate hours following any murder are regarded as crucial hours by investigators. The laneway and surrounding areas were canvassed that night. Local residents were quizzed. "Did you notice anything out of the ordinary this afternoon? Any stranger lurking about? Did you know the victim? Can you tell us anything – – anything at all — that could help us in our investigations?" Parks, backyards, pathways, carparks were combed. Madge Pahud's relatives were notified and invited to shed any light on why anybody would want to kill the elderly widow and grandmother. Lane Cove police station was chaos. The media milled about firing questions at the police media liaison officer, specially appointed to allow the investigators to do their work unhampered by the press and TV and radio reporters. The phones rang wild in the cramped and stuffy office. Often it would be the Commissioner's office or police headquarters in Sydney demanding updates, or a politician trying to deflect some electoral heat. Detectives grappled with running sheets, the vital record of any investigation. Soon after midnight someone decided it would be a good idea to get something to eat, but all local takeaway outlets had long closed. Some investigators stayed the night at the police station, others trudged home at 2am to snap up a couple of hours sleep. As dawn broke, the emergency room at Lane Cove was once more in full operation.

Living an hour and a half away, at Gosford on the Central Coast of New South Wales, Miles O'Toole got even less sleep than his colleagues that night. Two hours after collapsing into bed, O'Toole was back on the road again, back to Lane Cove for Day Two of the Pahud murder hunt. Not that he was nodding off. By now adrenalin had taken over. O'Toole was a good man in a crisis. With his overflowing nervous energy, steel-trap mind and capacity for the hard slog, he had become one of the state's leading detectives. An effective weapon in his armoury was his genuinely friendly nature. Because of his ready smile, deferential demeanour and boyish features, many criminals had made the mistake of believing that he was a soft touch. O'Toole was anything but.

As he powered down the Sydney-Newcastle freeway under a lightening sky, responsibility weighed heavily upon him. Convinced now that there was a serial killer out there in suburbia, his mind raced back to the earlier killings of Gwen Mitchelhill and Lady Ashton and the attempted murder of Doris Cox. He fast-forwarded through the investigations. Had a vital clue been missed, had he slipped up in not catching this maniac earlier? If he had, if he'd somehow stuffed up, he was in part responsible for the death of Madge Pahud. No doubt about that.

O'Toole was learning all about the particular hell of hunting for a serial killer. In a normal murder investigation the pressure is all in catching the killer. With a serial killer, you have to cope with that, but also with the certainty that your quarry plans to strike again. The man from the Central Coast had brown hair as he drove back to Chatswood that November morning. Five months later it would be tinged with grey.

The detective knew that he was embroiled in what would probably be the biggest operational investigation of his life. Aged 45, he had been a policeman for 24 years. After leaving Gosford High School he worked for an insurance company and the North Shore Gas Company then joined the New South Wales Police Force. He was assigned to uniformed duty in the City and at Ryde before being transferred to the Police Special Branch, investigating politically-motivated criminals and activists and sometimes playing the minder to visiting dignitaries. After six years of that it was off to Ryde-Eastwood, North Sydney and, ironically, Mosman for criminal investigation duties, then back to Gosford as a member of the Drug Squad. After five years there, in 1989, O'Toole was transferred to Homicide. However, although working in Sydney, he preferred to commute from the central coast, where he had grown up and where he now lived happily with his wife Evelyn and four daughters. O'Toole pulled into the driveway at Lane Cove police station at 8am. It was November 3.

The day was long and gruelling. Hagan, O'Toole, Mayger, Byrnes and Detective Sen Const Barry Keeling formed the core of the investigation unit, but they were backed up by numerous other police who had been assigned to the manhunt. They had their work cut out. All of yesterday's investigations had to be followed up, more people interviewed, scientific and forensic reports had to be checked and checked again. Any connections between victims had to be looked into. The saturation canvass of the area included talking to scores of schoolchildren and shop owners, and residents of the retirement village. All this against a backdrop of dread whipped up by a media who had already started referring to the attacker as the "Granny Killer".

Later that afternoon Miles O'Toole drove to the Regional Crime Squad headquarters at Chatswood, where the hunt for the murderer of Gwen Mitchelhill and Lady Ashton was being co-ordinated, to file a report on the past 26 hours of the Pahud investigation. In spite of the fact that he clearly looked dead-beat, a couple of the police there, including O'Toole's namesake, Detective Sen Sgt Dennis "Doodles" O'Toole, and Geoff Wright, roasted their colleague for slacking on the job, then asked with a grin would he like a beer before returning to Lane Cove. Would he, what! Wright took the frosty can from the fridge and handed it to the grateful Miles. The two sounds were simultaneous. The cheery hiss of the ring top being ripped from the top of the beer can and the jangle of the telephone.

Doodles O'Toole answered it. He listened to the message then put the phone down quietly. Something in his face froze the policemen on the spot. "We've got another one," he said.

CHAPTER 2

Task Force

Miles O'Toole had hoped against hope itself that Doodles was having another joke at his expense. But this was no joke. Just one day after the killing of Madge Pahud, the body of Olive Cleveland, 81, was found lying face down across a concrete path in the grounds of the Wesley Gardens Retirement Village at Belrose, a middle-north shore suburb of Sydney. There was the residue of blood near her head. Her dress had been pulled up past her knees and her legs left splayed apart. Her pantyhose had been removed and tied around her neck. The dead woman's glasses and shoes had been placed neatly by her feet and her handbag was nearby. Once more, the murder scene had been washed down, this time by nursing staff concerned about the distress the blood might have caused to other elderly residents of Wesley Gardens. Mitchelhill, Ashton, Pahud and now Cleveland; this was the fourth "granny killing" and, as with the first three, again there were no concrete leads for the investigating detectives led by Geoff Wright who had been placed in charge of the investigation.

Up until then, there had been talk of setting up some kind of special task force to catch the serial killer but police resources were stretched to the limit and Detective Insp Mike Hagan, head of the Regional Crime Squad North which had responsibility for investigating the four murders and the bashing of Doris Cox, had been ordered to carry on as best he could. Clearly now, however, as the murder toll rose and with it political, media and community hysteria, all stops had to be pulled out.

Next day, Saturday, November 4, 1989, the North Shore Murders Investigation was deemed a Major Investigation by New South Wales Police Commissioner John Avery and the North Shore Murders Task Force was established. Major Investigations, unlike normal crime probes, have access to all available police resources in the state and unlimited finances — whatever is required whenever it is required.

When the task force came into being it comprised 35 investigators. On March 23, 1990, when it was terminated, it was 70-strong. After considering setting up in a public hall, council chamber or school of arts in the Mosman area, the investigators decided to stay where they had been probing the earlier murders, in the command centre at the Regional Crime Squad office on the first floor of the State Bank Building on the corner of Victoria Avenue and Bertram Street, Chatswood. The task force bristled with expertise. It boasted experienced homicide investigators, skilled analysts, pathologists and forensic specialists, surveillance teams, intelligence experts and computer whizzes. Each member was individually selected because of his or her training, competence and ability.

These men and women were about to embark on an inquiry which became the most extensive, demanding and heartbreaking investigation of its type in Australian police history. Their brief: to catch the world's only recorded serial killer of elderly women. Their quarry was a monster who murdered and maimed old ladies in broad daylight in the busy garden suburbs of Sydney's north shore, who left no clues – – until the very end of his reign of terror — and who blended into his surroundings like a chameleon. At times in the investigation frustrated police were convinced they were hunting for the Invisible Man.

The task force command structure was established immediately. Responsible for the official administration of the force from police headquarters in Sydney, that is, for the operational overview, were Executive Chief Superintendent Joe Parrington who was named Acting State Commander, Assistant Commissioner Charlie Parsons who was Region Commander, North, and Chief Superintendent, now Assistant Commissioner, Norm Maroney, who was Commander of the State Investigative Group.

However, the man who led from the front, the man with whom the buck stopped, the man with day-to-day overall control of planning, organising and directing the investigation, was Mike Hagan, who was appointed Commander of Operations of the Task Force. Hagan is bald on top, but his resplendent set of dark brown muttonchop whiskers and moustache more than make up for this. Highly intelligent, unfailingly polite, bespectacled, he could pass for a university professor. In his 12 years in the Homicide Squad, he has investigated around 50 murders. He has a Diploma of Criminology, has specialised in the legal aspects of criminal investigation, done a senior crime manager's course in the UK and trained with Scotland Yard. He has been married 25 years and is the father of three.

Hagan, today a detective superintendent, had been, until the slaying of Olive Cleveland in November, 1989, when the task force was established, the detective supervising the manhunt for the murderer or murderers of Gwen Mitchellhill, Lady Ashton and Madge Pahud, and the attacker of Doris Cox. A man whom his crack homicide investigator Miles O'Toole praises as a superb leader, he was the natural choice to continue on as commander of the task force.

Hagan's deputy commanders Geoff Wright and Ron Smith, both detective senior sergeants, were the chief investigators responsible for daily operational control and co-ordination of all investigations. They allocated the assignments, disseminated the information, and made sure all enquiries were followed up. The pair, both men of vast policing experience, were also in charge of staff, budgeting and records. Wright is known as "Dad" because of his relaxed, fatherly demeanour. Over the length of the Granny Killer investigation, if a young task force detective was feeling the strain, had something he wanted to get off his chest, or was just on for a chat, he came to Dad. Twenty-six years a detective, the 54-year-old Wright in 1989 was rapidly losing what grey hair he had left. He had the bowed legs of a bush horseman and in fact had spent many years in plain clothes in the New South Wales country town of Parkes. Wright is the father of a daughter and a son. The long hours Wright has habitually spent on the job throughout his career did not discourage his boy from joining him in the police force.

Wright's fellow deputy commander, Ron Smith, is nicknamed "Brown Eyes" after his most prominent feature, a set of deep, dark, piercing eyes, and not, he tells you, for any other more ribald reason. Smith is in his mid-40s and has short, dark, curly hair. He is a superb police negotiator, cool, calculating and very smart. His soft voice belies his toughness. For much of his 23-year detective career he was a scourge of Sydney's big safecracking gangs. Talking to him, you quickly come to the conclusion that he knows his stuff. Like his partner in crime prevention, he is the father of a grown son and daughter.

Each morning for the duration of the search for the Granny Killer, Wright and Smith would stand before the assembled investigators and assign them their work for the day: take a statement from a particular witness, canvass this retirement village, probe the background of that suspect, issue a press release giving safety advice to the elderly, check out dry cleaners for bloodstained clothing, dress up like a surfie and spend the morning wandering around the shopping centre, contact a psychiatrist to put together a psychological profile of the bloke who could be committing these atrocities on our senior citizens, attend a post mortem of his latest victim at the City Morgue.

Miles O'Toole's namesake Detective Sen Sgt Dennis O'Toole, known as "Doodles", was the supervisor of surveillance in the North Shore Murders Task Force. Doodles? "Don't make me tell you why they call me that," he laughs. "Let's just say my brother lumbered me with the name when I was a teenager, and it's stuck." The 41-year-old has hair turned prematurely grey by years of hard play and harder work. Of medium build, he is well tanned, spending what spare time he has sailing, playing cricket and golf and attending surf lifesaving carnivals on Sydney's northern beaches with his son. O'Toole has a dry wit and is famed for his street cunning. When Gwen Mitchelhill was murdered he had been a policeman for 23 years. He was one of the first detectives assigned to catch her killer but was transferred shortly afterwards to the Armed Hold-up Squad and became involved in Task Force Top Cat, an operation aimed at stemming the flow of blackmarket illegal weapons. However with the slayings of Madge Pahud and Olive Cleveland he was transferred straight back into the North Shore Murders Task Force. His role was to supervise the surveillance people and monitor the operational investigative teams out in the field on a daily basis.

Doodles O'Toole developed an excellent working relationship with Detective Sgt John May who headed a 10-person surveillance team from the State Intelligence Group. Five months later, when at last the net was descending on the serial killer, the surveillance police found themselves in the eye of the storm. May, strangely for a man whose business was not to be noticed, stood out in the crowd. He sported a trendy haircut — his brown hair was long at the back but cropped short at the sides — and favoured brightly coloured clothes, in wild contrast to his soberly-dressed, well-groomed colleagues.

Aged around 40, he is a hard man and he looks it. His face is tanned, rugged-looking and on his brow is a permanent furrow. Super-fit, he keeps people at length and impresses as a bloke not to underestimate or cross.

Another who would feel the heat in the dramatic last days of the investigation was Detective Sgt Paul Mayger, Miles O'Toole's second in command. Mayger, 40 at the time of the task force, joined the police force relatively late at the age of 27 and was a plain clothes detective early on, after wearing a uniform for just three years. He became a homicide specialist in 1986. Tall, fair-haired and imposing looking, he is a man who knows he is good at his job. His manner is brusque. He tolerates no nonsense and can be impatient with fools. His boots 'n' all style has been known to intimidate criminals.

For men such as Mike Hagan, Miles O'Toole and their colleagues, long days — often lasting 20 hours or more — were the norm. In those months of November and December, 1989, and January, February and March, 1990, their family lives suffered, their health failed, they bickered and groused among themselves. The pressure upon them – – from the public, the media, politicians and police hierarchy — was unrelenting and enormous. They had to catch the Granny Killer, and catch him now, because they all knew there was nothing more certain than that he would strike again. They were not wrong. As late spring became summer and summer turned to autumn the killer's tally of victims mounted, and mounted.

Miles O'Toole, who would be there amid the death and the horror when the Granny Killer was at last brought to book, cannot remember a more committed team of investigators. "When Mike Hagan briefed us all we realised the enormous bloody job we had ahead of us," he says. "I really, sincerely, believe this, that I've never worked on a better task force. Everybody pulled their weight and got stuck right into it. Over the next five months we followed up literally thousands and thousands of leads.

"And, yes, I've got to say it. I know detectives are supposed to be cool and detached at all times, but we were motivated to a great extent by the nature of these crimes. It was an outrage that this killer was preying on these defenceless old women. It struck a chord with us all. Everybody has a grandmother. I felt for every one of those women, and I was not alone. These poor ladies had survived all that this century could throw at them, world wars, the great Depression. And then to have their lives ended this way. It was a tragic, terrible waste."

Mike Hagan says the North Shore Murders investigation was the most intense manhunt in all his long years as a policeman. He remembers the dedication and camaraderie of his task force members, the brilliance of much of the investigative work, the sense of euphoria that built up when things at last began to run their way. But he also will never forget the long, gruelling hours, the boredom and frustration, the mistakes that were made, the media and political carping, the numbing despair of arriving at yet another murder scene, the repeated trips to the City Morgue. "Going down there and seeing for yourself just what these poor helpless women endured affects even the most hardened policeman," he says today. "Nobody who ever saw them will forget the sight of these old ladies, the matriarchs of society. We are all taught to respect the elderly, but when you saw what this man had done to them... you'd never forget it, never forget it. It was as though the whole structure of our society was under attack.

"We had to return again and again to the morgue because, while in other crimes the victim is alive and can tell you what happened, in a murder investigation the victim is dead, but that victim can still speak to you — through his or her body. That body can relay to a detective familiar with the many wounds that can cause a person's death, and to the doctors and the forensic experts, vital information that can lead to the arrest of a killer. I insisted that a homicide detective attend every post mortem right throughout the investigation."

* * *

The job confronting the North Shore Murders Task Force was a massive one. And to keep track of the reams of information that poured in each day, a new computer programme was set up at Task Force headquarters. That programme was MIIRS, or Major Investigation Information Retrieval System. MIIRS is the brainchild of Detective Sen Const Gordon Green, a man with a vast knowledge of computers, who wrote the programme to fit this particular probe. Its great value was in replacing the old manual index card system of keeping running sheets, the essential printed record of every aspect of a case. The new programme allowed the running sheet information to be stored in a micro-computer and retrieved as desired. Investigators would punch the relevant information into the computer and the running sheets, records of interview, statements and so on were in turn transferred into two master computers donated especially for the job by Olivetti that were housed in the incident room. There, every single entry, totalling the equivalent of 10,000 A4 pages, was read by detectives who then categorised, classified and indexed the information. A printout of the entry was then made and locked in a safe place, just in case the computers went down.

A copy of the information was made, read and reread by Geoff Wright and Ron Smith who allocated an investigator to follow the running sheet through. The entry and the action taken by the investigator were recorded in the micro-computer. A numerical rating code then allowed the task force to establish the information's position, relevance and importance in their hunt for the murderer.

Gordon Green, 44 years of age, is known as "Agent Orange" for his Vietnam service, and "Glass And A Half" because with his bushy hair and eccentric scientist manner he reminded colleagues of the late Professor Julius Sumner Miller whose TV ads extolled for years the virtues of the glass and a half of milk in every Cadbury's chocolate. He is one of the foremost computer minds in the police State Intelligence Group.

In 1986 Green had become interested in micro-computers with their word-processing ability, their spreadsheets, data bases, graphics and so on. After fiddling around with one for a while he realised that micro-computers could make crime investigation more accurate and efficient. By 1988 one of his programmes to compile abridged running sheets was being used by the Organised Crime Squad. Bob Myers of the Regional Crime Squad South West approached Green and asked if his programme could have an application in investigating homicides. Green said he'd see what he could come up with. What he devised made Myers ecstatic. But, he asked Green, could he extend his programme even further? "I'll give it a go," said Glass And A Half.

After Green made further refinements, following discussions with Detective Sen Sgt Bob Myers, MIIRS was being routinely used by Myers and other South West Region detectives to help them streamline homicide investigations. The South West investigators learned then, in mid-1989, what the North Shore Murders Task Force would soon find out for themselves: that MIIRS reduced the manpower requirement in the incident room by up to 75 percent; computerised running sheets caused the turnaround in information processing to be reduced from three weeks under the old manual indexing system to a single day; and tracking the different aspects of the probe was now much easier. Freed of an estimated 40 percent of their paperwork, detectives were left to get on with the job of investigation.

Gordon Green woke on the morning of November 3 with a thumping hangover. A day's boating had been topped off with a marathon drinking session that stretched until 3am. A radio news item pierced his headache. An elderly woman had been found murdered at Lane Cove the previous afternoon and police thought there were similarities between it and the other killings of aged women. At work Green and Myers conferred and decided to offer MIIRS to Miles O'Toole, the Regional Crime Squad North homicide detective who was investigating all three murders. O'Toole accepted gratefully.

By 4pm Gordon Green was fading fast. Tongue dry and spinning out, he headed home for bed. Just as he was about to sink into oblivion, the phone rang. It was Myers. Says Green today, "Bob told me, 'Get over to Chatswood and start the computerised running sheet right now.' He said we might have another murder. I thought he was stirring and suggested he engage in some sex and travel. But he was fair dinkum. Mrs Cleveland had been killed. I got some gear together and drove straight to Chatswood." When Green arrived he took over a micro-computer. After erasing everything superfluous to the job at hand, he loaded the computer and prepared it for running sheet use.

Green and Myers, who would both be seconded to the task force when it was set up the following day, found themselves alone in the office at seven that night. "Bob kept saying, 'How are we going to manage this? We have to be able to put all four murders on one machine and have them loaded in such a way that we can cross-match and compare them. How are we going to manage this?' I replied, 'She'll be right. We'll start on one and come to the others and cross any bridges when we come to them.' But secretly my mind was elsewhere. I was thinking, 'God, this room's hot since they turned the air conditioning off, and I wish my headache would stop. And why won't Bob stop talking?' We sat there and pondered and answered the phone, shared a Chinese takeaway, and then Mike Hagan and the boys got back from the Cleveland murder scene at Belrose and more work was done. We went home at 2.30am. It was one of the longest days of my life — and my monumental hangover didn't help one bit."

Green and Myers were back on the job at 8am next day, the day the task force officially began operations. After a formal briefing the two, with their assistants Detective Sen Const Vince Valente and Detective Sen Constable Annie Langford, set up their computers in the incident room, converted that day from the superintendent's meal room. Lockers were moved out and tables and chairs brought in. They formed a rectangle of tables with a square hole in the centre. They put micro-computers on each of the tables and dropped all the wires into the square well. "This," laughs Green, "is where I made a big mistake. There were not many power sockets in the building so I jumped on a table and reached up and pushed one of the ceiling tiles up off the grid and grabbed one of the light sockets. I plugged an extension cable into this socket and then a power board on the other end of the lead. I plugged all the computers and printers into this board and started up one main computer to commence on the running sheets." Green's haphazard installation, done to save time as the investigation got under way, would cost precious hours later when Bob Myers walked next door to turn off a light and brought the entire computer system crashing down.

Green recalls that first day of the task force. "Bob Myers sat down and started on the running sheets for the Pahud murder while I sat at another computer and took out the source code for the programme and went through it and altered it, so that automatically it would cross-match more than one inquiry. I then exchanged the execution files on Myers's machine and left him to sit and type. I altered other programmes and started up another computer and loaded it with programmes. By the end of the morning I had six micro-computers up and away with running sheet software on them so police could start the massive task of back-capturing the running sheets from the other murder inquiries.

"I spent the afternoon writing the software to exchange the running sheets and move them to Myers's central micro-computer. Then through the evening I started loading some of the back-captured running sheets from the other murders into Myers's machine and we kept at it, classifying, categorising, indexing, checking, analysing the data and information.

"I ate before Myers that day. I had lunch at 5.30pm for 10 minutes. He ate about an hour later and we had a 10-minute supper at about 11pm. We finished work at about 1.30am and went home. For the first week and a half of the task force's life that was our work conditions: 8am start, lunch at 3pm for 10 minutes, dinner at 11pm for 10 minutes then a 1am knock-off. On Melbourne Cup Day we went to the pub and had a 45-minute lunch — no beers, computers and alcohol don't mix — watched the race, then went back to work. We went home early that night — at 11.30."

When it was in full swing, MIIRS became an index to every single aspect of the north shore murders investigation. A detective could search the entire running sheet for particular pieces of information simply by inputting key words such as "suspicious vehicles", "deceaseds' injuries", "skateboard riders", "victims' recovered property", "murder scenes" or whatever. In a short time the computer would flash up every single reference to the key words and the investigator could select and print out the information he was seeking.

After certain events that took place in January and February, 1990, the task force had cause to search the computer for references to a middle-aged, stocky, conservatively-dressed, grey-haired man. What the computer told them chilled their souls.

CHAPTER 3

"A Deeply Evil Man"

When John Walter Glover arrived in Melbourne from the UK in 1957 on board the *SS Strathnaver* his hair was not yet grey. Photographs taken days after his arrival show him to be a muscular, robust, almost-handsome 24-year-old with light-brown hair. In one photo the T-shirted young macho is quaffing a mug of beer. In the other he is wearing a broad-brimmed bushman's hat and is squinting into the middle-distance like a movie cowboy scouring the horizon for redskins. Shortly after this photo was taken, the wide boy from Wolverhampton changed his name from John Walter to John Wayne Glover.

Glover's own horizons at that time of his life were, he believed, limitless. He had arrived in this new country — "where I could *be* John Glover" — after turning his back on his homeland of England, a place where he felt sentenced to a life of "going from job to job, parent to parent, girlfriend to girlfriend".

John Glover was born in Wolverhampton, on November 26, 1932. His father Walter was a locksmith, a handsome, easygoing man without ambition who played the piano in the pub at night. Walter would try without success to have his son take up the piano. Perhaps the boy had been soured by an experience when, before his voice broke, the father secured his son a spot as a soloist in the church choir. Glover was paid one shilling and sixpence for each solo he sang, of which his father would take a hefty chunk as commission for getting him the job.

Glover's mother Freda, on the other hand, was a strongly-built, fierce-willed, hard-working woman who, Glover recalled when interviewed for this book, "had a will of iron and a sharp tongue when something upset her". Freda Glover tried, and succeeded, to provide a good home for her son, but had difficulty showing him affection.

Freda Glover, however, had no such difficulty with men. She would marry four times in her life and, according to her son, had many lovers outside marriage.

When the boy was nine, his parents split up after their marriage had grown increasingly acrimonious. On more than a few occasions, says Glover, he had surprised one or the other parent in bed with a stranger. Glover remained with his mother and three-years-younger brother Barry. In 1944, at the height of World War II, Freda Glover married again and had two more children, Patricia and Clifford. Her third son was fathered by another man not her husband. Although profoundly disgusted by what he considered his mother's promiscuity — "she was fast and loose, or becoming that way" — John Glover bottled up his discontent and remained outwardly respectful to this woman whom he both loved and loathed.

At this stage Glover was on an emotional merry-go-round, being "flitted" from his mother to his father and back again whenever each found it inconvenient to have him around, and sometimes being sent to live with aunts and uncles. However, when he turned 14 and left school, he says, "My mother welcomed me home with open arms because I was old enough to earn a quid." Although living with his mother was difficult, he stuck it out "because she always seemed to have more money than my father".

He is derisive of his schooling which was continually interrupted as he moved around living with different relatives. However Glover, then as now, considered himself unusually intelligent, quick-witted and with a flair for languages and music. That he never had the opportunity to realise this potential at high school and university rankled him all his life.

His first job was as an electrical apprentice but this fell apart because, he says, he was still traumatised by his unstable family life. His apprenticeship cast aside, he worked spasmodically, sometimes as an electrician's mate and others as a joiner or a tradesman's offsider.

At 16, he left home and lived with young friends. Glib, roguish, good-looking and always dapperly turned out, he discovered the opposite sex was attracted to him and he had a succession of girl-friends. He was an ardent lover and claims that he never had an unsuccessful sexual experience. He remains proud of his sexual prowess and boasts of a string of amorous conquests in his youth. He swears that even in his middle teen years he was constantly under pressure from girlfriends to marry. But much more fun, to him, was the single life. He filled his days with swims in the country, cycling, a little weightlifting and a lot of drinking. Although never a great sports fan, he would watch the soccer on TV. At night he would take his girlfriends dancing, to the pub and to bed. "I was a mad rooter," he boasts today.

When he was 13 his best friend fell out of a tree while stealing apples. The friend landed on his head and died soon afterwards. This upset the young Glover greatly.

Although not an unusually aggressive youth, he was known to get into fights, one in particular when he fell out with another boy at a dance and punches were thrown. His mother, who had long wondered where her son got the money to support his rakish lifestyle, wondered no more when Glover began racking up a series of convictions for theft. He was up for stealing five times between the ages of 14 and 22. He explains these offences away, "Stealing was just something everybody did. We were all bohemians and if somebody had something that I wanted then I'd take it."

One of Glover's siblings remembers the youth as being always out for himself: "He'd look after himself first, second and third. Even then, he was always putting on airs and graces and of course when he came to Australia he just got worse."

In March, 1947, aged 14, Glover stole goods from a house in Wolverhampton and was bound over to his father and made to pay 35 shillings compensation. The same year, in October, he stole tools and date stamps from his employer and remained bound over to Walter Glover. In May, 1952, he stole a raincoat and other clothing from a Lincoln City club and was fined four pounds and made to pay one pound compensation. Seven months later he stole an overcoat from a van and then drove off in the van. Again he was fined a few pounds, and was also disqualified from driving for 12 months. In 1954 he stole a woman's handbag and when caught was placed on probation for two years. Between these convictions Glover committed a number of other similar offences but was never brought to account.

When he was 18, Glover did his national service. "At first, like everybody else, I wanted to get out as soon as I got in. But I came to enjoy the army." After his six-week training period he'd settled in and was enjoying life as a soldier. "For the first time I got a glimpse of the real world." He enjoyed the camaraderie of his mates and says that never again in his life has he encountered such a good bunch of blokes as these.

For a youth who had led such a disrupted, unstable life, the security and order of the army were a godsend. Glover thrived on knowing that every day he would be fed, housed and clothed. He responded to the discipline and became an excellent marksman and climbed the ranks to become a drill instructor and a radar operator/ bombardier. "I'm sorry I ever left the army," says Glover today. "Although it wasn't like now when army men are always leaping out of helicopters, I enjoyed piling into the back of a truck with my trusty Lee Enfield slung over my shoulder and travelling up to Hull for exercises. I've never forgotten my army training. Even here in gaol I'm always the first bloke up, showered and dressed."

At 20, he returned to civilian life but found it hard to cope with freedom. He returned to a life of bus conducting and delivery van driving, of petty crime and frequent, loveless sex. In his own words, he was a "misfit". He was getting on with his mother no better than he had before, and he grew depressed at what he saw as the aimlessness of his existence in England. Then, in 1957, aged 24, while working as a bus conductor, he noticed in a local Wolverhampton paper an advertisement that had been placed by the Melbourne Metropolitan Tramways Board calling for tram drivers and conductors. Glover applied and was sent the application forms. He filled them in and quickly posted them back to Australia. Soon after receiving notification that his application was successful he packed his bags, bid a hasty farewell to his family, and left England forever.

John Glover paid his own one-way fare on board the *SS Strathnaver* — "I was proud not to emigrate as a 10-bob Pom" — and arrived in Melbourne with only a suit on his back and 30 shillings to his soon-to-be-altered name.

The Tramways Board organised lodgings for their new employee at a boarding house in Shakespeare Grove, Hawthorn, run by a Birmingham woman. The house was a temporary home to many newly-arrived Englishmen. Most would move on as soon as they established themselves, but Glover liked the place and stayed for some months before taking a flat in Burke Road, Camberwell.

He adapted quickly to the Aussie way of life. The people on the trams were open and friendly and responded well to his happy line of patter, funny stories and smutty Benny Hill-style jokes that usually involved a toilet, knickers or some part of the female anatomy. The money was good, the beer cold and plentiful and, just like back home, there was no shortage of willing women. He grew a spivvy goatee and got a tattoo on his left upper arm. "I was knocking around with a little cockney bastard at the time and one night we were downing some cold Carltons at the White Horse Inn at Hawthorn when my mate decided he'd get a tattoo. Three parts pissed, I went with him and let him talk me into getting one done as well. I chose an eagle carrying a shield and flying over a mountain. It cost me 15 shillings and sixpence and I've regretted it ever since. The significance of the eagle and the shield? Fuck all!"

After he had served his time as tram conductor, Glover moved on and worked in a factory, as a warehouse clerk, and then driving delivery vehicles. His heavy drinking and prolific lovemaking continued, and so did his penchant for crime, but now his wrongdoing took a disturbing and portentous turn.

On September 11, 1962, 73-year-old Myrtle Ince was walking along Berrick Street, Camberwell, at 10.15pm. Suddenly she was attacked from behind by a powerful man who clamped one hand over her mouth, the other around her neck, and flung her face down into a flower bed. Before she lapsed into unconsciousness she felt a hand interfering with her clothing. When she came to, she reported the assault and the theft of some of her belongings to police.

On the fourth day of the following month a woman in her 20s, Valerie Bird, was walking near the intersection of Christowel Street and Stoddart Street, Camberwell, at about 10.30pm when she saw a man walking on the opposite side of the road. Presently he crossed to her side and followed her. As the girl picked up speed, so did the man. Suddenly she was grabbed from behind by the man who snapped one hand over her mouth, the other around her body. She thought the attacker was wearing gloves. She cried for help then passed out. She awoke in the front garden of a house and screamed for help. Her face was aching and her mouth was bleeding. There were scratches and bruises on her neck and legs. Her clothes, torn and bloodstained, were dishevelled and belongings were missing from her bag. She was assisted into the house by a passerby and called the police.

The young woman's assailant had been interrupted mid-assault by a man who shouted, "Stop!" John Glover left his victim where she lay and hid in the garden of a nearby house. Shortly afterwards and for reasons best known to himself he knocked on the front door of the house and woke the owner. Glover said there had been an assault nearby and the attacker might have been in the man's backyard. Together they searched the yard. Finding nothing, Glover bid the homeowner goodnight and walked to the front gate where he was confronted by two policemen. Glover had been seen to run into the garden by the man who had interrupted his attack and who called the police.

The girl identified him as her attacker and Glover was charged with indecent assault, assault occasioning actual bodily harm, and larceny. Glover admitted his guilt. Then, when questioned by police about the attack on the elderly woman in Camberwell the previous month, Glover admitted responsibility for that as well and was again charged with indecent assault, assault occasioning actual bodily harm, and larceny. He told police that both assaults had followed arguments with his girlfriend. On each occasion he had left her in a furious temper, seen the woman in the street, and attacked. He did not know why. He struck on an impulse that he could not explain. Glover was placed on probation for four years and ordered to undergo psychiatric counselling.

As Glover's list of addresses mounted — Camberwell, Toorak, Middle Park, Prahran, East St Kilda — so did his criminal record. Just three weeks after his assault convictions, Glover, now working as a TV antenna rigger for the Australian Broadcasting Commission, stole two spotlights, an electric drill, a fan and a kerosene heater from his employer. He also stole a set of bongo drums from a workmate. A year earlier a stolen trombone and its case, a tape recorder and an amplifier had been found in his flat. The year after the twin assaults he stole a surfboard. When caught out for all these thefts he was fined small sums of money.

In 1965, Glover, the man who boasted endlessly to friends of his ability to win any woman he wanted and numbered among his many conceits the belief that he resembled the actor Paul Newman, was discovered in a garden in St Kilda Road, Windsor, peering through the windows of a house at two girls as they dressed. He was seen from the house, police were called, and he was apprehended in the garden. He received a three-month suspended sentence.

On his record sheet he was described as 5ft 8in tall, solid build, ruddy complexion, fair/grey hair, blue eyes, sometimes wearing a ziff beard, tattoo of eagle and shield on left upper arm. A personality profile of Glover in 1965 was compiled by police psychiatrists. "The defendant is a quiet type of person and is 32 years of age. He was born in England and has lived in Australia for approximately eight years. He came to Australia by ship and arrived at Melbourne where he has lived all the time he has been here. He is not married and lives by himself at 229 Canterbury Road, Middle Park. He has been going with a girl for the last three years but she has now gone to New Zealand for approximately three-six months with a girlfriend. Glover admits that he cannot stop himself from stealing and he is the type of person who would steal just out of sheer compulsion. When he is not with his girlfriend he becomes very depressed and looks for female company. He is very truthful once you break through to him and the best way to do this is to appeal to his better sense and suggest that he needs medical treatment for this behaviour, and he will admit that he committed the offence. He is likely to offend again in circumstances arising because of women and also he is most likely to start stealing. He is a television installer by occupation. The defendant is not a violent type of person and will offer no resistance to police in their arrest."

Friends at this time would have disagreed with the assessment that Glover was a non-violent man. Behind his dapper and easy-going facade, it was increasingly clear, he was an angry man with strong opinions on a range of subjects. He lost his temper frequently and was known to lash out with his fists. In September, 1967, a tram collided with his car. A noisy argument with the tram driver ensued. The tram driver reached for a steel lever in his cabin, but Glover was too fast and rained punches on the man. Charged with unlawful assault, Glover was ordered to pay $6.44 costs.

Glover's brother Barry and his step-brother Clifford came to stay with him for a few years in 1966. Glover and Barry were inseparable until Barry ran his motor scooter into the back of a Buick and suffered severe physical and mental injuries. The younger man then became a burden to Glover who told him he couldn't stay at the flat any more and would have to return to England. "I couldn't afford to get on with Barry after his accident," says Glover coldly. "I wasn't going to look after him. I'm not my brother's keeper."

The young Englishman's shiftlessness and propensity for violence had not prevented him from having a string of girlfriends during his time in Melbourne. In 1968 he was having a relationship with a French-Belgian woman. "All was wonderful," he says, "until she started pressuring me to marry her. She already had some kids from a previous marriage and I could see the danger signals. I didn't want to get tied down with children. Things were rocky between us when my girlfriend introduced me to one of her friends named Gay who was on the rebound from a broken relationship."

Glover broke off with the French-Belgian woman and started going out with Jacqueline Gail Rolls, who was known as "Gay". Gay Rolls came from a wealthy family who lived in the very establishment Sydney suburb of Mosman. The pair hit it off at once. Glover revelled in Gay's class, intelligence and vivaciousness, and luxuriated in the fact that she came from respectable stock; while she enjoyed his jokes and his charm and believed she could see in him an enormous untapped potential to succeed as a salesman. She felt she could bring out the best in him.

Remembers Glover, "One day Gay said to me, 'I know what you've been like with women in the past, now what are we going to do about it?' I told her next time I was in Coles I would pick up a cheap ring and give it to her as a symbol of my faithfulness. But Gay beat me to it. She went out to a jeweller and bought an expensive engagement ring. All of a sudden we were engaged."

Gay Rolls could not wait to introduce her fiance to her mother Veronica, known as "Essie". Says Glover, "Essie came to Melbourne to meet me with rings on her fingers and bells on her toes and was delighted with her daughter's choice of husband. The two of us got on well in Melbourne. It was only when Gay and I moved to Sydney a year or so after our marriage that things went bad between my mother-in-law and me."

Glover's family greeted the news of his impending marriage with scepticism. "When we heard the lad had landed himself an only child with wealthy parents and a big house she'd inherit, we thought, 'There he goes, he's done it again,'" laughs one relative. "He's a sly one. He can look you straight in the face and tell you a lie and you believe him every time."

Shortly before his marriage Glover was sacked from his job as a driver with a wine and spirits merchant. In a rage, he stole liquor from his employer, was caught and placed on a bond to be of good behaviour for one year and ordered to pay $30 into the poor box at Prahran.

This latest addition to his by-now lengthy criminal record did nothing to spoil Glover and Gay Rolls's plans and on June 1, 1968, a bleak and drizzling Melbourne day, the two wed at the little yellow-brick Church of Christ, South Yarra. Glover, wearing a dinner suit with a carnation on the lapel and a snappy black bowtie, beams out of the wedding photograph. His hands are behind his back. His hair is noticeably greying at the temples. He resembles a prosperous young business executive. Gay Glover, attractive, round-faced and beaming too, her dark hair swept back from her face, stands at her husband's left. She is about to plunge a ribbon-bedecked knife into a thickly-iced, two-tier wedding cake.

Under Gay's influence, Glover set about fulfilling his destiny as a successful salesman in the liquor industry. He worked hard and completed sales and wine appreciation courses and landed a job with another wine and spirits company as a salesman. Glover would later tell a psychiatrist of his career transformation: "I became John Glover, sales representative. Instead of driving a delivery truck I was driving a company car. It was a fillip to me, the result was good. I became the collar and tie brigade. I was very successful at it, wines and spirits initially, later a wider range — wine casks, palletisation, discounting. I was always a gentleman in my business dealings and maintained good relations with the opposition." Of his wife's influence on his life, he denied to the same psychiatrist that she had ever dominated him, rather she "directed" him.

Now brimming with confidence over his success as a salesman, Glover was all for it when his wife suggested they up stakes and start a new life in Sydney. They would live with her parents, Essie and John, in their two-storey home on the high side of Wyong Road, Mosman, with its sweeping views of Quakers Hat Bay and the leafy streets and staid, pricey homes of the upper-middle-class garden suburb. For the working class lad who had dared to forge a new life in a new land with no friends or money, the prospect was music to his ears.

The move to Mosman was the catalyst that changed John Glover into a different person. From the first, Glover became what he believed a Mosman man should be. He became inordinately proud of his suburb, his street, his garden and home, as proud as only someone who secretly believes he really doesn't belong there can be.

The one-time drunken lout, thief and womaniser took to speaking slowly and deliberately, pausing between each word in what he considered to be a cultured way. Although he had been in Australia 13 years now, there was still a trace of Britishness in his speech and he played on this for all he was worth. He threw away his flashy shirts and shiny, coloured trousers and took to dressing conservatively, guided in his clothes choices by his wife, and let everybody know he listened to and watched the ABC. He was careful not to let his Mosman neighbours see his tattoo. In the garage was his company car, to him a symbol of business success. He would wash it every weekend, out in the street so the neighbours could see. And like the car, the clothes and the lordly demeanour, his shock of prematurely greying hair and thickening waistline were convincing window dressing in John Glover's transformation from petty criminal to pillar of society.

Glover had just one problem. Essie Rolls. She could see right through him. Although later the parents-in-law would build a third storey on the house in Wyong Road and move into the new living area themselves, in the early '70s Essie, Gay and the two Johns lived together in the second storey. Sparks flew from the beginning when Essie Rolls decided that Gay had made a dreadful mistake and that John Glover was simply not suitable for her. She would hector her son-in-law every day. Nothing he did was any good, he was bogus, a lazy waster, he had no money and less upbringing. John Glover learned early that there was a price to pay for his newfound respectability, and that price was having to live with Essie Rolls. And the worst thing about it was she had the upper hand. There was no way he and Gay could afford to buy a place of their own, certainly not anything as grand as No.18 Wyong Road in such a good suburb as Mosman. So he took her abuse in silence, hung in there, and waited for her to die. It would take 18 years.

What Glover did not know was that he was not the only target for Essie Rolls's venom. She was known throughout Mosman as a bad-tempered, querulous woman who did and said exactly as she pleased. One neighbour described her as "a nasty version of Dame Edna Everage. She'd have her hair done regularly, the same wisteria rinse and swept back, and she'd wear big coloured glasses like Dame Edna. Essie was a real Mosman matriarch, a domineering, angry woman right until the end of her life. And her voice, it was so loud that when she shouted at John you could hear her up and down the street and into the valley."

Only once — that anybody knew about anyway — in those early years in Sydney did the old John Glover emerge. In 1978 he was caught shoplifting in a North Sydney department store and given the choice of paying a $100 fine or doing 20 days hard labour. Glover paid the fine. He had to. By that time his assumed identity was in place and this misdemeanour could not be allowed to put that at risk. He had an excellent job as a salesman with Nestles and, Essie apart, everything in the garden was rosy. Married life with Gay was good, and he was the father of two beautiful and intelligent girls, Kellie, born in 1971, and Marney, born in 1973. Even in the dark and terrible days that followed, Glover was never less than an excellent provider and loving father to his daughters, gentle, kind and caring. The girls were, simply, the best thing that ever happened to him.

In 1981 Glover applied for the position of sales representative with the Four 'N Twenty Pie Company, based in Bourke Street, Alexandria, an inner southern suburb of Sydney. He was successful. Although he had never sold pastries before, he took to his new job quickly. His brief was to travel all over the north shore in his company car calling on clients in supermarkets, shops, hospitals, clubs, retirement villages and nursing homes. He would take orders for the range of Four 'N Twenty pastries and pass them on to a distributor for fulfilment. As a sales rep, too, he was expected to play his part in company public relations and hospitality to clients at Sydney Swans games at the Sydney Cricket Ground, Four 'N Twenty being a sponsor of the Australian rules team. In this role the gregarious Glover dined in the company of such luminaries as the future premier of New South Wales Nick Greiner, John Blackman of TV's *Hey, Hey It's Saturday!*, entertainer Barry Crocker and the Swans then-owner Dr Geoffrey Edelsten. He is remembered as a hearty dinner companion, always full of jokes and good fun, even if he tended to become smutty and embarrassing with a few drinks under his belt. Often he would be accompanied at such company functions by his wife Gay and one who dined with them recalls the pair's one-liners and witty repartee would have done credit to Laurel and Hardy.

Glover was considered by company management to be a diligent and hardworking salesman, nothing brilliant, but a good operator and a pleasant enough bloke. Those who dealt with him on a day-to-day basis, however, had a different opinion. Glover and his immediate supervisor Morris Grant hated each other from the outset. Their personality clash lasted for as long as Glover was employed at Four 'N Twenty. Glover despised Grant and claimed he could have risen far up the corporate ladder at Four 'N Twenty if Grant had not conspired to hold him back. Glover claimed Grant was jealous of his high intelligence. "Morris was far below me in every way. But especially," Glover says grandly today, "in the matter of intelligentsia!" Interviewed for this book in gaol, John Glover still expressed the hope that some terrible fate had befallen Morris Grant in the time since they had last met.

Glover's workmates, too, according to former Four 'N Twenty state sales manager Jim Keddie who knew Glover at Nestles and later at the pastry company, had little time for him.

"Oh yes, management didn't mind Glover because he could put up a good front and was always sucking up to them, but as far as I am concerned he was a thief, a bully, a coward and disgusting in front of women," says Keddie. The first Keddie knew of Glover was when a Nestles customer reported the salesman for stealing $50 from a cash register. "Keep that bloke away from me," the shopkeeper had said,

"I don't want him in my shop any more." Then word filtered through to Keddie, who was then Nestles' national sales manager of industrial products, that Glover was not only dishonest, but lazy as well. When Glover applied for a position with Four 'N Twenty Pies, the pastry company asked Keddie for a reference. "Don't touch him," advised Keddie, "he's a bludger and a thief." Glover got the job regardless.

The pair's paths crossed again when Keddie too joined Four 'N Twenty in the early '80s as one of Glover's bosses. "Nothing had changed," says Keddie. "I found him just as unpleasant as before. He was one of those blokes who would niggle at you, try to get under your skin, but always with a smile on his face. He'd keep wearing away at what he considered to be your weak spot to try to get a reaction." Once this backfired painfully on Glover when he pushed another sales representative too far and the man punched Glover hard on the face two or three times. "Glover backed off. The man was a coward, a real mouse, when anyone stood up to him," recalls Keddie.

Glover had a reputation for being smutty in front of women. Once he went to expose himself at an office party and horrified female employees reported him to management who rebuked him mildly. And Jim Keddie remembers how Glover had once touched the breasts and bottom of a female sales representative and she had rounded on him and said, "Get away from me, you horrible little man!" Glover had grinned and said he was only having a little harmless fun.

Keddie says he had been shocked by Glover's behaviour on a number of occasions when the pair called on customers. "We'd go into a milk bar to take an order for our pastries and Glover would say to the woman behind the counter, 'Gee, you've got nice tits!' He thought he was irresistible and comments like that were a big come-on. I'd say, 'Oh, God!' and cringe and chastise him when we left the shop. Then he'd go all stupid, just like a naughty little boy, when I'd tell him off. After a while nobody wanted to be with Glover. He was what I'd call an 'optic', a man who couldn't keep his eyes or hands off women, young or old. He was always leering and passing smartarse comments at them.

"A couple of times when I was supervising him on the road we'd drop into one of his clubs for lunch and a game of snooker. He was a member of Mosman RSL, North Sydney Rugby Union Club, and South Sydney Businessman's Club. He was a big drinker who could hold his booze and a good snooker player. He even had his own cue at Norths' rugby club."

Keddie once noticed a claw hammer under the front seat of Glover's company car. When he asked him why he kept it there, Glover replied that he liked to have it handy in case he ever had trouble with another driver. "I'll pull it out and get stuck into any bastard who hassles me on the road," Glover told Keddie.

Glover had a chip on his shoulder, says Keddie, who often had to reprimand him after he had been overbearing to other Four 'N Twenty employees, particularly female van drivers. The rep also incurred Keddie's ire for swapping Four 'N Twenty products with the products of other salesmen at trade fairs. "He was always disappearing with our sample packs and returning laden down with tins of tomatoes, sets of chef's knives and so on. He was into freebies in a big way, and was suspected of pilfering company products as well," says Keddie.

For all of Keddie's opinion, Glover led a charmed life at Four 'N Twenty. He was considered a solid, dependable salesman and because he so clearly enjoyed being the life of the party, was often chosen to drive the company's mobile pie, a car done up to resemble a huge meat pie, at trade fairs and such occasions as the Festival of Sydney parade along Macquarie Street.

Glover was badly put out when his mother and sister Pat and Pat's husband emigrated to Australia, expecting to move right into Wyong Road with the Glovers and the Rolls. Glover would have none of it. Apart from his ongoing deep resentment of his mother's "loose" lifestyle, he believed he had risen far above their station in life and that they would prove an embarrassment to him if they were set loose in his Mosman. Glover pulled no punches with his mother when she arrived in Sydney. "There's no way you're going to move in with us. The closest either of you are coming to me is Gosford — 100 kilometres up the coast!" One Christmas Day Glover relented and allowed Freda and and her last husband Roger Underwood to drive to Sydney and visit him and his family for lunch. However, once the uncomfortable meal was over, instead of inviting them to stay the night and get an early start home next morning, he packed them off to a nearby motel.

The Glovers did travel to Gosford to visit his relatives from time to time, but although he tried to be respectful — "show due deference" as he puts it — it was clear by Glover's antagonistic behaviour towards his mother and by hers to him, that there was no love lost between them and that there never would be.

One Wyong Road man remembers his time as John Glover's neighbour well. "Your first impression of Glover would be that here is Mr Average Suburban Man. When I was a teenager in the '70s I thought he was very much part of the Mosman establishment, the way he'd swagger around the neighbourhood. Then, as I grew older I recognised signs that everything was not quite what it seemed."

After one particular incident Glover was held in awe and not a little fear by his neighbours. Gay Glover was in the house one evening when she looked out the window and saw a prowler in her backyard. She called out for help. The prowler, a youth, took fright at the commotion and ran into the street where he was apprehended by neighbours who had been alerted by Gay Glover's cries. The easily overpowered and by-now distressed young man was made to sit in the gutter surrounded by his captors to await the arrival of the police. Suddenly John Glover exploded through the ring of neighbours. Red-faced-furious, he was shouting obscenities and wielding a cut-down baseball bat. The neighbours could only watch shocked as Glover attacked the abject youth with the bat, crashing it down on his head and shoulders. The terrified prowler leapt to his feet and ran off into the night. Alarmed neighbours exchanged embarrassed looks and then drifted uneasily back to their homes, leaving John Glover panting heavily alone in the middle of Wyong Road.

Over the years, Glover became obsessively territorial about his street and considered it his own. He would lecture residents if their gardens became untidy or their lawns overgrown and testily refer recalcitrant gardeners to his own grounds, pointing out how neat his lawns and gardens were and boasting that even the leaves on his trees and plants were kept spotless.

Although unfailingly courteous and always quick with a perfunctory pleasantry, this self-appointed guardian of Wyong Road had no true friends in the street that meant much to him. People knew him, passed the time of day with him, and often came to him in a crisis, but there was something about him that unsettled them and, like his workmates, Wyong Roaders kept John Glover at arm's length.

Glover's neighbour remembered, "John would rave on to me about his pet hates, and he had plenty of them. There was a seething anger underneath his urbane exterior. He especially hated the wealthy young people, yuppies, I guess, who were moving into the area. And he also said to me often that there were too many old people in Mosman. 'The place is full of old people and young people with too much money!' he'd fume."

Glover saw red when a young man who drove a black Porsche bought a small house across the road and rebuilt it into what to him resembled a giant orange castle. Glover complained to the council that the building was lowering the tone of the street then waged his own urban guerilla campaign against the owner. He tried to whip up the ire of his neighbours against the new house and then one night someone scrawled on the wall of the house in large red letters "Friendly?!" "John told me it wasn't him who'd painted the graffiti but I remember him laughing at the sign. I believe he was responsible," says his neighbour. Glover also stormed into the office of the then-mayor of Mosman, Dom Lopez, and lost his temper over the orange house. "What the hell are you people doing in council? Letting houses like that be built in my street! I don't have to put up with this nonsense!" he shouted, his face the colour of blood. Lopez was shaken by the pyrotechnics.

Another time, someone broke the streetlight in front of the house next door. Glover told his neighbour, "I'll catch this bastard if it's the last thing I do." Glover roamed the streets at night searching for the streetlight smasher. One night while on the hunt for this bloke he saw an innocuous-looking young man, decided he was the one, and accused him noisily and offensively of being the vandal.

The neighbour, who as a child had been shouted at by Glover for landing a frisbee on Glover's car, remembers how Glover had "done his block" that day. "He screamed at me and threatened to make me cut back and polish his car from bonnet to boot. But I wasn't scared. I always thought that for all his bluster he was a bit of a wimp, all talk and no action. I altered that opinion later."

The more this neighbour got to know John Glover, the more he believed the man suffered from a giant inferiority complex. "John would never admit it, but he clearly felt he wasn't of the same class as Mosman people. He was very aware that he came from a working-class background. I remember him telling my father about his life in England and saying that when he married Gay, he married up."

Essie Rolls gleefully fuelled her son-in-law's insecurities. She would regularly rub it in that he was not good enough for her daughter. Neighbours could hear her browbeating Glover night and day. Another Wyong Road resident retains a clear image of Glover working in the garden one afternoon while Essie, her head sticking out of the upper-storey window, berated him at the top of her voice. Glover had cowered from the verbal attack and not responded to the abuse. He just kept digging in his precious garden, an expression of absolute hatred on his red face, distractedly plunging his spade into the earth.

The mother-in-law also made it clear to Glover that No.18 Wyong Road was *her* house, not his. No matter how fastidious he was about the gardens, no matter how spotless he kept the place, she left him in no doubt — and in front of his wife and daughters — that he didn't belong, that he was an imposter, a gypsy in the palace. Essie Rolls castrated John Glover with her barbs and abuse just as surely as if she had held a knife.

One neighbour remembers Gay Glover joking that "We would all like to strangle Essie" but does not believe the wife was really aware of the effect the elderly woman had on Glover. "John bottled up his feelings well most of the time and to this day I believe that he mostly managed to hide his hatred of his mother-in-law from Gay. He was very controlled. But often when we talked it was obvious that he was seething inside and hated Essie. Gay and John were chalk and cheese. She was very open and outgoing and always saw the best in everything, while he was cold, guarded and controlled. His cheerful front was just bunged on. I reckon that the jokes and good humour were just a defence and that inside he was a deeply evil man spinning out of control."

In the face of Essie's criticism, Glover for a long time seemed to be the perfect husband and father. He gave the impression of being faithful to his wife, brought home his wages, was considerate and even-tempered. To his daughters he was super-protective, a friendly companion, and he fostered their academic and musical gifts. Those who knew him said he was happiest when with Kellie and Marney, who attended Loreto Convent at Kirribilli. Glover himself took up the electric organ and was a passable player. When alone, he would sing — in a good, strong baritone, too, according to the neighbours who could hear him in their yards. As for interests around the home, he had few. Just the garden and cleaning his company car, his organ, a bit of TV. He was not particularly interested in sport, but watched a little Australian rules on television after his company became a sponsor of the Sydney Swans.

Although also a member of North Sydney Rugby Union Club and South Sydney Businessmen's Club, the Mosman RSL Club was Glover's refuge from "the unbearable Essie". An imposing, modernish building in Military Road a couple of hundred metres down from Spit Junction, the RSL became the beleaguered man's home away from home. It was a place where he would go every day but Saturday, to drink his wine and play the poker machines. Glover would arrive at the club mid-afternoon — having started his working day at 6am or 6.30 he was entitled to finish early. He was known as a big loser on the pokies and members there can recall him dropping hundreds of dollars in a single afternoon on many occasions. Many considered him a poker machine addict. Glover denies this today. "No, I wasn't addicted. The club and the machines were just a social outlet for me. I liked to stand there and watch the passing parade. You wouldn't believe the number of women who made passes at me in that club," says Glover, "but naturally I turned all of them down."

Club stalwarts, however, believe differently. They swear Glover had a series of affairs with women from the club. They also say he was an amiable, but rather shadowy, figure. He was friendly, but reserved. He didn't let anybody too close. He never caused trouble and was part of a syndicate of two or three acquaintances who occasionally played the machines together. Often he would unload quantities of his unsold pastries on kitchen staff, no charge. An abiding memory for many members is Glover dancing with his daughters to the music of veteran rockers Digger Revell or Roland Storm on the club's regular Thursday rock 'n' roll nights. "What a great father he is," people recall thinking, "so proud of his daughters."

Such was John Glover's life as he passed from youth to grey-haired, paunchy middle age. Gay — although, he later told police, they had ceased being intimate around 1982. Kellie and Marney. Essie. His suburb, street and home. Freda and Pat in Gosford. Selling pastries for Four 'N Twenty. The club and the poker machines. Glover's only police conviction between 1970 and December, 1988, was the North Sydney shoplifting charge. (It is possible, some police say probable, that he committed other crimes in this period, but if so, he escaped detection.) Then, at the end of 1988, two events changed everything.

On October 7, Glover's 79-year-old mother, known then as Freda Underwood, was admitted to Neringah Hospital in South Wahroongah on Sydney's upper north shore. She was suffering from breast cancer. Four days later she was dead. According to family members Glover joined his step-sister and her husband in his mother's hospital room on the day before she was reported deceased. There was no warmth between mother and son, and the two were seen to exchange glares. As the family departed the hospital Glover was left alone at his mother's bedside. Next morning she was found dead in her bed. Freda Underwood was cremated without an autopsy. All John Glover will say about the passing of his mother is that when she died "it came as a relief".

Shortly before his mother died, Glover too contracted breast cancer, an unusual but not unknown condition in men. He had the cancerous tissue removed in a modified mastectomy. He was embarrassed by this problem and thought it "unmanly". He blamed his mother for passing it on to him.

Essie Rolls's health had deteriorated since the recent death of her husband John, however her grief had not toned down the 83-year-old woman's vitriolic harangues. So it came as a major relief to her son-in-law when on September 21 she was admitted to the Mosman Nursing Home. After suffering her nonstop bile for 13 years, finally John Glover was free.

Those who knew Glover at the time remember him undergoing a marked personality change during the period when Essie Rolls was in the nursing home. A neighbour recalls asking Glover to play *Happy Birthday* on his electric organ when his son had his first birthday that October. "Once Glover would have relished the opportunity to show off his musical skills and given a wholehearted rendition, but now he just glumly agreed and played a very doleful version of the song. John was obviously depressed with something weighing heavily on his mind."

Of more sinister significance was a series of sexual assaults in the Mosman Nursing Home at the very time of Essie Rolls's confinement there. The matron suspected John Glover immediately, having seen him loitering in the victims' rooms around the time of the attacks. However no action was taken against him except for a dressing down and a demand that in future when visiting his mother-in-law he park his car at the front of the hospital and walk directly to Essie Rolls's room. More than a year later, however, police had cause to show a photograph of Glover to patients at the nursing home. When the Polaroid was produced, one 84-year-old woman immediately became distraught at the sight of the grey-haired man, although, because her medical condition made verbal communication impossible, no action was able to be taken against Glover.

Essie Rolls was transferred to the Bradleys Head Nursing Home on January 21. She died there the same day.

By then, however, John Glover had snapped. Driving in Hale Road, Mosman, on January 11, 10 days before his mother-in-law's death, Glover saw 84-year-old Margaret Todhunter walking on the footpath. The woman was visiting from Queensland. All he knew, he says today, was that he had to hurt and humiliate this old woman. He couldn't say if his rage was triggered by the death of Freda and the clearly-impending death of Essie, just that the impulse to lash out hit him on the spot and he was powerless to deny it.

Glover parked his car and walked towards the woman who was carrying a white vinyl clutch purse. As he passed her, he turned and bludgeoned her to the ground with a blunt instrument. The blows to the back of her head sent the old woman to her knees. Looking up, she saw Glover running away with her purse containing around $200, various tickets and papers and a bank passbook. Margaret Todhunter did not scream for help. She directed what energy she had left toward abusing her attacker. "You rotten bugger!" she cried as Glover disappeared around the corner. Shocked and with blood flowing from her head, she staggered to a nearby private hospital where two deep, four-centimetre-long gashes in her scalp were stitched. Later she was interviewed by police. She described her attacker as a grey-haired man in his late 40s or 50s with a large upper body, big shoulders, chest and waist. He was clean and well-dressed in an immaculate white shirt and tie and cream slacks.

Later, back home in Queensland, Margaret Todhunter provided police with sufficient information for them to compile an artist's impression of the assailant. The drawing would prove crucial in bringing to a halt one of the most savage killing sprees in Australian criminal history. But that would not be until much, much later.

CHAPTER 4

Blood On The Rose

John Glover finished work in the middle of the afternoon and drove straight to the Mosman RSL. Although it was the first day of Autumn, 1989, Sydney's summer lingered and the pie salesman took his tie off after his last call and tossed it on to the back seat of his white company Ford station wagon alongside his order book and clipboard. The car, like its driver with his luxuriant grey-white hair, open, ruddy face, grey slacks and black shoes and short-sleeved cream shirt, would not have attracted a second glance. Nobody could have guessed the demons that danced in this man's mind, just as nobody could have known the reason why a heavy wooden-handled, metal-headed Stanley Hercules claw hammer rested under the front seat of this spotless vehicle.

Glover parked in Military Road near the RSL and climbed out of the car. Inside the air-conditioned, cavernous club he bought a glass of wine that he would make last as long as he stayed, stood, he would always stand, never sit, in front of a poker machine and began inserting coins. A practised player, an addicted player, he found his rhythm quickly. Coin in, finger poised on the button, snap it down, fruit spins and whirrs, come on, *pay*, click — a pineapple, click — a pineapple, click — a cherry, no pay, oh well, coin in, button down... The rhythmical sounds of the poker machine, lulling and soporific, drowned the voices, the female voices, that rang in his head, taunting him, telling him off, bossing him about.

For a frail 82-year-old who needed a walking stick to get around these days, Gwen Mitchelhill packed a lot into her life. That morning the well-preserved and sunny-faced widow dressed in a blue floral dress, striped blouse, white shoes and pearls and was ready at 10 when her taxi picked her up outside her unit block, Camellia Gardens, at 699 Military Road. She collected a friend, Jean Howard, and the two travelled up the Pacific Highway to Killara where they attended a matinee performance at the Marion Street Theatre. The show over, the friends returned by train and bus to Spit Junction where they said their goodbyes.

Gwen Mitchelhill continued on to buy notepads and a magazine at a newsagent then kept her 2.30pm appointment at the Silhouette Skin and Beauty Salon in Military Road. During her facial, waxing and tint she chatted happily to the proprietor about how she planned to stay with her daughter at Tamworth over the coming Easter break. Her mood darkened when she recalled how six bottles of whisky and a brass table had recently been stolen from her garage. The table had been mysteriously returned in a weathered condition, but as to the whereabouts of the whisky she had not a clue. She didn't know what the world was coming to, there were certainly some odd people about. After her hour-long beauty treatment she left the salon, crossed the road to make an appointment at Raymond's Hair Salon, and then walked home.

John Glover sauntered out of the RSL into the glare of the afternoon light. It was 3.50pm. As he prepared to get into his car he saw Gwen Mitchelhill, handbag, shopping bags and silver-handled black walking stick in hand, approaching slowly. The sight of the old woman awoke the demons. Glover's mind boiled. He opened the car door and reached under the front seat. The metal head of the claw hammer was cool to the touch. He took it out and bundled it down inside his trousers, the head held fast in his belt. Shadowing slowly at first, Glover picked up his step as he followed the old woman into the grounds of the units. When Gwen Mitchelhill stopped to take her door keys out of her bag at the entrance to the foyer of the flats Glover came at her fast, from behind, wielding the hammer.

Swinging the hammer high, Glover brought it down on the back of the woman's head, once, twice. As she staggered he punched her viciously on the face and then in the chest, smashing seven of the woman's ribs. She crashed to the pathway, bleeding profusely.

Glover neatly arranged his victim's shoes and walking stick near her body then picked up her handbag, snapped it open and removed a purse that contained a $100 bill. He placed the handbag near the shoes and the stick, stuffed the purse into his pocket and at that point, according to Glover, he walked briskly back to his car. Police, however, suspect that the sound of a lift descending to the ground floor of the unit block disturbed the attacker before he was able to further defile his victim. Back at the car, he opened the door and slipped the bloody hammer under the front seat then eased his vehicle into the flow of traffic heading north up Military Road. Nearing Wyong Road, Glover diverted down a street leading to Jolls Boatshed and after taking the money out, hurled the purse into a bush at the side of the road. He then drove home, threw his shirt and socks into the dirty washing basket, hung his trousers in the wardrobe and changed into casual clothing. His day's work done, he settled down in front of the TV to wait for the police reports on the ABC 7pm news.

As Glover departed Camellia Gardens two brothers, aged nine and 11, alighted from the lift in the foyer of the unit block. They had been visiting their great aunt and now were off to try to retrieve one brother's boater which he had left on the school bus earlier that afternoon. They saw Gwen Mitchelhill sprawled face down in a pool of blood just outside the front door. A walking stick, shoes and an open handbag were placed nearby and a woven carry bag lay further away.

The horrified boys raced back into the unit block and banged on residents' doors crying for assistance for the old lady downstairs. Accompanied by a neighbour of their great aunt they returned to the foyer where they saw that the battered woman had somehow dragged herself to a sitting position. She now sat slouched, her head slumped forward onto her chest with her back against the entrance doors. An ambulance was called and another neighbour attempted to talk to Gwen Mitchelhill and staunch with a towel the blood that was streaming from horrendous wounds on the back of her head.

"Gwen, what's happened?" soothed the neighbour, putting her arm around the elderly woman's tiny shoulders. "Keys," the victim gasped weakly, and the neighbour could see she was grasping her door keys in her hand. Gwen Mitchelhill remained semi-conscious until the ambulance arrived five minutes later. One ambulanceman, taking in the woman's wounds and noticing the neat placement of her handbag, walking stick and shoes — an island of order in a sea of carnage — suspected that she had not fallen down, as everybody was thinking, but was the victim of foul play. He rang the police and told them so.

The medicos put a bandage on Gwen Mitchelhill's head but the feisty woman attempted to take it off and told the ambulancemen to carry her upstairs. One ambulanceman replied that she was on her way to hospital then they lifted her into the ambulance. The vehicle then hurtled off to Royal North Shore Hospital, siren screaming. Before the wail of the siren had faded neighbours had washed away the blood that had covered the pebblecrete path and was seeping into the garden beds. When detectives arrived the assault scene was sterile.

"Damaging, extremely damaging, to the investigation" was how Detective Sen Const Paul Mayger, one of the detectives called to the unit block, summed up the effect of the washing down of the scene. "Many, many cases are solved purely and simply on physical evidence such as footprints and fingerprints. The well-meaning neighbours put paid to our chances of finding any of these, and when Mrs Mitchelhill died before she could tell us anything about her attacker, the investigation was up against it from the outset."

The attack did not make that evening's news, but any disappointment John Glover might have felt at that was assuaged next morning when he read on page seven of *The Sydney Morning Herald* that Gwendoline Mitchelhill had died last night after a "particularly brutal" attack at a Mosman unit block. A smile may have crossed the killer's face when he read on and discovered that the police's No.1 suspect was a man seen earlier that afternoon offering to tell the fortunes of Mosman shopkeepers by analysing their handwriting. By chance that man was in the beauty salon at the same time as Gwen Mitchelhill and it was thought he might have seen that she was carrying a considerable amount of cash when she paid for her treatment. A week or so later the handwriting analyst was traced to a boarding house at Cremorne Point. After a thorough quizzing he was rated an unlikely suspect.

The following night Paul Mayger attended the post mortem examination of Gwen Mitchelhill. It was conducted at the City Morgue by forensic pathologist Dr Johan DuFlou, deputy director of the NSW Institute of Forensic Medicine. Detectives are expected to deal with death, it's their job. But no matter how many post mortems a policeman attends they never lose their impact. They are harrowing and deeply saddening experiences, but they are vital in any murder investigation. It is as if the corpse there on the mortuary slab actually *talks* to the police and doctors present. The investigators learn much of what happened to the victim and how it happened. Whether the victim has been struck from the front, from the back and with what type of object. Often bruises do not reveal themselves on the body for days after death. This means that investigators must keep returning to view the corpse. Over the next 12 months, Paul Mayger and his colleagues would beat a path to the doors of the City Morgue.

The detective's role at the post mortem is to watch closely and listen for any clue that could help in the investigation. He points out the various injuries to the doctor performing the examination and asks questions: "How do you think this or that injury occurred? How much force was used? What type of weapon?"

Looking at the small body lying there in the morgue on that night of March 1, Mayger was left in no doubt as to how dreadfully Gwen Mitchelhill had suffered. Dr DuFlou spoke his observations out loud and his words were captured on a cassette tape recorder that dangled from the edge of the steel tray where the body lay: "Severe bruising to the right eye consistent with a fist; severe bruising to the right shoulder consistent with a blunt object; two wounds to the back of the skull consistent with a blunt object; extensive fracture rear of the skull, seven broken ribs consistent with a fist." Mayger thought to himself, "He didn't have to do that, he didn't have to hit her with such incredible force just to pinch her bag." Dr DuFlou believed that the murder weapon was blunt and rounded, like the leg of a chair.

With nothing concrete to go on, police embarked on an intensive canvass of the whole area. Residents, shopkeepers, workmen, all had to be interviewed. The questions going through the investigators' minds: did a crazy neighbour do this, a druggie out for money to supply his habit, a mugger who went too far, a homicidal maniac on day leave from a psychiatric centre? Hundreds of people were questioned and the victim's relatives notified. This last task calls for special skills: on one hand to winkle out possibly helpful information from those who knew the deceased best, and on the other to give solace to the heartbroken and horrified recipients of the terrible tidings.

After dredging up cases of similar attacks in the area down through the decades, police paid a call on two boys aged 17. Three years before, they had knocked down an old lady virtually across the street from Camellia Gardens and tried to steal her handbag. One lad had an alibi but police were unable to clear his mate, a large and powerful youth who had become severely retarded since the assault on the woman. Police doubted his guilt but were unable to eliminate him as a suspect. Senior officers demanded that he be grilled at length and his home searched. Not surprisingly, his parents, "very, very decent people" according to investigators, took umbrage at the invasion of their privacy. It was hard for police to explain to such people that they were just doing their job.

As March and April passed, with still no breakthrough, police were running out of leads to investigate; the inquiry was losing momentum. Then, on May 9, the killer struck again.

CHAPTER 5

Death Of An Angel

Lady Winfreda Ashton was a character in a suburb rich with characters. A kindly, garrulous and concerned 84-year-old with a sharp, pretty face, she had lived alone in a Raglan Street home unit since the death 15 years before of her husband, the noted impressionist painter Sir William Ashton. Although suffering now from cancer of the spine, a bad hip and a liver ailment, frail and unable to walk without a stick, she kept busy seeing her many friends, doing what she could for the sick and infirm of her suburb and encouraging aspiring artists. She was a frequent letter writer to Mosman mayor Barry O'Keefe on community matters. O'Keefe remembers her letters as succinct, relevant and couched in the gracious phraseology of an earlier age. One close friend, Barbara Hancock, considered Lady Ashton "an absolute angel who walked on earth".

Another elderly woman had been a good friend of Lady Ashton for the past quarter century. The two now lived in the same unit block in Raglan Street. Though remembering her companion as a generous person, kind to everybody, the woman tells how "Freda" would grow angry at mention of the man who had killed Gwen Mitchelhill, who was an acquaintance. "Once Freda was sounding off in a bus, 'Whoever this dreadful killer is, he should be caught and hanged!' and a young man stood up and said loudly to Lady Ashton, 'You're nothing but a so-and-so!' 'Well!' I said to Lady Ashton who was shocked at this, 'You shouldn't say those things in public!' But that was Freda, she would say exactly what was on her mind.

"Lady Ashton was devoted to elderly people and worked tirelessly to help them, taking them on outings and dropping in with a meal or to make a cup of tea. And she knew so many people in the area. She

knew all those women who were killed, Mrs Mitchelhill, Mrs Falconer. We'd all lived here for years and were all friends together. And
Freda was a fanatical bingo player and would play at Mosman RSL
or Manly RSL three times a week. Oh, and she was always on jury
duty. Even though she was elderly and not well at all, she was
mentally very alert and saw jury duty as a way of helping the
community. We were to have dinner together the night she died."

On her last day alive Lady Ashton dressed in a brown and white
striped dress, black shoes and bundled on gloves, a brown scarf,
brown woollen beanie and a red nylon raincoat to ward off the wintry
winds and showers predicted for that day, Tuesday, the 9th of May.
She left her Raglan Street home unit complex and caught a bus to the
Sydney Eye Hospital in Sir John Young Crescent near the Domain.
After having a glaucoma problem treated, she left the hospital mid-
morning and was next seen in typically high spirits playing bingo at
Mosman RSL where she was an active member. The popular old lady
was also a hearty participant in the various fund-raising raffles and
competitions held by the RSL. Only recently she had won a roast in
a club raffle and given it away, to a grateful neighbour in her unit
block.

Lady Ashton left Mosman RSL at 2.30pm and slowly made her way
south down Military Road to the shops near the Raglan Street
intersection. There she did her banking at the Commonwealth before
filling two supermarket carry bags with groceries. Shopping done as
4 o'clock approached, she hobbled the hundred metres or so to her
home.

John Glover was driving up Raglan Street to the RSL when he saw
the diminutive red-raincoated figure check her letterbox then turn
into the grounds of the home unit block at 186 Raglan Street. The
demons danced. He parked his white station wagon near the driveway, pulled on a pair of gloves and moved toward his quarry with a
lightness and speed that belied his bulk. None of the shoppers,
schoolchildren or commuters who milled around the busy junction
remembered seeing a thing.

Lady Ashton passed through the entry foyer and went to a rubbish
bin room on the ground floor. She was unaware that Glover was hard
on her heels. In the room, he grabbed her from behind, one hand
clapped to her mouth to stifle her screams and the other over her head

pulling her toward him. Glover jerked his victim backwards with such ferocity that he fell too, the pair crashing heavily to the concrete floor. Flailing at her in a homicidal fury he broke ribs with his punches and battered the old woman with her walking stick. He then took Lady Ashton's face in his hands and banged the back of her head on the floor until she ceased struggling and lay still. Glover would later revolt police by quipping, "Yes, for a little woman, she put up a good fight."

Removing her pantyhose, he tied the garment so tightly around her neck that fragments later were found embedded in the soft creases of Lady Ashton's throat. A post mortem showed that asphyxiation was the primary cause of death. Before fleeing, the killer spreadeagled the victim's legs and snatched a wallet and purses from her handbag. He then returned to his car, walking neither too fast nor too slow, pulled out from the kerb and disappeared into the traffic.

Incredibly, it was to Ashton Park near Bradley's Head, named after Lady Ashton's late husband Sir William, that he drove. There he got out of the car and walked into the bush. He removed money, more than $100, from the purses and threw them into the undergrowth. When questioned by detectives almost a year later, Glover could not remember whether he drove straight home after disposing of Lady Ashton's belongings or whether he continued his journey to the RSL for a bout with the pokies.

At 8 o'clock that evening John Ferke, a resident at 186 Raglan Street, heard a sound like garbage tins rattling below in the bin room. Thinking it was a friend from another unit, he started downstairs for a chat. At the bottom of the stairs he saw another neighbour coming from the direction of the bin room. The ashen-faced man ignored Ferke's cheery greeting and hurried past. Ferke continued to the bin room. There he saw the body of Lady Ashton lying diagonally across the room. Beneath her head was a small pool of blood. Strewn around her were a walking stick, a handbag, a gas bill and plastic grocery bags. Her shoes were placed neatly near her wooden cane. Ferke rushed to raise another neighbour. It was David McKinnon, the man to whom Lady Ashton had given the lucky RSL roast just days before.

* * *

It was at once clear to detectives of the Regional Crime Squad North at Chatswood, the team in charge of the investigation, that there were marked similarities between Gwen Mitchelhill's murder and that of Lady Ashton, although the first victim had not been strangled. Both were elderly. Both suffered horrific head injuries. Both were attacked in the foyer of their home units on arriving home from shopping. The two murder scenes were less than one kilometre apart. The purses of both victims had been stolen (although the extraordinary and excessive violence inflicted on the women seemed to rule out robbery as a primary motive). The possibility had to be faced that the same person or persons had killed both women.

Scientific and forensic examinations of the rubbish bin room and outside turned up no clues, so a massive-scale search and canvass of the district was mounted in the weeks that followed the Ashton killing. The parks, streets and beaches of Mosman were combed and more than 2000 premises visited and the residents interviewed. Several suspects were investigated and kept under surveillance. The community cowered in anticipation of another murder. Residents were counselled to beware, to travel in groups, not to take unnecessary risks. The district's locksmiths did record business as people reinforced their doors and windows. Miles O'Toole, interviewed by reporters, warned the elderly to be on their guard at all times because of the brazenness of the attacks.

Concerned and frightened residents assisted police all they could, but there are always oddballs. Paul Mayger shakes his head at some of the characters he encountered in that mass canvass of the area. "Once I knocked on the door of a house and it was opened by an extremely arrogant bloke aged about 18 or 19. I told him we were investigating the murders of Gwen Mitchelhill and Lady Ashton and this fellow just laughed and said he found it quite amusing that all these old ladies were being bumped off because they're only a drain on society anyway. I wanted to punch his lights out. I restrained myself, but it was a pleasure to add this person to the red-hot suspects list."

The fear and loathing was not confined to Mosman. Never before in Australia had a serial killer like this been on the loose. All over the country in homes, offices and factories people were talking of the way evil had come to, of all places, pleasant, leafy, middle-class Mosman. Workmates of John Glover can recall him dropping his jokey, knockabout facade for a moment to curse and say, "This bastard just *has* to be stopped." He had made the same pronouncement to his own family in the living room at Wyong Road.

Prime suspect at this stage was a man in his early 20s, 180 cm tall, slim, with a mop of blond hair. Police had been on the lookout for the man since April 26 when at 11.30pm he had crept up behind 60-year-old Raymond Roper, an SBS Television employee, in Raglan Street and struck him several times on the back of the head with a heavy object. However, in spite of lacerations that would need extensive stitching, the victim did not go down. Instead he turned on his attacker and yelled at him. The blond youth ran off into the night. What was of particular interest to police, in the light of the murders of the elderly women, was that Roper was wearing a long coat and a hat and to someone approaching in the darkness from behind, he may have looked like an old lady.

While detectives followed this line of investigation, Geoff Wright contacted Dr Rod Milton, a specialist forensic psychiatrist, and requested his assistance in composing a profile of the killer of Gwen Mitchelhill and Lady Ashton. After studying the information at hand Milton responded in writing. His report included the following points:

- While it was possible that the offender was a grossly mentally disturbed person, for example a schizophrenic, he believed it was more likely that the killer was not psychotic.
- The degree of violence exhibited pointed to the offender being male.
- The murderer was likely to be young, possibly of late teen age or in his early 20s. This conclusion because, in view of the lack of provocation, it was more probable that the degree of violence and the emotion underlying the violence would come from a younger, rather than an older, person.
- The proximity of the crimes suggested the offender lived in the vicinity. Possibly, considering that the crimes were committed midweek around 4 pm, he was a student at the local high school.
- Very violent crimes were often committed by men who felt vulnerable and who were themselves afraid of violence directed towards them, possibly by a dominating, angry and violent father. Boys so exposed to such a father could act paradoxically and identify with their tormentor. In the process the boy tended to look down on

anyone vulnerable, particularly women, and often the same women who had tried to protect him and indulge him, for example his mother or grandmother.

- Therefore the killer might be a lad in his late teens, attending the local high school, with a dominating, brutal and probably successful father and a protective and indulgent mother. The father might be of an orderly nature, perhaps from a military back ground, and this might account for the neat arrangement of the shoes and walking sticks at the murder scenes.

- The lad was likely to be living still in the family home, although possibly his parents were separated and he lives with his mother, though in conflict with her.

- Police would be advised to approach the principal of the local high school who might be prepared to talk to the staff individually to see if they might be aware of any male students in the 16-18 age range who seemed unhappy, who tended to be daydreamers, not doing too well at school, who were known to be having difficulties in their relationships with their fathers or mothers, and — because of the powerful blows delivered to the thorax of the victims — might have an interest in or have been trained in boxing.

- The offender would present reasonably well at interview, although the interviewer would get no feeling of openness or honesty from him. He would not show much feeling, probably be reasonably tall, possibly be stooped as evidence of his own fear of attack. He might sweat freely. He was likely to be afraid of police as authority figures while having a degree of admiration for them, perhaps identifying with them.

- The act of strangling victims with their own pantyhose might be interpreted as an insulting act of defilement.

- The offender would be unlikely to make close friends, and probably not have regular girlfriends, though he might make a relationship with a girl who adopted a submissive attitude towards men. He was unlikely to be an obvious bully, but would more likely be regarded as "creepy" by other students. If he had male friends, they would be acquaintances rather than close mates.

- He would probably not seek counselling or therapy help for his inner thoughts would be so secretive and violent that he would be afraid to reveal these to anyone.

- The violence shown in the crimes, the risks taken by the offender and the likelihood of extremely powerful underlying emotional conflict, suggested that if the offender were not apprehended he would commit further offences.

* * *

Two months after the murder of Lady Ashton, Margaret Dickson, an accountant from Glebe, was walking with her family through Ashton Park near Bradley's Head. They came upon a maroon leather wallet lying in the bush near a stone wall. Investigating, they saw that the wallet contained papers identifying its owner as Lady Winfreda Ashton of Raglan Street. Assuming the wallet had been lost or stolen Margaret Dickson that afternoon deposited the wallet in the letterbox that had once been Lady Ashton's.

Since the death of Lady Ashton in May, her neighbour Nelune Rajapakse had regularly cleared the letterbox of her much-missed old friend. On July 15 when she checked the box she found inside a red leather wallet. She took the wallet immediately to Mosman police station. Police made a public call for the person who had put the wallet in the letterbox to come forward. Margaret Dickson did so and accompanied police to Ashton Park where she showed them where she had found the murdered woman's belongings. Police found the remainder of Lady Ashton's property in bushland nearby.

CHAPTER 6

Assault
And Battery

J ohn Glover's job as a sales representative for Four 'N Twenty Pies gave him the freedom to roam. Up until July 10, 1989, his territory was Sydney's north shore area which extended from Neutral Bay and Mosman on Sydney Harbour up through Lane Cove, Chatswood, Belrose and on to Killara, Hornsby and the Central Coast areas such as Gosford, Woy Woy and Ettalong. Then, when another sales representative resigned in July, Glover was allocated his territory as well which made him responsible for collecting orders, dealing with customer complaints and maintaining accounts all over the Sydney metropolitan area. However Glover continued to stick pretty much to his home turf, the north shore.

His working day would begin at six or 6.30am. An early start meant an early finish and so more time to play the poker machines in the afternoon before heading home to the family. Always first out of bed in the house, he would shower and dress in one of his two work outfits: black shoes, grey trousers, blue shirt, tie, and a company-supplied blue Sunbuster spray jacket, or brown shoes, brown trousers, white or light-coloured shirt, tie and the spray jacket or a brown leather sports jacket with patches on the elbows. After wolfing down a quick breakfast and catching up on the news on ABC radio he was on the road. Glover drove a white Ford Falcon company station wagon until September 5, 1990, when Four 'N Twenty replaced it with a blue Falcon station wagon.

Glover was not directly accountable for his movements during the day, and checked in at Four 'N Twenty's Alexandria headquarters only when he had to, but he was expected to put in 40 hours work a week canvassing the catering staff at retirement villages and nursing homes, as well as the proprietors and stock purchasers of milk bars, grocery stores and supermarkets. He never kept a log.

The grey-haired pie salesman was well-known and accepted by his clients. They considered him a jovial man, smart-witted and pleasant, at times a little risque, perhaps, but not pushy like some of the reps. Many of the women he called on admitted that they found him attractive, a fine figure of man, always neatly-dressed, nicely-spoken and an altogether decent type.

Carrying his order book and clipboard which contained all the prices of the assorted pies, cakes, donuts and pizzas that comprised the Four 'N Twenty product range, Glover would drop in, ask for a moment of the customer's time, and take any orders, writing them on foolscap sheets headed with the words "Four 'N Twenty Pies, John W. Glover Area Manager". At the top right hand corner of the sheet was an overweight cartoon blackbird in a red and white checked bib licking his beak. On obtaining an order, it was Glover's duty to pass the details on to private delivery contractors who would stock up at the Alexandria store and deliver to the customer.

The job, to Glover, was not the be-all-and-end-all, but it paid the bills, fuelled his poker machine addiction and provided plenty of opportunities to placate his demons.

* * *

At 12.45pm on June 28, 1989, the month after the violent slaying of Lady Winfreda Ashton in Mosman, Sister Margaret Whitehead, a nurse at the Wesley Gardens Retirement Village at Belrose, observed a stocky, silver-white-haired man wearing grey slacks and a blue spray jacket staring intently at an elderly patient who lay in one of the beds in the room. Sensing something was wrong, she approached the man, whom she had never seen around the village before.

"Are you looking for Mrs Pople?" she asked.

"No," replied the man, "I've come to see Rob in the kitchen, but I've lost a very valuable gold pen with a chain on it."

"Well," said the nurse, "you go and look in the car park and I'll put an announcement over the loudspeaker."

"Fine, that's a good idea," said the man and he left the room.

Sister Whitehead, deeply suspicious, made her way to the kitchen to check the stranger's story with the chef, Robert Murrell.

Meanwhile John Glover, clipboard in hand, continued to stalk the corridors. Halted by two cleaners who asked him what he was doing wandering about, he repeated that he was looking for Rob the chef and could they please tell him where the kitchen was. The pair gave directions and Glover walked off.

A short time later the cleaners encountered Glover back where they had first seen him. When they asked him had he located Rob, he replied that he had not, but that he'd lost his gold pen and was searching for it. He then left the building and made towards the village carpark. Minutes later the cleaners saw him walking slowly around the carpark, which faces on to Forest Way. The deputy director of nursing at Wesley Gardens, Lorraine van der Linden, also saw Glover leave the building and stroll to the carpark, where she knew that one of the elderly residents of the hospital was taking a daily walk.

When questioned months later about his reign of terror, Glover always claimed that he could not help himself. The urge to damage and humiliate elderly women was irresistible. Don't blame him, blame the demons. He said such was the case this day.

"How are you?" Glover asked the 77-year-old walking in the carpark. She was wearing a pink tracksuit. He put his arm around her shoulder. Then he touched her on the breast.

Terrified, the old lady could mutter only, "I'll be alright," as she tried to escape. Then, "No... no... no!" as he followed her towards the village church. Glover turned on his heel, climbed into his car and drove away.

Safely inside the building, the elderly woman went straight to the nursing station where she found Sister Whitehead. "Oh Marnie," she cried, "you'll never believe what just happened to me. I was up in the top car park and a man touched me on the breast." The victim, a manic depressive with many physical disorders and at the time undergoing shock treatment, could shed little light on the appearance of the man who had menaced her. The assault, like other assaults that Glover committed in nursing homes in the months of June, July, August and September, 1989, was not reported to police.

* * *

All salesmen have to cope with knockbacks and so it was for John Glover when he ran into a brick wall in the shape of cook Helen Roe at the Caroline Chisholm Nursing Home in Lane Cove on July 24. In spite of his best efforts to convince her to place an order for his sausage rolls and pies, she would have none of it. "Then how about some lamingtons?" persisted Glover. Again he was told no. Taking up his clipboard, he patted Helen Roe on the shoulder, said, "Thanks anyway, love" and walked out of the kitchen.

Later she remembered how she had thought the pie salesman well-dressed, well-spoken and extremely good-looking with his neatly-cut white-grey hair and his light brown leather coat, brown slacks and brown shoes. She could not, however, when later asked, remember which company the salesman was representing and he had left no paperwork behind.

Glover had come to the kitchen by a circuitous route. Shortly before, he had been surprised on an upper floor of the nursing home by diversional therapist Stephanye Holden who demanded to know what he was doing lurking in room 45. "Which patient do you want?" she asked.

"I want the kitchen," Glover replied.

"Then follow me," said the therapist as she led him back down the stairs to where the meals were prepared. Glover was presented to Helen Roe and Stephanye Holden went about her business.

Some time later, around 2.30, the therapist was working in the area where Glover had been and entered a resident's room, No.32. The elderly woman looked at the nursing home staffer with terror in her eyes. "I'm frightened of the man," she said.

On leaving the kitchen Glover had returned upstairs. He walked unopposed into room 28, where he saw a 69-year-old resident alone in the room lying on her bed with her back to the door. The woman had returned recently from lunch and was wearing a black winter frock. Glover crept up behind the dozing woman, lifted her dress and placed his hand on her bare buttocks. She swung around but her attacker was gone. Moments later she saw through the door a "well-groomed man with excellent carriage" passing along the corridor.

The well-groomed man marched straight to room 32 where an 85-year-old woman lay alone. He plunged his hand down the front of her nightie and touched her breast then left without a word. The woman remained on the bed, scared and stunned, until Stephanye Holden came in half an hour later.

Glover's first victim, the 69-year-old woman, also reported her incident to Stephanye Holden. "Gee, Stephanye," she said when the therapist entered her room, "I just had a funny experience. A well-dressed man just came in and pulled up my skirt and looked at my bottom."

"What did the man look like?"

"A tan jacket — leather, brown pants, white hair and good-looking," the old woman replied.

Realising this was the exact description of the man she had earlier escorted to the kitchen, Stephanye Holden returned to the 85 year old's room. "Tell me about the man," she said.

"He put his hand down the front of my nightie," she said and indicated her breasts.

"What colour coat was this man wearing?"

"Brown."

Stephanye Holden reported the incidents to the matron of the nursing home. Police were not called but the Caroline Chisholm staff were given a description of the man and told to report him at once to the matron should he show his face on the premises again.

Three days later Glover was back. At 2.45 a nurse, Susan Roughton, saw a man who answered the rogue salesman's appearance striding along a ground floor corridor. She followed him into the lounge of the nursing home and saw him take a look around before walking back to the corridor that led to the patients' rooms. Susan Roughton confronted the visitor. "Do you want any help?"

"I'm looking for the public telephone," Glover replied pleasantly.

The nurse led him to the telephone and stood with him until he picked up the receiver. She then withdrew but continued to watch him from around a corner. Glover stood there, the telephone handset raised to his face, but he did not speak and he inserted no coins. She watched his eyes dart about and settle on a patient's room near the phone. Glover then replaced the handset and walked straight upstairs.

Susan Roughton raced to Matron Borton and the pair set off after the intruder. They stopped him in a corridor near the top of the stairs. "I'm the matron. Can I help you?" said Matron Borton. Glover feigned confusion and indicated he was looking for a neighbouring retirement village. The two women escorted Glover out of the premises and last saw him crossing the car park.

* * *

When Euphemia Carnie first saw John Glover he was about 10 metres away, a distinguished-looking, middle-aged gent walking in her direction up Treatts Road, Lindfield, near the entrance to North Haven Retirement Village where the 82 year old was a resident. The gent looked like a company man taking care of business, which is in fact what Glover was: he'd considered North Haven a likely customer for Four 'N Twenty products but had not entered when he discovered it was a self-care establishment and so not in the market for pre-cooked pastries.

As Glover approached, he came close to the elderly woman, so close she was sure he was about to ask her a question. But no alarm bells rang until she saw him, right upon her now, form a fist with his right hand. Next thing Euphemia Carnie knew she was flat on her back on the footpath, a searing pain in her chest where he had viciously punched her and the back of her head throbbing from where it had bounced off the concrete path.

Glover prised the woman's handbag and her groceries from her grip and, leaving the woman floundering on the ground, calmly returned to his car and drove away. This was August 25, 1pm, the middle of the day in a busy suburb, and nobody saw a thing.

Euphemia Carnie dragged herself to her feet and staggered the short distance to the retirement village. Police were notified.

Meanwhile Glover rifled through the handbag. Inside were keys, glasses, a library card, bank books and a brown leather purse containing $80. Glover took the money, put it in his own wallet, then drove to Soldiers Memorial Park in Tryon Road, Lindfield, where he hurled the other stolen goods into the bush. He then drove down the Pacific Highway to Mosman and the RSL club where he fed Euphemia Carnie's $80 into a poker machine.

* * *

Phyliss McNeill was blind but nevertheless knew something was wrong. She had been alone in her room at Wybenia Nursing Home, Neutral Bay, when someone entered.

The male voice was deep and soothing, "Now, what are you doing in here all alone?" It was a voice she had never heard before. Something in the man's tone disturbed the woman.

"I'm eating my dinner. Who are you?" she said.

"I'm Dr Brown."

"I don't think we need you here," Phyllis McNeill snapped. "We have our own doctors."

There was silence, no sound for five minutes, then a rustle as John Glover lifted the woman's nightie and dressing gown and touched her on the thigh. Although 86, frail and unable to see, she rounded on this person who was taking such liberties with her. "How dare you do that to me! Who *are* you?"

"I'm a doctor," came the soothing reply. "It's alright, it's alright."

His voice betrayed his lie. Phyllis McNeill reached out to where she knew her security button was and pounded on it. Glover rushed from the room and left the building. By the time a nursing sister answered the buzzer and found the blind woman in a highly-distressed state, Glover had entered his blue station wagon which he had parked in Wycombe Road outside the nursing home and was speeding up towards Military Road. A nurse at the home, Tess Diaz, saw his departure and made a mental note of the man's appearance and the date, September 6, 1989. Later she would be able to help police with their enquiries.

* * *

When the demons danced, as they did again on October 18, just the sight of an elderly woman was enough to trigger John Glover's murderous fury and the sickness commanded nothing less than immediate action. His urge to hurt and humiliate was irresistible.

Around 4pm the salesman was making a telephone call from the post office at Spit Junction, just across from the Garrison Retirement Village in Spit Road. Mid-conversation he caught sight of 86-year-old Doris Cox, a resident of the village, making slow progress along the footpath outside the Garrison. He burst out of the post office, crossed the road and slowed as he approached the woman. The need to vent his rage on her was urgent and all-consuming and left Glover no time to fetch the claw hammer from under the front seat of his car. It was this oversight that saved Doris Cox's life.

Drawing level with the old lady, Glover made pleasant small talk. To anyone passing by, he could have been her son, a study in solicitude as he led the aged and ailing woman into the grounds of the village, along a secluded walkway. When they reached a flight of steps, like any gentleman would, he let the lady proceed first.

At the bottom of the descent, Glover exploded. He charged at Doris Cox from behind, pounding her head with his fists. Then taking the back of her head with both hands he pushed her face into a brick wall with all his force. He kept pushing, as if to ram her head clear through the bricks, until she collapsed on to the ground and lay motionless.

Glover stormed through the fallen woman's handbag in search of money but found none and discarded the bag on the path near the victim. He then returned to his car parked near the post office and drove the kilometre or so home to Wyong Road.

At the same time that Glover was changing out of his work clothes and preparing to settle down for a relaxing evening, perhaps an hour or two on the pokies at Mosman RSL, dinner with the family and TV, two passing women, Mere Savu and Kui Harris, heard a feeble cry for help coming from the grounds of the Garrison. They immediately investigated and found Doris Cox sitting on the path at the foot of the steps. Her arms were extended toward her rescuers and she continued to cry, "Help, help." Her head and body were bathed in blood and in one hand she held her dentures. The pair assisted the battered woman into the foyer of the Garrison where staff took over.

At first it was thought that the dazed and incoherent woman had fallen down the stairs, but on examining her injuries ambulance officers became convinced Doris Cox was the victim of a vicious assault and summoned police. Miles O'Toole, investigating the incident, saw at once that there were similarities between Doris Cox's wounds and those of Gwen Mitchelhill and Lady Ashton, both of whom were murdered within walking distance of the Garrison. Although residents of the village hosed down the blood-spattered pathway before police arrived, so obliterating any clues, police at last, as they said, had "a live one". O'Toole and his fellow investigators had high hopes that when recovered she may be able to supply a description of her assailant and give them the breakthrough they needed.

As soon as Doris Cox was able to talk the following day, Miles O'Toole and Detective Sen Const Dave Forbes of the Physical Evidence Section sped to her bedside at Royal North Shore Hospital. The old woman was a distressing sight. The attacker had knocked out five of her teeth, broken her nose, fractured her cheekbone and inflicted many other cuts and abrasions, including two wounds on her head that required 11 stitches and eight stitches respectively. O'Toole rounded angrily on one doctor who insisted the injuries had been caused by a fall, then introduced himself to Doris Cox and asked the woman did she remember anything about what had happened the day before.

"Yes," she replied, "of course I do." You beauty, thought the detectives.

"Go ahead, Doris," said O'Toole, "tell us."

"Well, I'd been to my sister's and came back home."

"Your sister, what's her name?"

Doris Cox told her sister's name.

"Where does your sister live?"

The battered woman gave an address, reeled off her sister's telephone number, and said, "I had morning tea with her and then we had lunch and later I caught the bus home to the Garrison at Spit Junction and I walked up the path."

The detectives were impressed by her prompt and concise answers and excellent recall for one so old and in such a condition.

"What happened on the path?" O'Toole honed in.

"Well, I went home."

"No, no, what happened on the path?"

"I *told* you, *nothing* happened on the path, young man. I just went home."

It was clear to the detectives that something was drastically amiss. While Dave Forbes photographed Doris Cox's injuries, O'Toole left the room and returned with a mirror. He held it up in front of her face. "Look, *something* happened on the path, Doris. *This* happened on the path!"

The woman looked into the mirror and calmly replied, "What are you showing me her for? She's not me."

By now at his wits' end, O'Toole tried another tack. He telephoned Doris Cox's sister. An Asian woman answered the phone. In halting English she explained that she and her family had lived at that address for nine years. Doris Cox's sister had lived there 13 years ago but the old woman had been dead for a decade.

Later that evening Miles O'Toole perused Doris Cox's medical records at the Garrison and discovered that the woman suffered from senile dementia, Alzheimer's disease. For her the attack that all but claimed her life had never happened. John Glover's luck was holding.

Two days later Doris Cox was moved back to the Garrison, to the anger of some staff members who believed her still-grotesquely swollen features would frighten other residents. Forensic pathologist Dr Johan DuFlou and his assistant Dr Lilliana Schwartz arrived to examine the wounds on Doris Cox's head to see if they were consistent with those of Gwen Mitchelhill. As the doctors prodded and scraped and measured the cuts, Doris Cox squirmed in discomfort and fired insults at them. "You're a queer-looking doctor," was one barb she directed at DuFlou. The detectives stifled a smile when DuFlou, most of whose examinations were performed on corpses at the City Morgue, quipped to the wriggling woman, "This is a change for me. Most of my patients are not ticklish at all!"

"It did take us a long time to examine Mrs Cox," says DuFlou, who would oversee the post mortems of all of the killer's victims. "We had to look for all the wounds. When we have to examine a corpse we automatically shave all the hair off so any head wounds are immediately apparent. But because she was still alive, we were unable to subject Doris to this indignity. So we had to comb through her hair very, very carefully and didn't she get impatient with us!"

Although the forensic pathologists were able to confirm that Doris Cox's injuries were caused by an assault and not a fall, they could not say with any certainty that the wounds were caused by the same blunt instrument that had inflicted similar damage on the other woman.

In the end, all that police investigating the attempted murder of Doris Cox were left with was the description of a youth of medium build with dark hair, shorn at the sides and long on top, who at around 4pm, the time of the assault, was seen bursting out of the bushes at the Garrison on a skateboard and startling a group of old people. The woman who reported the youth to police was affronted by the fellow's behaviour and bemoaned the lack of respect shown to the elderly by young people these days.

CHAPTER 7

The Gathering Storm

Madge Pahud was the scourge of Lane Cove Council. As a resident of the graceful old middle north shore suburb for many years, the 85-year-old took a fierce pride in her suburb and loved nothing better than a dust-up with the local aldermen whenever they displeased her. Her daughter Elaine Avis laughs today about how her mum, "a feisty old bird", was outraged when the council put a pedestrian plaza in the middle of the Lane Cove shopping area. What particularly irked Madge Pahud was the way people would sit on the benches in the plaza and eat their lunch then leave their rubbish behind. Lane Cove was beginning to resemble a garbage dump, she griped. One day she became so annoyed that she had her son-in-law accompany her to the plaza with a camera and take photographs of all the papers lying under the benches. She then stormed into the council chambers and threatened to release the photo to the press if something was not done to curb the littering.

"Oh, those councillors must have hated it every time they saw Mum burst through their doors," Elaine Avis chuckles. "She was a strong and independent woman, always telling people exactly what she thought of them. She'd never let anybody stand over her. If she'd had her umbrella handy she would have really laid into the man who killed her."

Although clearly not to be trifled with, Madge Pahud had many friends. She was a plump woman with a beaming smile and people were attracted by her sense of fun and lively wit. She was also heavily involved in Legacy and often organised visits to the theatre for Legacy ladies. Madge Pahud was always out and about, invariably preferring to do business in person rather than use a telephone. She was a familiar figure walking the short distance from Lane Cove shops to the unit behind the Kamilaroi Retirement Village in Longueville Road where she had lived alone since the death of her husband Sid some years before.

One of Madge Pahud's best friends was Dorothy Beencke, an elderly woman who lived in the same unit block but on the floor above. The pair visited each other frequently and Madge would always water Dorothy's plants when she was away.

About 2pm on Thursday, November 2, Dorothy Beencke told police later, she was returning home from shopping, laden with bags, when she was approached by a man she described as "65 years old, medium build, and healthy for his age" who offered to help her carry her groceries from Longueville Road down the 100-metre-long private laneway to her unit. "Can I carry your bags? They look too heavy for you," he said.

The woman at first declined but when the man insisted pleasantly she let him have his way. "Well, alright. It's nice to know there are still some gentlemen around."

"And it's nice to know there are still some ladies around, also," the charming stranger replied. "Now where are you going?"

"I live down by Kamilaroi."

"Well, I don't know that way. I'll follow you."

Dorothy Beencke, who would later tell police that this friendly, well-dressed man could never have done anyone any harm, led the way and he followed behind carrying the parcels.

Passing the front yard, the man commented, "You have a nice pool there, I suppose you swim in it?"

"No," replied the woman.

When they reached the entrance to her unit block the man put the shopping bags on a telephone stool by her front door and said goodbye.

"Thank you so much," said Dorothy Beencke as the man disappeared back up the laneway.

John Glover would later tell police that he had singled out Dorothy Beencke as his next victim but somewhere in that laneway his demons had subsided, he didn't know why, and he had decided to let her live.

Like Madge Pahud, who had been out and about since the early morning chatting to friends, banking, buying groceries and borrowing two books from the library, John Glover had had a busy day. Clipboard in hand he'd called on a number of Four 'N Twenty clients on the north shore before finishing just before 2pm at Lane Cove. After helping Dorothy Beencke with her parcels he returned to his blue Ford Falcon station wagon parked in Longueville Road. There, claw hammer at his feet, Glover, once more in the mood to murder, waited and watched.

At about 3pm he saw Madge Pahud, wearing a red and brown floral skirt and top and carrying a shopping bag in each hand, walking toward him. She moved briskly, in spite of the fact that she was still recuperating from broken ribs suffered in a car accident just weeks before. Glover reached down for the hammer and tucked it into his trousers, then set off in pursuit of the woman. When she turned into the leafy walkway that led to her unit block, the same walkway down which he had accompanied Dorothy Beencke just an hour before, he made his move. Glover swung his hammer with unrestrained ferocity, bringing it down hard three times on the back of the head of Madge Pahud. The blows sent her sprawling to the pathway where she lay in a widening pool of blood.

Glover put the blood-flecked hammer back in his trousers, coolly unconcerned by the fact that schoolchildren were streaming out of the Lane Cove Primary School grounds just metres away on the other side of the walkway fence. Amazingly, as with his other murders, no blood stained his clothes. He picked up the handbag that had fallen by Madge Pahud's grocery bags and returned up the walkway to his car.

Minutes later the mortally-wounded woman was seen lying face down on the path by a nine-year-old schoolgirl who tore off to fetch her mother. Doctors were summoned and neighbours tried to stem the bleeding with towels. One passerby, familiar with first aid technique, sat Madge Pahud in the coma position. But it was too late. By the time the ambulance arrived she was gone. After the body was taken away but before the police arrived, neighbours brought hoses, hard-bristled brooms, detergent and bleach and washed and scrubbed the bloodstains — and any clues — away. Among the cleaners was Dorothy Beencke.

John Glover put the claw hammer back under the front seat of his car and drove along Longueville Road to River Road where he pulled into the Lane Cove Country Club. He parked the station wagon near the entrance to the club, took more than $300 cash from the purses contained in the handbag and shoved the bag into a stormwater drain. Days later a jogger found the waterlogged bag after rain had washed it down the drain and into the open and notified police that it belonged to Madge Pahud. Police cordoned off the area. Twenty officers from the Tactical Response Group combed the surrounds but found nothing. Police conducted forensic tests on the bag but the tests were fruitless.

After dumping the handbag John Glover made a final call that day — to the Mosman RSL Club where he drank some wine and played his poker machine into the early evening. Thursday night at the club is rock 'n' roll night and the Glover family often made an evening of it, and none of them were slouches on the dance floor. Many members recall often seeing the paunchy figure of John Glover dancing, feet kicking, arms flailing, with his daughters Kellie and Marney, although none questioned later could recall whether he kicked up his heels on this particular night.

The savage wounds inflicted on Madge Pahud erased any thoughts that she had fallen down or suffered a heart attack. As police gathered after the post mortem to co-ordinate their investigation they knew — in spite of the fact that the murder scene had once more been washed clean of clues before their arrival — that the murderer of Gwen Mitchelhill and Lady Ashton had found a new killing field.

As twilight fell and Mike Hagan, Miles O'Toole, Paul Mayger and their colleagues swung into action in the just-commandeered Lane Cove police station, Elaine Avis's telephone rang in her West Killara home. Madge Pahud's only daughter found herself being questioned by a doctor from Lane Cove. He wanted to know who her mother's regular doctor was and what medical problems she suffered from. When Elaine Avis asked was her mother alright, she was told that she was in excellent health. The doctor rang back 20 minutes later and told the concerned woman to make her way to Royal North Shore Hospital. There was no rush, he said.

When Elaine Avis arrived at the casualty ward she noticed many uniformed police hanging about. She asked the nurse on duty if she could see her mother, Madge Pahud. She was taken immediately to an interview room. Police, a social worker and a nurse were there.

The nurse hugged her. "My mother is dead, isn't she." Elaine Avis learned how her mother had died. She identified the body then, too shocked to drive, was taken home by her husband.

Even today, she says, just hearing or reading a news report of a murder is enough to freeze her to the marrow and bring flooding back the dreadful events of November 2, 1989.

* * *

"We've got another one," Doodles O'Toole informed the stunned detectives in the little room at Regional Crime Squad North headquarters at Chatswood the next day, November 3. While Miles O'Toole and Paul Mayger returned to Lane Cove and the Madge Pahud murder investigation, detectives including Geoff Wright, Murray Byrnes and Barry Keeling sped east to Forest Way, Belrose, to the Wesley Gardens Retirement Village. They were led to the village mortuary where they saw the body of Olive Cleveland. The dead woman lay on a trolley, her head and face horrifically bruised and lacerated. Her features were distorted. Detectives become hardened to death and suffering but they'll tell you that nothing ever prepares them for sights such as they encountered that day.

Olive Cleveland had never married and this, she had once joked, was the reason why she had lived so long. Just recently however she had begun to show her 81 years. She was growing increasingly vague and becoming dogged by a variety of illnesses. To other residents of Wesley Gardens Retirement Village she fretted that it was getting harder and harder to look after herself. She was a thin woman with shortish frizzy hair, a high forehead and prominent teeth set in a wide mouth. She wore pink-framed glasses.

She was, remembers her brother William today, a stenographer – – "and a very good one, too" — with the Institute of Engineers in Sydney until she retired, aged 60. "Oll never married because she devoted her life to our parents. Mum was blind. My sister was never interested in marriage. She went out a bit with boys when she was younger, but not much. She was a bit self-conscious about being tall and flat-chested in an era when such a look wasn't fashionable and maybe that had something to do with it. But, no, right from the early days she decided to be an old maid. She liked that sort of life. Right up to her old age she was a very private person who liked to mind her own business and she didn't take part in any social activities at all.

She kept to herself. Oll had a very definite sense of what she wanted to do and how she was going to do it."

On the Sunday before she died, William Cleveland and his wife Merle visited Olive Cleveland at Wesley Gardens. The three old people sat in the garden on a seat by a fish pond. Olive Cleveland gazed at the silver and orange fish while William, a staunch Baptist, read to her from his Bible. The seat in the garden was one of Olive Cleveland's favourite places in the world. She was sitting there shortly after lunch the following Friday, when fellow residents last saw her alive.

On that day, November 3, Olive Cleveland left her room in the south wing of the village at 12.15 and walked slowly to the dining room. After a lunch of chicken casserole with peas, carrots and rice, then steamed pudding and custard, she handed her empty plates to Jan Penicka the kitchen hand and at 12.45 walked out into the grounds. She was sitting on the seat by the fish pond in the garden when John Glover joined her.

The salesman was at Wesley Gardens on business. He knew he'd been recognised after his indecent assault of the elderly shock treatment patient in the car park there on June 28, but brazenly, and typically, he'd returned to try to sell his wares at Wesley Gardens a number of times since. Although so far he'd had no luck in coercing the chef Robert Murrell to buy his pastries he was back again today for another try. However the chef had left early, leaving Glover at a loose end.

He sat there on the seat close beside Olive Cleveland, a charming and amusing maker of smalltalk. Dressed in slacks, shirt, tie and spray jacket, he had with him his clipboard but not, this time, the hammer. The weapon, with bloodstains upon it not yet 24 hours old, remained in his station wagon in the car park. He'd come to Wesley Gardens to sell pies, not kill, but when the demons called, Glover answered.

He told police when it was all over that he decided to murder Olive Cleveland only when the old lady got up off the seat and made to return inside the village building. He related how just as she was about to enter the doorway leading inside he pushed her around the corner. Once in the side passageway, the heavyset attacker savaged his 46kg quarry to the ground. As she lay there face down he leapt astride her back and took her head in his hands and crashed it repeatedly on to the concrete path. When Olive Cleveland was still, he pulled her dress up around her thighs, stripped off her grey pantyhose and tied them tightly in a bow around the right side of his victim's neck, strangling her. Glover then removed $60 from the woman's purse, walked nonchalantly back to the car park, climbed into his vehicle and drove away.

At 4.25pm a resident saw the body of an aged woman lying, legs wide apart, in a puddle of blood in the passage. Her face was so badly battered as to be unrecognisable, but the resident identified the woman's distinctive dark-green, light-green and white-striped dress as one often worn by her occasional shopping mate Olive Cleveland. Before crying for help the thought registered that her friend was not wearing stockings.

The hostel manager of Wesley Gardens, Anne Moyle, on hearing the resident's cry that there was a "lady laying down" in the grounds feared a serious accident had taken place and in turn summoned Jan Penicka from the kitchen. As she approached the corner of the building Jan Penicka saw a pair of feet protruding from the passageway. Closer investigation revealed the body of Olive Cleveland lying on her left side with her left cheek on the ground. She thought then that the blood that haloed the old woman's head had been there for some time as it had seeped into the concrete. The kitchen hand touched one of the deceased's feet and it was cold. She placed a blanket over the body which was then lifted on to a trolley and taken to the mortuary. It was only then that the pantyhose, an obscene bowtie, was seen knotted tightly around the victim's throat. This was no fall or, as some had at first suspected, a suicide. The police were called.

CHAPTER 8

On The Edge

With the murder of Olive Cleveland, the New South Wales Government gave police hierarchy the go-ahead to deem the North Shore Murders probe a Major Investigation, thereby making all funds, resources and expertise available to the newly-formed task force which set up headquarters in the Regional Crime Squad office in Chatswood, the geographical heart of Sydney's north shore.

The workload of the hand-picked investigators, led by Detective Insp Mike Hagan, was massive. Among the assignments allotted to the team of homicide detectives, surveillance police, computer experts, analysts, medical and forensic officers throughout the five months of the task force's operation were:

- Take detailed statements from all those in the vicinity of the murder and assault scenes, from witnesses to incidents, from informants, and from relatives and friends of victims.
- Canvass all north shore retirement villages, nursing homes and surrounding areas.
- Conduct scientific and forensic examinations of murder and assault sites and attend all post mortems of victims.
- Probe prior movements and associations of victims.
- Determine if there are any common denominators between victims.
- Issue regular press releases to the media and pamphlets giving safety advice to the elderly.
- Uniformed and plain clothes officers to patrol retirement villages, nursing homes, shopping centres and all places frequented by the elderly.
- Enter all details of past murders similar to those currently under investigation in the task force computer for comparison.
- Canvass transport systems and delivery services.

- Investigate releasees from prisons and psychiatric institutions with a history of assault or murder.
- Institute and maintain the MIIRS computerised running sheet programme.
- Canvass dry cleaners for bloodstained clothing.
- Brief and commission forensic psychiatrist to compose a profile of the offender.
- Liaise with Neighbourhood Watch, aged persons organisations, community groups.

Seven days a week, task force Commander Hagan and his deputy commanders and chief investigators Geoff Wright and Ron Smith would meet at 7am and, using MIIRS, the computerised running sheet system, sift through what had happened the day and night before. Considering existing assignments that needed follow-up along with new developments and information, they would then allocate priorities to all the jobs that needed to be done that day. At 8am the investigators — 35 when the task force began on November 4, double that when the workload burgeoned out of control after the serial killer claimed yet another victim on November 26 — would arrive and form a circle around the three commanders.

Each morning that bleary-eyed throng would include the crack homicide detectives Miles O'Toole, Paul Mayger, Murray Byrnes, Barry Keeling and Paul Jacob; the surveillance supervisor Doodles O'Toole; John May and his surveillance team; Dave Hughes, Dave Forbes and Phil Flogel of the Physical Evidence Unit; and Detective Sen Const Kim McGee, a policewoman seconded from the Sexual Assault Squad. They and their fellow investigators would brief colleagues and commanders on work in progress and then Dad and Brown Eyes would load up the already sorely-overburdened task force members with new jobs to do. These daily briefings became a focal point of the task force's activities.

Much of Wright and Smith's day was spent reading the running sheets to gather information on the murders and assaults that would be loaded into the computers in the incident room and end up as assignments to be allocated next morning. Because no detail, no matter how small or seemingly insignificant, on those computer printouts could afford to be missed, as one would read a sheet he would pass it to the other for a second look. Thus the equivalent of

10,000 A4 pages of data were digested by Wright and Smith. The weight of their reading duties often kept them in the dingy, window-less interview room at Chatswood from seven in the morning until 10 or 11 o'clock at night. The room became known variously as "the bunker", "the dungeon" and "the bridge".

"I nearly went berserk in that room, mate, I can tell you," grimaces Geoff Wright today. "Just reading and reading. You can only read for so long before your mind begins to go and you start glazing over and that's when things get missed. But we kept at it every day, sitting down so long at a stretch that the chair would cut off the circulation at the back of our legs. I'd go home at night to try to get a little sleep and the pain in my legs would keep me awake. Then because there was no natural light in the bunker, just fluorescent light, we suffered from dreadful eye strain until we had special reading lights in-stalled."

"Often," says Ron Smith, "I just had to get up and go for a walk, anywhere. To the shops, buy a sandwich, anything for a bit of relief. What kept us going was the chance that each new day might bring a clue to the identity of the murderer."

Close by the bunker was the incident room with its desks, whiteboards, computers and their attendant tangle of cables and leads, where Bob Myers and Gordon Green and their team of Vince Valente and Annie Langford supervised the MIIRS computer system which stored and retrieved all the data of the investigation. MIIRS replaced the time-consuming and unwieldy old-style manual run-ning sheet system that tied up investigators with paperwork when they could have been out on the job. It was their brief to feed the computerised running sheet data from the incident room, nicknamed "the engine room", to Wright and Smith in the bridge.

Now and then Ron Smith would break up the investigators by standing outside the bridge with an electric microphone and yelling, "Bridge to engine room, bridge to engine room. Less speed! Less speed!"

The beauty of MIIRS was that it could cross-reference. Any previously-entered detail in the computer, no matter what aspect or category of the investigation it pertained to, could be searched for, found, and linked with associated details, therefore opening a line of investigation or allowing the compilation of a flow chart. Given the hundreds of thousands of pieces of data entered during the investigation, this was to prove a blessing.

As the investigation ground on, there was recorded in those computers, on disk, a growing number of references to a middle-aged, grey-haired man. Witnesses had seen him in the vicinity of the various assaults but often, when questioned by police, had included him in their recollections of the scene almost as an afterthought. Says Bob Myers, "We had a very vague description of the man who ultimately turned out to be the killer in the computer system from the start but we had no way of knowing who he was until later when the pie salesman became a suspect." Gordon Green remembers saying to Ron Smith just days after the Pahud and Cleveland slayings, "Have you noticed that a grey-haired bloke appears in both murders?" Smith had answered, "Yes, I have noticed that. Trouble is that every second bloke in these areas is grey-haired." They left it at that.

"That's the thing about computers," says Bob Myers. "They can record and retrieve vital data, but they can't solve crimes. Only investigators can do that. The crimes would have been solved MIIRS or no MIIRS, but our programme was invaluable because of the time it saved. We back-captured all of the running sheets for the unsolved murders that stretched back nine months or so within the first two weeks of getting up and running. So a fortnight into the investigation we were about an hour behind recording the latest data that was coming in from the field. In the old days of keeping your running sheets on hand-typed or written index cards you could find yourself with weeks and weeks of backlog to record."

Green remembers the singlemindedness of Bob Myers and the MIIRS team to provide a base on which the killings could be solved. He recalls watching Annie Langford at work at the height of the investigation. "She had RSI in her hand. It was strapped, but she continued to type and boasted that she'd get through 100 running sheets that day. She powered away until very late at night then stood up from her computer. 'That's it!' she announced. 'I'm buggered.' She had completed 92 running sheets, a phenomenal number, and her hand literally could type no more. I've also seen that girl struggle on despite a blinding migraine headache. This is how it was day after day and even then the team would take work home with them."

There were hiccups. "In our rush to get the computers up," laughs

Bob Myers, "Greenie had plugged some of the leads into a fluorescent light socket in an adjoining room. One night I walked out of the incident room and into that other room. When I finished there I switched off the light to try to reduce the temperature in the office. That flick of a switch brought all the computers down in the incident room and damaged the electronic data base. Although the data was still on the disk, access would have been difficult because of the computer's damaged reference table. Thank goodness we'd kept the hard copy locked in a safe. All the same, it took us four or five hours to type the data back into the computers."

The temperature in the task force offices at Chatswood often soared into the 40s. The air conditioning was set on a timer that cut the power off at 6pm, often six or seven hours before many of the investigators knocked off. With everybody's nose to the grindstone it would be 6.30 before anybody noticed that the temperature was on the rise. Then the air conditioning would be switched on manually, but with scores of detectives working feverishly, not to mention the computers humming away, it could be two hours or more before the rooms cooled back down to comfort level.

In contrast to Dad Wright, Brown Eyes Smith, Bob Myers and Glass And A Half Green, the surveillance police, known as "the dog squad", spent their days and nights out of doors. But in its own way, their task was just as gruelling. "For the majority of the investigation we had no profile on who we were looking for," says Detective Sgt John May who headed the surveillance team. "We were just photographing or tailing Tom, Dick and Harry. Anybody who looked a bit odd, strange or out of the ordinary we'd take their picture or follow them to a car or an address and log the surveillance in the running sheet in case it became important later in the investigation. Everything was speculation. All we could do was be there in the key areas keeping an eye on things and trying not to let anything crucial escape us. What with the dog squad, uniformed, plain clothes and under-cover police on the streets, we seemed to outnumber the citizens."

Although Madge Pahud had been slain in Lane Cove and Olive Cleveland at Belrose, Mosman remained the focal point of the investigation. "We always felt that the murderer would show up in Mosman," says surveillance supervisor Doodles O'Toole. To this end, three fixed cameras were set up to photograph at random people walking in the shopping area. One was in a bank opposite Mosman High School in Military Road, the second, to cover the eastern side of the shopping centre, was set up above a real estate office on the corner of Military Road and Avenue Road, and the third was installed above a shop at the Raglan Street and Military Road intersection.

"All the shopkeepers co-operated. They were very, very good to us," says Doodles O'Toole. "They put themselves out by clearing furniture away to give us room to set up and allowed us 24-hour access to their premises so we could carry out our surveillance duties."

The cameras were manned during shopping hours and about 100 photos a day were taken, ordinary shoppers as well as anybody deemed by the police to look a little strange or to be acting suspiciously. Says O'Toole, "We hoped that these photographs would come in handy if there was another murder by providing proof that the killer, if we had him in our photo file, was at a certain place at a certain time on a certain day. Each photo carried a time and the date.

"We believed the murderer stalked his victims and the common denominator in three of the four killings to date was that the victim had been shopping in a shopping centre. So these were the logical locations for camera surveillance. As we sifted through our shots each day, we realised just how many weird people there are in Mosman."

Nobody was safe as the candid cameras clicked away. Task force members who sneaked off to the pub or a restaurant or just to snatch a milk shake in a hamburger shop were gleefully photographed from the vantage points and the photographic evidence was left on their desk. There was great hilarity, too, when undercover cops turned up in the weirdo photo file.

Miles O'Toole also remembers those first three months without leads when the task force was grappling with the huge amount of information resulting from the canvass, hoping for a lucky break. "All we knew was that the killer blended into the community because in the execution of all his crimes, committed in busy places in daylight, only a relatively small number of people who saw him actually remembered him and included him in their recollections to police, usually as an afterthought. Back in those early days of the task force we were clutching at straws. So we had surveillance police strolling around likely strike areas dressed as beach bums or casually in shorts and T-shirts. We had uniform police patrolling areas frequented by the elderly. We had detectives probing the murders, and police, community groups, school children, the army and council rangers giving protection to the aged in a bid to prevent any more. There was also a permanent police caravan set up in Mosman."

On November 5, New South Wales Police Commissioner John Avery weighed in and ordered an around-the-clock police guard on every nursing home and retirement village in Sydney and called on Sydneysiders to report to police any disturbed relatives they thought might be capable of the killings. He also urged the elderly to carry personal alarms and make straight for Neighbourhood Watch safe houses if they thought they were in danger. All over the city, north to Hornsby, west to Penrith, south to Sutherland, police and civilians sought out the elderly, offering comfort and advice and urging them to take care.

State Police Minister Ted Pickering on November 8 approved Commissioner Avery's request that the reward for information leading to the arrest of the Granny Killer be doubled from $100,000 to $200,000, or $50,000 for each murder.

Elderly liaison co-ordinator Brien Gately of the police Aged Services Division organised a series of meetings at Mosman Council, Warringah Shire Council, Kuringai Council, Lane Cove Municipal Council and Hornsby Council to advise old people about commonsense safety precautions. Elderly people filled the halls to bursting point. "Unlike a lot of private security companies that leapt on the bandwagon and tried to make a buck out of people's terror, we had the old people's interests at heart, and they responded to this. We backed up these meetings with special protection patrols and, with the assistance of the Mosman Council, a volunteer bus service to ferry them around.

"At these meetings, on TV and 2UE and 2GB talkback radio and in a series of articles for newspapers and mass circulation magazines such as *Woman's Day* as well as in our own brochure "Safety Advice For The Elderly", we'd teach the aged to remain calm and look out for each other. Adopt a signal system with their blinds. If the blinds are up in the day and down at night, all's well. If they're the other way around, pay a call or telephone just to check that everything's OK. We urged them to become aware of each other's routines."

At Christmas, Gately, wearing full uniform, addressed church congregations of all denominations in the Mosman and Lane Cove areas. He expected only to get up at the end of the service and say a few words to the worshippers about safety precautions, try to allay their fears, and tell what the police were doing to catch the murderer in their midst, but he was urged to speak first, at the very beginning, so that his message would not be missed.

"I spoke at a service at Lane Cove, just 500 metres up the road from where Mrs Pahud was murdered, and that day, in addition to my usual message, I asked the congregation to say a prayer for all the victims and that if they had any information that could lead to the killer's arrest to please notify the police."

Gately believes the media portrayed the elderly incorrectly at the time. "The TV and newspaper reporters had the old people down as useless, fearful people peering out from venetian blinds. They weren't like that at all. The elderly I dealt with had a lot of pride and remained very level-headed and defiant in spite of the fact that a serial killer was stalking them."

Gately has dealt with the aged long enough to know that you should never underestimate them. Respect them, yes, underestimate them, never. He tells the story of the Boggabri Boys Brass Band. A young fellow knocks on the door of an old gent and tells him he's collecting money to send the Boggabri Boys Brass Band to an eisteddfod in Sydney. The old man cups his hand to his ear and says, "What?" The young man repeats, "We're collecting money for the Boggabri Boys Brass Band. Would you like to donate some?" The old man, hand over his ear, says, "What did you say?" At this, the young fellow loses patience with the old man and storms back down the path. The old man calls out, "Don't forget to close the gate." The angry young man mutters softly, "You know what you can do with your bloody gate." And the old man responds, "And you know what you can do with the Boggabri Boys Brass Band!"

* * *

As the months dragged by, the demands on the task force members became almost intolerable. The killer was still on the loose and the state government, police hierarchy, the media and the community were growing impatient for a result. This relentless pressure, when coupled with the frustration of pounding their heads against a seemingly impenetrable brick wall for up to 18 hours a day, seven days a week, inevitably took its toll on the team.

"Even the most hardened policeman would have been affected, both emotionally and physically, by investigating the savage deaths of these defenceless little old ladies," says Mike Hagan today. "Here were grandmothers who had suffered horrendous injuries at the hands of a serial murderer. I know I will never get over seeing such sights as a 93-year-old woman viciously beaten and strangled with her own pantyhose and degradingly left half-naked and bleeding to death in her own home.

"Our only escape valve was to talk among ourselves and honestly tell each other how we were feeling. We bounced off one another in a positive, therapeutic way. Sometimes we'd release the pressure by playing practical jokes, going for a swim or a walk or a jog. Quite often we'd head to the pub for a drink and a bit of frivolity. I'm sure many people saw us laughing and joking around and thought we were not taking our responsibilities seriously, but this was just our way of staying sane."

The frustration of working so hard for no success led to friction and the occasional blow-up between task force members. Says Mike Hagan, "One of the attributes of a good investigator is a strong determination to solve the crime. This single-mindedness to succeed can make a detective overly aggressive, especially when he is achieving little headway. Strong people have strong opinions and stick up for them. Put a whole lot of fiercely-professional and strong-willed police together in a tense atmosphere and sparks are going to fly.

"My main job was to solve the north shore killings, but my second priority was to look after my staff. When the going was tough, especially in November '89, when we had three murders in 24 days, and the cracks were beginning to appear in a few of the task force members' composure, it was essential to foster camaraderie among the troops. Happily, the team responded wonderfully. In spite of all the pressures and differences of opinion, I've never known such *esprit de corps* in any group of people I have ever been associated with."

One day John May received a message on his beeper to contact a man he had never heard of. Puzzled, the surveillance expert returned the call and asked the man what he wanted. "I have to tell you in person," the man said. May said OK, and could they meet somewhere, say, outside the fish shop at Balmoral, in an hour and a half. "Sounds good," said the stranger.

When May arrived at the rendezvous it was bucketing with rain. He ran to the shelter of the shops where he saw a man waiting. "Now what's this about?" demanded the drenched May.

"Are you John May?" asked the man.

"I am."

"Then I have these papers for you."

"Oh yeah, what are they about?"

"Just read them," said the man.

May did. They were documents from the Family Law Court. John May's wife was seeking a divorce.

"That Granny Killer cost me my marriage," says May sadly today. "I don't blame my wife. I was working long hours and it was so hard on her and our two small children. I was so preoccupied with the case I'd stopped talking to my wife. And I'd be leaving for work before my kids woke up and arriving home long after they'd gone to bed, so I lost contact with them, too. It was a strain."

Homicide detective Murray Byrnes' wife was pregnant during the hunt for the killer. In spite of the sometimes almost-unendurable daily work pressures, he tried hard to give her emotional support whenever the investigation allowed and to continue being a good father to his kids. Byrnes, stout with short, wavy, dark-brown hair, meticulous and good-natured, would play a key role in solving the crimes, but he found being on that task force the most harrowing experience of his life. "Being macho is one of the ways we cope with homicide work. You tend to bottle things up and never betray emotion to your colleagues. You know, 'Solving murders is just another job. Let's have another drink'. But sometimes the work we do does get to you. Those north shore murders affected me more than any others I'd been assigned to in my career. When the investigation was finally wound up, I got out of Homicide." Today Byrnes is with the Internal Affairs Branch.

Geoff Wright and Ron Smith were towers of strength who went far out of their way to nurture the morale of their investigators. "Long hours away from the home and family led to domestic problems for many of the team," says Smith. "Arriving home late every night, seven days a week, some of the blokes didn't see their kids for weeks on end. A few of the team regularly worked for 48, 60, 72 hours at a stretch.

"Occasionally we'd hear of someone experiencing strife on the home front and have a quiet word with him, maybe give him a little time off if absolutely necessary. We couldn't have a situation where a bloke burned out, or became so distracted by trouble at home that he could not do his job properly. We had to sort them out for the sake of the task force."

The commanders encouraged their investigators to wind down when they could. "We didn't mind if they had a few beers when the opportunity arose or sneaked out for a bit of lunch together. We joined in. If we hadn't, we wouldn't have been able to keep going," says Geoff Wright.

"We could understand how the men and women were feeling because we were in exactly the same boat," says Wright. "Our own home situations weren't the best at times, either. At one stage we worked six weeks straight without a day off and would arrive home at midnight, sleep a few hours and be back at Chatswood headquarters at the crack of dawn next day. There was a fair bit of strain."

"It was a fairly ordinary Christmas for all of us, believe me," says Smith. "The task force being fully operational 24 hours a day for as long as it took to solve the murders, we naturally had to show up on Christmas Day. Although we did try to roster off a few fellows with young families so they could spend the day with the wife and kids. Boxing Day was business as usual for everyone."

As more investigators joined the team, swelling it to 70 in January and February, 1990, it became a little easier to allow the task force members their permitted two days off a fortnight. Even so, says Wright and Smith, "It was a wonder nobody went over the edge."

Mike Hagan introduced a donut feast to provide a little light relief after the regular Wednesday morning briefings. Hagan is an aficionado of donuts and ordered his troops to tuck in too. Everyone looked forward to the bosses' donut morning and for 15 minutes or so once a week attention turned from post mortems, surveillance and suspects to who'd get the sugar-coated or the iced donut that day. At the beginning three dozen donuts were sufficient for a session, but as the investigation gathered momentum with the new year six or seven dozen was the order of the day. The Wednesday morning donut feast remains a tradition at the Chatswood Regional Crime Squad office.

Doodles O'Toole, who at one point himself became so distracted that he wrote on his police petrol requisition form "$50 worth of murder", was quick to spot the warning signs of an impending crack-up in some of his surveillance people and, like Hagan, Smith and Wright, encouraged them, if they were working around Mosman, to take a quick break and head down the Raglan Street hill to Balmoral Beach for a swim and a jog beside the water. At times during that summer a dozen or so investigators at a time would be running up and down the picturesque beachfront. O'Toole remembers constantly greeting fellow task force members — "G'day, g'day, g'day" — as he ran his laps on the sand. If in Mosman, the Buena Vista Hotel, just near Mosman police station, was the favoured watering hole, while task force members working from Chatswood would frequent the Willoughby Hotel, just a couple of hundred metres from Regional Crime Squad headquarters.

Joe Sands is the publican, licensee and owner of the Willoughby Hotel, known jokingly as "Box No.1" to the police. He is tall and fair-haired with a rugged face. "The pressure on those men was unbeliev-able," he says. "I wouldn't see the task force members for a week or two at a time, but when they came in they really unwound. They'd walk in strained and drawn and after one drink they'd be acting like they'd had seven or eight. A single beer would change their personality, they were just so tired. In fact, they probably should not have been drinking at all, they should have gone straight home to bed. Some of them had not been home for three days. But they had to, as they termed it, 'de-tense', just relax among themselves.

"Sometimes they'd order a meal and they'd fall asleep at their table before it was even served. A couple of times I walked into the snack bar and found half a dozen blokes at a table snoring their heads off. I'd offer these fellows a bed in the hotel. They looked terrible, worn out and haggard, and often they'd wear the same clothes for days in a row. At 6am next morning I'd go to their room to wake them up and offer them some breakfast but they'd have left long before, back on the job.

"Occasionally, after a few drinks they'd be short-tempered with each other, and I'd have to say, 'Hey gentlemen, let's not unwind *too* much.' Then they'd have a go at me. The combination of tiredness, frustration and alcohol saw them behave in ways that might shock the bloke in the street. They'd wrestle and carry each other around on their shoulders, maybe headbutt a fan. But I pretty much left them alone because I knew what they were going through.

"Some of the detectives had become familiar faces through the TV news reports and occasionally customers would go up to them and say things like, 'Keep up the good work' or 'Have you caught the Granny Killer yet?' Most of this was well-meaning, but the detectives didn't take kindly to amateur detectives who'd demand, 'What's wrong with you guys? Can't you catch anybody?' and then try to tell them how to do their job. These people were met with an angry silence. The police were copping enough flak from the media, they didn't need it from the public, too."

To try to take his mates' minds off the job and give them something else to talk about, Joe Sands formed a fishing club. To his wife's displeasure he would remain behind at the hotel drinking and swapping yarns with the detectives. "She said I may as well be in the police force myself because I was spending so much time with them at the pub and so little time at home. It was a bad period, a bad period for everybody, but particularly for them."

Later, when their work was done, Joe Sands remembers many happy celebrations. "Only then," he says, "did they start to look like human beings again."

One night, after two straight days on the job, Miles O'Toole had a drink at the Willoughby Hotel and set off on the long drive home to Gosford. Near Hornsby, his car had a flat tyre. The exhausted detective cursed and heaved his jack and spare tyre out of the boot. Shortly afterwards, a police squad car was driving through Hornsby when they saw a dishevelled and grease-caked man crouched down beside a car having all kinds of problems changing his wheel. The squad car stopped. "I can't get the nuts tightened up," complained Miles O'Toole when the officers asked what was the trouble. When they took a closer look they saw that the dog-weary O'Toole was trying to put his wheel on back to front.

As much as the task force appreciated the co-operation of the responsible media, much of the press reporting of the investigation caused fury among the men and women who were risking their health, family life and sanity in their quest to catch the Granny Killer. "I know a lot of these reporters were only following their boss's orders," says Miles O'Toole, "but some of them would follow you everywhere, asking questions and getting in the way of your work. A couple of the more unscrupulous reporters, when we were either unable or unwilling to speak to them, just made things up. Things improved when it was made clear that the only person who was authorised to talk to the media was the task force commander Mike Hagan. That freed up the rest of us to concentrate on the investigation. Having just one high-echelon spokesman also put a stop to a lot of the innuendos, rumours and general garbage being printed by some newspapers. When the new chain of information was established, the media was forced to become a lot more responsible."

"Although the media was generally very helpful and responsible," says Mike Hagan, "there was some media input that caused hassles at times. One particular time was when the press needed a new angle and came up with speculation that a copycat killer had murdered Mrs Pahud, that there were in fact *two* offenders out there. We knew this was nonsense and that the same person had committed all the murders. There was never any reason to believe that there was a copycat killer. But these reports were leading to pressure being put on us to open a second line of investigation to try to apprehend this non-existent second killer and this would have been a waste of already sorely-stretched time and resources. I asked the press to drop the speculation and happily they did." There continued, however, a mocking, cynical tone to much of the press coverage of the North Shore Murders Investigation. This muckraking increased as the months wore on and still there was no arrest, and when finally there *was* an arrest press criticism of the task force reached a crescendo.

The detectives also had to live with criticism from the community. Paul Mayger remembers encountering hostility from citizens while canvassing houses in the Mosman area. "It was frustrating to know that there were plenty of citizens who were knocking you and holding you personally responsible for the killer still being on the loose. You'd be asking them questions and you could see they were thinking, 'What are you blokes *doing*? Why aren't you doing more? Why haven't you caught him yet? Why are you making me live in fear?'

"This kind of stress and pressure was with us 24 hours a day," says

Mayger. "You can't just close the door on the problem when you arrive home and make it go away. A happy home life became a thing of the past. Mate, that inquiry lasted almost 13 months from first murder to arrest and my family life, social calendar, household duties, everything, went out the window for the whole period. When you are required you have to drop whatever else you may be doing, just drop it, and get on the job.

"What kept us all going was the knowledge that the killer would keep on killing until he was caught. I can remember saying to a couple of my workmates after the Ashton murder, 'This isn't the end of it. We're going to have more.' And of course we did."

Before he murdered Lady Ashton the so-called Granny Killer had slain Gwen Mitchelhill. After, he savagely ended the lives of Madge Pahud and Olive Cleveland on November 2 and 3 and it was then that the search for the killer escalated into a Major Investigation. For the first three weeks of the task force's life the killer was quiet. Then, as November drew to a close and Mosman began to deck itself in the trappings of the festive season, he struck again, right in front of the investigators' noses. Until then, the men and women of the task force had been working harder than they ever had before, in circumstances more demanding than they had ever experienced. But the ferocious November 23 slaying of 93-year-old Mosmanite Muriel Falconer meant the investigators were set to learn what real pressure was all about.

CHAPTER 9

False Steps

Since the bashing of Doris Cox, Muriel Falconer had been hearing noises in the night. She complained to her good friend and neighbour Maggie Hughes how for the first time in her long life the wind whistling in the trees outside would keep her awake, and that there were other strange sounds coming from her garden. Maggie Hughes put it down to the nervousness that had gripped all of Mosman. Many times the elderly woman had conceded that the serial killer must be a very clever man to continue to get away with his crimes.

However, nervous or not, Muriel Falconer was 93 years of age and not inclined to change her ways for anybody. Certainly not this Granny Killer chappie who'd managed to turn her Mosman, her sedate, charming, friendly Mosman, into a frightened, whispering place where even old friends held each other in suspicion. She was a woman every bit as proud, fearless and independent as her regal bearing and patrician features suggested and if she wanted to go to the shops alone then that's exactly what she was going to do. She was a familiar sight as she carried her bags, never resorting to a trolley, home from the shops.

A widow for 18 years, Muriel Falconer was totally blind in one eye and partially without sight in the other. This and a little high blood pressure aside, she had enjoyed lusty health all her life until the June just past when she suffered a stroke which impaired her hearing and confined her to bed for a time. But before long she was again seen in the shopping centres of Mosman, a walking stick one of only two concessions she made to her illness. The other was to take her doctor's advice and accept Meals On Wheels, the service where citizens donate their time to deliver prepared meals to elderly and infirm people and stop for a chat when they make their regular rounds.

Muriel Falconer enjoyed the food and the friendship of the women who called on her at her home in Muston Street, the first road that bisects the eastern slope of Raglan Street as you leave Military Road and head down to the shimmering waters and yellow crescent beaches of Balmoral.

In spite of her grand age and mounting health problems, Muriel Falconer had staunchly resisted moving into a nursing home, much preferring to carry on alone in the house where she had had so many happy times. No.3 Muston Street was, with its dark brick and carved wood exterior and the high ceilings, ornate polished furniture, cut glass bowls, candelabra, umbrella stands, ornate vases and expensive rugs within, a rich evocation of days past. Sweeter days, gentler days, days before the Granny Killer.

Muriel Falconer was a woman people cared about. She was especially close to her son John and his wife Margaret and their three children. She doted on her grandchildren and often worried about the world they were growing up in. Margaret would telephone her mother-in-law regularly and John would drop in on his mum at least three times a week just to check up on her and make sure that all was well. Since the reign of the north shore serial killer began earlier in the year they had been very concerned for the elderly woman's welfare, even asked her to leave the suburb, but whenever they cautioned her not to walk around Mosman alone as much as she did and to keep an eye out for trouble, the nonagenarian would laugh and refuse point blank to change her ways.

Maggie Hughes from two doors down in Muston Street was another with the welfare of her elderly neighbour very much at heart. Although Muriel Falconer was more than twice Maggie Hughes's age, the pair had been good friends ever since the younger woman had moved into Muston Street 16 years before. The two first met when Maggie Hughes was gardening and suddenly Muriel Falconer had popped her head over the fence to lecture, "That's not the way to tie a shrub to a stake!" From that day on the two girls from the bush became firm companions, their friendship fuelled by a mutual love of gardening and antiques, and a desire to solve together the political problems of the world over a cup of tea. Muriel Falconer was fond of calling her friend "the daughter I never had". This meant a lot to Maggie Hughes whose own mother had been murdered in the 1960s.

"Mrs Falconer was a very private and dogmatic person. She wasn't intimidated by anybody," says Maggie Hughes. "I remember one day we went to a gardening show and she recognised the TV gardening expert Don Burke in the crowd. She marched up to him and said, 'Listen, stupid. I don't always agree with you. You're not always right!" He gave her a pot plant."

Maggie Hughes would drop in on Muriel Falconer several times a week, talk to her on the telephone often, and carry her rubbish bin from the rear lane up to her back door on garbage collection days. She would also take her companion to auctions, to such places as Vaucluse House, and to plant nurseries once or twice a month, outings the aged woman prized as special treats.

The pair had a security system of sorts. If Maggie Hughes had not seen Muriel Falconer's side door open and the old woman watering her garden and feeding the birds in the backyard by late morning or lunchtime, she'd check up on her. Maggie Hughes always knew that she would be the one to find her neighbour passed away, "but from natural causes or a stroke, never the way she went".

On the morning of Wednesday, November 23, Maggie Hughes noticed Muriel Falconer watering the plants in her back garden. A few hours later, about 2.30pm, she saw her neighbour at her front gate with her sister from Melbourne — "She called her her 'baby sister', she was only 88" — and another woman and stopped for a chat with the three. Muriel Falconer announced that later in the afternoon she'd be off up to Military Road to do a little shopping.

* * *

Sean McGovern was losing patience. A lighting consultant, he had been despatched to Muston Street, Mosman, to pick up some Italian lights from a distributor. The address he had been given was a number at the northern end of the tree-lined street but when he knocked on the door he was told that there was no lighting distributor there and he must have the wrong address. As he returned to his vehicle he noticed a grey-haired, middle-aged man "with a bit of a gut" standing outside a construction site across the road.

The lighting consultant then drove to Military Road and telephoned his office. He was advised that the distributor had just called to say that he could be found at an address at the southern end of Muston Street and he would be waiting outside in the street. McGovern returned to the opposite end of Muston Street, eyes peeled for his contact. To his surprise, when he reached the south end of the road he saw the same grey-haired man who just minutes before had been loitering outside the construction site at the northern end. "No," McGovern thought, "that bloke's not my man", and drove slowly back to the other end. There was no sign of his distributor anywhere. Finally, the exasperated McGovern pulled up beside the middle-aged man who this time when he saw him had moved again and was now standing aimlessly on the corner of Muston and Raglan streets. When McGovern enquired whether he was a lighting distributor, the man shrugged his shoulders, replied "No" in a deep voice, spun on his heel and walked briskly up Raglan Street toward Military Road.

Soon afterwards, McGovern located the distributor and collected his order of lights. While waiting at the Raglan Street-Military Road traffic lights to change on the way back to his office, he looked across and again saw the grey-haired man, standing outside a milk bar, doing nothing.

* * *

Like any husband and father trying to make his wages go that little bit further in difficult economic times, John Glover was always on the lookout for a bargain. When he first saw Muriel Falconer hobbling with her grocery bags along Middle Head Road on November 23 he was comparing whisky specials in the bottle shop of the Buena Vista Hotel, across from Mosman police station. It was nearing 5pm and Glover had long knocked off work. The appearance of this elderly woman, however, meant that he was not quite finished for the day.

As the demons stirred, Glover noted how slowly his quarry moved. There was no need to rush. Leaving the hotel, he returned to his car which he'd parked right outside the police station. He took a pair of gloves from under the front seat and put them in his trouser pocket and tucked the hammer inside his shirt, the clawed head supported by his belt. Closing the car door — Miles O'Toole, working inside the police station at that very time, would have, had he been listening, heard the door slam — Glover returned to Middle Head Road. He had no trouble picking up Muriel Falconer's pink cardigan and brown floral dress among the late afternoon pedestrians. He shadowed her slowly at a distance along Middle Head Road. He was dressed in his work outfit of light shirt, brown slacks and brown leather brogues.

Glover picked up pace as the elderly lady turned into Muston Street and was only a metre away as she passed through her front gate. Inserting the key into her front-door lock, Muriel Falconer, blind and scarcely able to hear since her stroke, had no idea that the grey-haired killer, the only serial murderer of elderly women in recorded criminal history, was close enough to reach out and touch.

When the old lady entered her house, John Glover was on her heels. He clamped one gloved hand to her mouth to stifle her screams then rained hammer blows on the back of the woman's head until she fell to the ground in the hallway. Muriel Falconer fought for her life like a lion. In a frenzy, Glover pulled the struggling woman's dress, blouse and cardigan up over her head, but still she shouted. He struck her again on the head with the hammer. Tearing her pantyhose off, he tied them tightly around his victim's neck, but still she screamed. He hit her again with the hammer. Muriel Falconer at last lay still. Groceries were strewn in disarray on the floor. The contents of a blue, two-litre container of ice cream seeped on to the floor. Blood splattered the walls and carpet.

Flustered and gasping for breath, Glover closed the front door then, after setting his victim's red and brown shoes neatly by her body, rifled through the woman's purse. Finding no money there, he searched various rooms before entering a parlour and coming upon $100 in a chest of drawers. He stuffed the money into his pocket, the gloves and hammer into a shopping bag, and departed the premises. He did, however, leave something behind. There, on the blood-saturated carpet and a Persian rug, were two prints of a male's right shoe, faint but discernible. If other, later, events had not played their part as they did, the shoeprints may well have been decisive in putting John Glover behind bars.

After murdering Muriel Falconer, John Glover drove home where he dumped his clothes into the dirty washing basket, put the bloodied gloves into the garbage bin — it was collection night in Wyong Road — and washed the claw hammer clean with hydrochloric acid and left it in his garden shed.

Next day at 11.30am the Meals On Wheels team knocked on the door of No.3 Muston Street. No answer. They returned at 1pm and knocked once more but again there was no response from inside the house. The food container was left to grow cold on the second rung of a plant stand outside the front door. At 4.55, concerned because she had not seen her neighbour all day, Maggie Hughes went to No.3 and knocked but there was no reply. She called out, "Mrs Falconer!" and looked through various windows of the house. Still no sign of life. Underneath a full milk bottle in the garden was a note in the elderly woman's handwriting. The worried neighbour read: "Milko, please shut the front gate." Then Maggie Hughes saw a key in the lock of the front security door. That was strange. Alarmed now, she used a spare key to open the front door. Inside on the carpet lay the body of Muriel Falconer. She had been dead for 24 hours.

"I saw her lying angled across the door in the hallway," says the victim's old friend. "I thought she'd collapsed unconscious, then I realised she was dead and that her clothes had been pulled up over her head and she was wearing no pantyhose. The pantyhose were tied around her neck. Then I saw the blood. Being a trained nurse I felt for her pulse but rigor mortis had set in and her whole hand was blue. I noticed the man's footprint then, pointing toward the front door, in the blood.

"At this stage I knew it was murder and that it was the Granny Killer. But somehow I stayed calm. It didn't even enter my mind that he may still have been on the premises." What did come rushing back to me as I stood in Mrs Falconer's house were memories of my own mother's murder 20-odd years before."

Maggie Hughes telephoned Muriel Falconer's doctor, telling him only that his patient's respiration had ceased and that her clothes had been interfered with, then she called the victim's son and daughter-in-law. When he arrived at the scene the badly-shaken doctor took one look at Muriel Falconer and called the police. First on the scene was the Manly patrol commander Graham Ferguson who knew this was task force territory. In minutes Mike Hagan, Miles O'Toole and his homicide detectives and Phil Flogel of Physical Evidence were at work at the perfectly-preserved crime site.

Muston Street was cordoned off and, after comforting Maggie Hughes, the task forcers asked her permission to use her home as an office. The request granted, the police took over and turned Maggie Hughes's home into bedlam.

Back in No.3 all eyes were focussed on the shoe prints, the first clue the killer had left in his nine-month murder spree. Phil Flogel summoned colleague Dave Forbes to photograph the prints then, taking a Stanley knife to the carpet, cut carefully around the two shoe prints. Next day he took the carpet squares to the Victorian Police Force's State Forensic Science Laboratory in Melbourne where there were facilities to electronically enhance the prints and provide more detailed photographs of them than could Forbes's Roleiflex SL66 camera. The prints, it was determined, were those of a leather Koller shoe, brogue-style, size 8, made in Poland, with a wear pattern on the outside right edge of the heel.

Unfortunately, this time, because the prints were fairly faint, the results were not a significant improvement on the ones already in hand. So Flogel delivered his carpet squares to a computer installation at Artarmon, near Chatswood, which was able to enhance the shots but, again, not significantly. They would make do with what they had.

Says Forbes, "Eventually when Glover was arrested, we got every pair of shoes he had in his house. Phil examined them all and he was pretty happy with one of the brown brogues. The wear patterns matched. In fact he was able to say in court with total accuracy that that was the shoe that made the print found in the hall."

On the night of the murder word somehow reached the media that a shoeprint, possibly the Granny Killer's, had been found at the house. Police were furious. If this appeared in the papers the first thing the killer would do was destroy the shoe. As an exercise in damage control, Physical Research chief Dave Hughes the following day went to a vacant block next door to the murder house and was photographed by the newspapers and TV stations taking a plaster mould of a shoeprint in the dirt there. The reporters leapt to the assumption that this was the shoeprint in question and that information along with the photo of Hughes ran on that night's news and the front page of several papers. Result: the media was lured off the track of the vital shoeprint *inside* the house and the killer, knowing he had never been in the vacant block, was lulled into a false security thinking that once more he had put one over on the investigators.

After photographing Muriel Falconer's body at the City Morgue, Forbes returned to No.3 Muston Street where his colleagues were combing the house for clues. This was the first time that the killer had struck inside his victim's home. "That examination took literally days," says Forbes. "We were there all through the night of the murder and went back next day and the next. We probed every centimetre of the house including the roof. You never know, the killer might have thrown his weapon up there or, for that matter, he might even have been hiding up there himself." While Forbes, Flogel, Hughes and their physical evidence team were examining the house, other detectives were cawling through the garden, under the house, in neighbouring yards, in the street. They found no leads.

Muriel Falconer's distraught son John made an emotional plea in the pages of *The Daily Mirror*. "This person must be stopped," he said. "The poor old things don't stand a chance. Nothing will stop whoever it is from killing again... The terrifying thing is this person leaves no clues. He strikes savagely and quickly. But someone out there must know something. What they must remember is it could be their mother or grandmother who falls next victim."

CHAPTER 10

Hysteria

After the murder of Muriel Falconer Mosman was gripped by a hysteria never known by an Australian suburb. From three to six in the afternoon, the once-hectic streets and shopping centres of Military Road and Spit Junction were virtually deserted. For a while it seemed that there were more police than citizens out and about, and what citizens there were appeared to scurry rather than walk, doing their business urgently, eyes darting, peeled to pick out anybody who looked like he might follow them home and kill them. Most people who ventured outside their homes *had* to do so. There was an inevitability in the air that the Granny Killer would keep murdering and that no task force, no matter how skilled or dedicated, could stop him.

Fear gripped this staid and prosperous suburb and the community grew restive. Citizens wanted an arrest and they wanted it now. Certainly one citizen, John Glover of 18 Wyong Road, made it known that he was getting bloody angry about the police's inability to catch the serial killer after all these months of taxpayers' money being spent on the investigation. Glover, known to many in the suburb as a proud and solid Mosmanite who took a strong interest in community affairs, was heard more than once by his family, neighbours, friends and workmates to say, "For God's sake, I wish someone would *catch* this bastard!"

Barry O'Keefe was mayor of Mosman at the time. "Mass murders just didn't happen in Mosman," he says. "The feeling at the time was that the killer had to be an outsider who had infiltrated this law-abiding and lovely suburb. It was a quiet place where many elderly people lived happily alongside the more recently-arrived artistic, literary, academic and professional residents. When the first two killings and the assault of Mrs Cox occurred here we had trouble accepting it, and I'm afraid when the next two were committed at Lane Cove and Belrose many people breathed a sigh of relief and thought, 'There, you see, we knew it wasn't a Mosman person. He's struck somewhere else, probably closer to home.' Then Mrs Falconer was killed in Muston Street.

"I knew some of the victims. Lady Ashton was a great supporter of mine, but she really gave me some stick if anything happened in council that she didn't like. She was an old-worldly lady. She would never telephone me to complain, always write these polite but very firm Margaret Rutherford-type letters. And, like everybody else, I had often seen Mrs Falconer going her independent way around the place. That a woman of her age did not get to die naturally in bed shocked a lot of people."

O'Keefe recalls the atmosphere when Mosman Council organised a public meeting after the Falconer murder to try to bring everybody together to confront the menace in their midst. "There were police, people from community organisations and clubs, service groups, the army and the navy, concerned citizens. Some of those present were in a state bordering on the hysterical, but unlike many public meetings, nobody was blaming others for the predicament we were in. This problem was too important for petty point-scoring and everybody was very constructive. We decided to set up a series of organisational moves that would help protect the old people in the community by bonding them to the young. Adopt an oldie, that sort of thing. An army bus would take the aged to and from shopping centres and senior citizens activities. The soldiers acquitted themselves very well at all times and the old ladies took a real shine to them. A lot of friendships were made that I'm sure have survived to this day. Mosman is a reserved kind of place but people really reached out to each other then. In spite of the terrible events, that period proved to me that there is a basic decency in people. Given the right circumstances, people come through."

O'Keefe, who is the brother of the late rock 'n' roller Johnny O'Keefe, offered the task force every facility, and in fact the Mosman Town Hall, as did Mosman police station, became an outpost of the Chatswood-based investigation. He and his colleagues on council found themselves working long into the night to administer the many safety systems they'd established. One day O'Keefe's secretary Nerida

McPherson took a phone call from a man asking to speak to the mayor. When she told the man that O'Keefe, a Queens Counsel, was in court and unavailable, the caller said to pass on the message that unless the mayor stopped trying to catch the Granny Killer, his wife would be the next victim. "From that day on," O'Keefe says, "there was a police and navy guard on my family."

The longtime councillor and present-day mayor of Mosman Dom Lopez remembers an air of unreality in his suburb. "None of us could believe that this was happening in our Mosman," he says. "There was the feeling all the time that a killer was on the prowl, and there was the very obvious police presence. The suburb was crawling with police. The community really rose to the occasion, with volunteers going out of their way to look after the elderly and drive them to bingo or their various senior citizens activities."

Lopez adds, however, that while most elderly people followed police advice to take precautions, lock their doors and go shopping in groups and so on, quite a few adopted a fatalistic attitude. "'Oh no,' they'd say to me, 'I'm not scared. If I'm going to die, I'm going to die. If the Granny Killer wants to murder me, then that's it. He will.' They were fiercely independent and resented being protected. They wanted to look after themselves. I think I'll be exactly the same way should I live to a great age."

Dom Lopez remembers the period from March, 1989, to March, 1990, as a terrifying time. "Two years on, Mosman still has not recovered from the serial killings. I don't think it will *ever* recover. Until the Granny Killings we had always seemed to be able to hold at bay the social pressures and problems that were destroying other suburbs and towns. Murders, drugs — none of these major crimes seemed to touch Mosman. 'It can't happen here' type of thing. Then everything changed. Now we know that crime does not respect suburban boundaries."

There was, however, one positive side effect of the hysteria that gripped Mosman. With so many police visible the crime rate plummeted to be almost non-existent. No break and enters, no muggings, car theft or loutish behaviour. For a time, the deeds of the Granny Killer excepted, Mosman was a crimeless society.

Task force commander Mike Hagan recalls how the November murders turned the suburb upside down. "The terror and paranoia was hardly surprising. We were faced with three murders in the one month. Mrs Pahud on the 2nd, Mrs Cleveland on the 3rd and Mrs Falconer on the 23rd. The Falconer murder took us to fever pitch. I've never experienced anything like the period after that killing. As well as the task force, every type of government department was involved in the hunt in some way, including the army and the Roads and Transport Authority who put on special buses for old people, plus service clubs, local councils, and even civilian volunteers who shepherded the elderly."

After the identity of the killer was finally revealed, there was more than one elderly Mosman resident who realised to her horror how close she herself had come to being a victim. Dom Lopez's 80-year-old mother declined Glover's offer of a lift home — "She gets shivers when she thinks about it today," says Lopez. And Muriel Falconer's friend and neighbour Maggie Hughes tells of an 82-year-old woman tapping her on the shoulder, then bursting into tears. "This woman told me how she was at Mosman RSL only days after Mrs Falconer's death and when it was time to go home, she looked about for an escort. She considered all the possibilities at the club and finally decided that John Glover would be her ideal protector. Glover gladly agreed to see her to her door. When they arrived at her home, the woman handed him the door key and he actually went in first to check the rooms and make sure that the Granny Killer was not lurking inside. He assured her that the coast was clear, said goodnight and left. How lucky was she!"

Also, after the identity of the killer was known and the list of offences released, Miles O'Toole received five phone calls from distraught relatives of nursing home inmates. The patients had complained to the relatives that they had been sexually molested by a grey-haired man but their claims had been dismissed by family and nursing home staff as senile fantasies. All five victims had since passed away. O'Toole had to confirm to the relatives that as Glover frequented the homes in question it was probable that their worst fears had been realised.

Few of his task force knew it, but for a while Mike Hagan took to patrolling the streets of Mosman himself. "I've always believed that to be well informed about any situation you have to experience it first hand. After the Falconer murder I would often slip away from

Chatswood headquarters in the late afternoon and drive over to Mosman where I'd park the car and just walk up and down Military Road. I was not only the commander running the show, I was also an investigator. I walked that street in the hope that my detective's eye might notice something significant that somebody less-trained might miss. I just fell back on my natural policeman's instincts.

"I'm a bloke with a strong faith and as I walked I prayed that good would eventually triumph over evil in this case. My faith and positive determination to solve these killings gave me a lot of strength. I've always believed that the combination of faith in God and a positive attitude is a powerful weapon," says Hagan.

Police made regular pleas to the public to come forward with any information, no matter how unimportant it might seem, that might help them in their hunt. An emotive appeal was made on the high-rating John Laws Show on Radio 2UE when the veteran broadcaster opened his airwaves to assist the investigation. A huge audience tuned in to the specially-produced programme. The segment began:

John Laws: Police believe a serial killer may be on the loose in Sydney. To date, four defenceless elderly women have been brutally murdered, another viciously attacked. Somebody knows who that killer is. You may not think so, but you could hold the key to catching the killer. You may have seen something, heard something, or know something.

Voice 1: Obviously we have someone out there who's got a very sick mind.

Voice 2: A task force of 35 of the state's top investigators is co-ordinating the hunt, but there are few clues.

Voice 3: All of them were bashed from behind. They were struck with a blunt object of some sort. All of them were very brutal attacks, they were very vicious attacks.

Voice 4: People involved in serial killings are typically people living on the fringes of society, people who aren't integrated, people who don't come from happy family childhoods, people who, for one reason or another, are ostracised or alienated from the mainstream of social life.

Voice 5: We believe there are similarities in relation to the other murders we are investigating on the north shore.

Voice 6: Somebody knows the north shore serial killer.

Laws then led listeners through the four murders and the attempted murder in detail in an effort to jog the public's memory and prompt them to provide the clue that could solve the crimes. He finished, "There is absolutely no doubt in the minds of investigators that the killer will strike again. This person obviously must be caught. Somebody has seen something, or somebody knows something that can make this capture possible. Are you that someone? Think long. Think hard." The broadcaster then read out the task force action line telephone numbers.

Police Minister Ted Pickering then came on the radio programme's talkback line and announced that he would approve that afternoon a $200,000 reward for information leading to the Granny Killer's arrest.

Next to speak to listeners was Ron Smith, on the John Laws open line from task force headquarters:

Smith: Hello. Good morning, John.

Laws: Have you made any progress?

Smith: We are making steady progress, but nothing really that we can point to at this point of time. There is just a huge volume of information that's come in through the public response which we've got to sift through, and it's going to take some time, obviously, but, as I say, the response has been overwhelming.

Laws: What is the best lead you've got?

Smith: Well, basically, any lead that comes in from the public so far as suspects or whatever, is a good lead as far as we are concerned. It all has to be followed through. I can't point to anyone at this stage. As I say, there's been a huge response and it takes some time for each of these bits of information to be thoroughly investigated.

Laws: Yeah, I can also understand that you wouldn't want to divulge too much of your internal activities, because by doing that you could well warn the killer.

Smith: Exactly.

Laws: And I certainly wouldn't want to press that point, but, out of interest, are you getting information that is matching up?

Smith: Our information is certainly strong in various areas, but once again each and every piece of information has to be thoroughly investigated... The enthusiasm of the investigators here is something overwhelming, really. They're clambering to get involved...

Laws: Yes, I believe that's the case. And I believe they're working extraordinarily long hours on it.

Smith: Exactly.

Laws: But obviously what you need is some matching leads. One that will point to another, so that you can head in a certain direction.

Smith: That's right. That's what it's all about.

Once more the task force numbers were broadcast and the switchboard at Chatswood burst into life. However, nothing concrete would come from any of the appeals to the public.

Before the Falconer slaying the investigation was in top gear. After it, the task force went into overdrive. More detectives were assigned and the force now numbered 70. Not a home in the suburb went uncanvassed, scarcely a resident unquestioned: "Did you know the deceased?... When did you last see her?... Have you seen anyone or anything strange, unusual or suspicious in the area?... Any person who seemed to be following another?... Are there any elderly ladies on the premises?"

Shop and office staff were sent police notices advising of the reward, which was increased from $200,000 to $250,000 with the discovery of the fifth murder victim, and requesting them to pay particular attention when serving the elderly and to be alert to anybody who appeared to be following aged customers. Any suspicious behaviour should be reported to police at once. The pamphlet went on, "It is also requested that special attention be paid to any person seen loitering in the vicinity of the shopping centre, or following elderly persons in the surrounding residential streets."

Reward posters were plastered all over Mosman, Neutral Bay, Cremorne and North Sydney: "Information Sought From The Public. Assistance is sought from members of the public who may be able to provide any information that would lead to the apprehension of the person or persons responsible for the murders and serious assaults in the north shore area. A reward of $250,000 has been posted by the NSW Government." The poster then outlined the details of the murder and noted that it was linked to the earlier killings. It continued: "It is requested that any person in that area on the afternoon of Thursday, 23rd November, who may have seen the deceased either alone or in the company of another person, contact police on the following numbers as a matter of urgency. All information will be treated in the strictest confidence." At the bottom were police telephone numbers, a description of the clothes Muriel Falconer wore on her last day alive, and a photograph of the victim.

The New South Wales Police Department published a brochure, "Safety Advice For The Elderly — Some Simple Crime Prevention Tips". The aged of Mosman, of all Sydney, began taking the following precautions:

- Talk regularly to someone you can trust.
- Maintain a signal with someone at a certain time each day, for example three rings on the telephone.
- If you become a victim of crime, seek help immediately. Don't be embarrassed.
- Have a peephole in your front door and a light just outside.
- Install deadlocks on all doors.
- Put safety catches on screens and windows.
- Never admit to anyone that you live alone.
- Don't let anyone into your home that you don't know or trust.
- Ask for identification and make a quick phone call, if necessary, to verify people claiming to represent gas, electricity and telephone companies.
- Travel and shop with friends wherever possible.
- Carry your purse or bag close to your body and never leave them on seats in buses and trains.
- If someone attempts to steal your bag, don't resist. If possible, tip out the contents.
- At night, walk along well-lit roads and avoid side streets.
- Consult public transport timetables before you leave home to avoid unnecessary waiting at bus stops and railway stations.
- Don't use back lanes, parks or vacant lots as short cuts.
- Carry a small torch.
- Try to get someone to see you to your front door.
- Don't go to the bank or the building society at the same time each day.
- Don't display large amounts of cash.
- Place cash in a purse before walking away from the teller or automatic teller machine.

The terror in the streets was fuelled by a number of TV reports and newspaper beat-ups based more on speculation than on fact. *The*

Sydney Morning Herald of November 11 ran a photograph of an elderly woman peeping fearfully from behind venetian blinds and accompanied that photo with an Identikit picture of a dark-haired man in his 20s and the heading "I Got A Terrible Shock. He Knew Where I Lived". The article told how an unnamed 64-year-old Ryde woman — not, incidentally, the one shown peeping through the blinds — had been followed home day after day for a week from a Top Ryde shopping plaza by a man similar to the one in the Identikit composite, and how on November 2 the man had sat outside her home unit block watching her window. He departed at 1.15pm. Two hours later Madge Pahud was murdered at Lane Cove. The reporter called the incident "the biggest breakthrough in the north shore killings" and then took it upon herself to claim that it gave police "their best lead in the hunt for the killer, or killers..." She continued, "An important part of the woman's story is that if the man is the killer, he may have known his victims, their habits, their addresses, and many other personal details before he bashed them from behind with a blunt instrument..." The reporter then indulged in a little psychiatric speculation, "He may also have enjoyed the victim knowing that he was stalking her", before venturing that the woman might have been the serial killer's third victim and that she only now realised how lucky she was.

There was no connection at all between the stalking of the Ryde shopper and the serial killings of the elderly women. The task force was irritated by the *Herald* article because of the way the reporter had linked the frightened woman's ordeal to the murders in spite of the fact that there was no real basis for such an assumption. Reasoned, level-headed community awareness of the danger confronting the elderly was what was required, not scare articles that only incited needless terror. The beat-up was published at the top of the front page of *The Sydney Morning Herald*, being given prominence over major stories on an East German Communist Party purge and how Australian manufacturing industry was in its death throes. Detectives were ordered to Ryde where they questioned a number of men who resembled the fellow in the Identikit but released them all and returned to their inquiry.

A bewildered and besieged community took police up on their exhortations to report suspicious people and a rash of "Granny

Killers" were sighted all over Sydney. Every sighting was investigated by local police and the task force and details were loaded into MIIRS. A number of Identikit pictures, all different and none resembling John Glover, of men sought by police for questioning over the serial killings had been published in the press and this added to the confusion and, consequently, to the investigators' workload. On a single day in November, for example, police squad cars zig-zagged the city when the killer was reported drinking in a club at Lakemba, lurking outside a nursing home at Mosman, driving west along Parramatta Road, playing squash at Collaroy, strolling in Hunters Hill, doing business at Dee Why post office, standing outside a nursery at Ryde, and waiting for a train at North Sydney station. The train and its irritated passengers were delayed until police arrived. Every one of these sightings could have been the crucial one, the one to break the case, and so had to be followed up, but, as it turned out, none proved fruitful.

The Granny Killings inspired many extraordinary reactions in the community. Citizens anxious to help deluged the investigators with letters and phone calls to the task force hotline offering advice, clues and encouragement. The mail bags at Chatswood headquarters were further swelled by less-welcome, time-wasting correspondence from clairvoyants, crackpots and mischief makers.

Says Mike Hagan, "A lot of useful information came in from the public, but too often you'd get a bloke who was blueing with his neighbour and he'd ring up and anonymously dob the neighbour in as the Granny Killer. People who wanted to settle a score with their boss or whoever would try the same trick," says Mike Hagan. "It sounds amusing now, but all of these tips had to be checked out at a time when there wasn't a policeman or a second to waste."

Task force members have kept some of the more memorable letters received at the height of the manhunt. Says one: "If you want to knou abaut the second north shore granny killer go to (address given) in Mascot — owner white Mercedes. A yellow Holden Gemeni (number plate given) — in particular check out the guy with the long black hair. M....y. Signed, A Friend 1590." And another: "The Coogee rapist and Mosman Granny Killer looks like a trained nurse (name given) at Prince Henry Hospital." A photograph of a man was stuck to the page. A third read: "(Name given) fits description of person following lady at Ryde — age more like about in his 30s. Drank pub here Lane Cove. Said he lived in Lane Cove. But told he now lives Mosman. Strange, secretive, sometime angry and persacuted type. Ref, or code for any reward RSX."

One person claimed that the victims had been chosen because their initials formed an alphabetical pattern. Break the code to that pattern and the killer's name would be revealed. Another advised police to view a recent British TV movie on Jack the Ripper starring Michael Caine. The murders, he said, paralleled those of the English serial slayer of last century. He directed police to go to local libraries and investigate all those who had borrowed books on the Ripper. Yet another citizen trying to assist said the north shore murderer was inspired by a character in ancient mythology called the Saga Killer. Mike Hagan read up on the old Norse heroes but could find little connection.

From Sydney's Long Bay Gaol came the following, written in block capital letters: "Sir, This letter is being sent from within Long Bay prison. I am writing because I know exactly who the north shore serial killer is. You may bleive this letter to be a hoax, but bleive me you would be very wrong. My concern is that the reward offered is no good to me, as I cant spend it in prison. I am prepared to devulge the killers identity, on the condition that if the killer is who I say, that a deal be made that I both recieve the reward money, and a release from prison. To make your decision a little easier, I have only 2 years left to serve before release. I watch Channel Ten news every day, so you can communicate your intentions through that network. I will say this much, the man you are looking for spent time both in prison and Morriset Phyc Centre, and has a short hystery for assault on old person, and that I both shared a cell with him, and in emediate contact with him, and he has told me what he has done, and that he wants to stop. It's your decision now, but remember this, he will strike again, cause he has told me he can not control himself. I will keep viewing Channel 10, but remember. I want 100% guarantee that in return for the correct information I am given both the reward and a special licence. No ifs or butts."

Another correspondent wrote asking whether police had considered that the murderer might be a supporter of euthanasia who may believe he is doing these elderly women a good turn by hitting them on the head. The author of this letter then helpfully named a person she knew who had started a euthanasia counselling group and with whom she just happened to have had a recent argument. The 69-year-old writer said she would be happy to help police locate this "baddy" but hoped they would not subject her to too much questioning as she was suffering from a "nasty dose of the sun".

A number of clairvoyants emerged, but proved no more helpful to the investigators than the woman suffering from sunstroke. Old men, young men, children, women, Englishmen, Americans, Yugoslavians and Italians, a teenage gang, someone with a gold tooth, an elderly lady in a red hat — all were variously exposed as the killer by psychics and soothsayers.

Once or twice, however, a clairvoyant came chillingly close to the truth. The murderer, wrote a person with an indecipherable signature on December 14, was about to kill again. "His emotions and stress are building up... he will strike sooner than you think... He has trouble with his mother and wishes she would die. She has created the mess he is in... he wants to kill, kill, kill... He won't be caught till after he has killed again... I see a house, No.81... I feel he lives near the seaside area. This man at the moment can't see straight, he feels so depressed, angry, confused... I am also seeing him in a grey suit... This man has a foreign background... He doesn't want to do it but (with the) excitement and anger he has no other release... I don't know if the papers said it was jewellery he took from each person but whatever it is he won't part with it. It is of no financial benefit, but it is of benefit to him... He will kill very soon, I see him as sort of within him waiting. He has also killed in another area before he moved to where he is now, but before his condition was more under control than it is now." The clairvoyant was correct on 10 counts and had a near-miss with the killer's house number. Reverse the digits and she would have been right 11 times over.

And there was the late night radio listener from Casula, south west of Sydney, who wrote to Mike Hagan: "I wrote to the police at Mosman a couple of months ago. I didn't sign my name to that letter because at the time I felt I might be taken for a ratbag. Concerning the Mosman Granny Killer, I have a feeling he is a person I've heard twice on talk-back radio shows late at night. The first time, about which I wrote, he called in to Mike Williams' show on 2UE between

12.30 and 1.30am. On that occasion he expressed sorrow at the killing of innocent old ladies. He sounded insincere and depressed. He kept on repeating how bad he felt about it... but there was something about this fellow's voice that wasn't right.

"He said on that occasion that his name was John, that he lived at Mosman, and I got the impression somehow that he said something about him working in TV or radio or on a newspaper. Well, I take a lot of notice of voices. I have a deaf son and I have spent a lot of time helping him to learn to talk, so how a person breathes, hesitates etc, how they express themselves, is automatically noted by me. And I think females are by nature more aware of nuances.

"Well, on Friday morning, December 1, I heard that man's voice again, this time on Andrew Harwood's show on 2GB, between 12.30 and 1.15am. Again he struck me as if there was a message in what he was saying because he had a very unusual attitude to the killing of the old ladies.

"He kept repeating that it would have happened anyway. I didn't know what his line of reasoning was. Andrew Harwood, the host of the show, wasn't as sharp as he usually is. Maybe he was tired that night, and just agreed with him and interpreted the man's comment as being a result of society today.

"Anyway, this fellow said he lived in Muston Street, Mosman. He hesitated over the pronunciation of "Muston", so I came to the conclusion that he was lying on that score... He said he had offered his services as an escort for the elderly, but had been rejected. But he kept repeating that those killings (or deaths) would have happened anyway.

"I know this letter sounds pretty stupid, but if it could help you, then I don't mind being regarded as foolish. I hope you can understand my writing. I have arthritis in my hand and have difficulty controlling the pen."

An interesting sidelight to all these letters received by police was that not one writer confessed to the crimes. Says Mike Hagan, "Normally with any killing you get crackpots writing in and telling you that they are the guilty party — nuisances wanting a bit of anonymous notoriety. It says a lot about the Granny Killings that not even people of unsound mind wanted to own up to them."

CHAPTER 11

Under Suspicion

The youth had come to Mosman to smell death. He was into death, he told task force homicide chief Miles O'Toole, and had read about the murders in the newspaper and he had come to the suburb to walk the streets but — great disappointment — he couldn't smell death anywhere. There was nothing else to do, he told the incredulous investigator, but catch a train to Rookwood cemetery and sleep the night on a grave. "This bloke just turned up in the office," says O'Toole, who was in charge of investigating possible suspects, "and he was one fellow we certainly kept an eye on, but he was eliminated fairly quickly."

Another fellow O'Toole was able to clear rapidly was an American pornographic movie star denounced as the Granny Killer by a 90-year-old Mosman woman. She had been at her octogenarian brother's home when a plain brown package was delivered to his door. The sister opened the package and found a video inside. She put the cassette into a VCR and found her sensibilities outraged by an X-rated movie which featured the freakishly-proportioned late US actor John Holmes cavorting with a number of women. After watching it all the way through, she called a friend and the pair viewed the video together for another 25 minutes, until they could stand no more. She then reported the movie star to Miles O'Toole, saying anybody capable of doing what the man in the video did to women just *had* to be the Granny Killer.

Running sheets were also generated on an American sailor who carried a bowie knife who was informed on as being capable of mass murder by a shipmate who himself had been picked up after being found wandering in a drunken stupor around Mosman. And a sheet was started on a youth who emerged from behind bushes and barked like a dog at an elderly woman in Frenchs Forest, and on another youth who made an obscene remark to an old lady at Bondi. Then there were the three Mosman boys, aged around 12 to 14, who thought it funny to brandish their skateboards at an elderly woman in Military Road. Sur-veillance police saw it all and summoned detectives Miles O'Toole and Barrry Keeling who bundled the children off to Mosman police station where they spent the most unhappy 20 minutes of their lives as the policemen gave them a grilling and a few pointers about respecting the elderly. Finally, in a desperate effort to get out of there, the boys suggested to the detectives that they thought they knew who was responsible for the killings and they informed on some rough-looking blokes in stubbies and board shorts they'd seen earlier in the shopping centre. The men they fingered were the very surveillance police responsible for landing the boys in their present predicament. Good to break the tension and not much else, all these incidents, and many others equally trivial, needed to be logged in the task force computers.

The tension was broken, too, when Stephen Shepherd, the licensee of the popular task force watering hole, the Buena Vista, just across the road from Mosman police station, was arrested. Shepherd had taken a break from work on November 24, brought a pie, and was munching away in nearby Muston Street when he saw a commotion outside No.3. Muriel Falconer had been murdered there the previous day and the street was alive with police. The curious publican peered over the garden wall to try to catch a glimpse of the feverish activity inside the house when he felt a heavy hand on his shoulder. "Who are you and what are you doing?" demanded the uniformed officer, a policeman not from Mosman who did not recognise Shepherd. The publican stammered out his name, said he ran the Buena Vista Hotel and that he was only taking a stroll. The policeman said he'd see about that and marched Shepherd around the corner to the Buena Vista. There, Shepherd approached an employee, a young fellow keen on practical jokes.

"Tell the officer I'm the licensee of this pub," demanded Shepherd.

"Sorry, mate," said the employee with a perplexed expression, "I've never seen you before in my life."

Just as the fuming Shepherd was being hauled out the door and across to the police station the young man decided he valued his job after all and set the policeman right.

Of the 740 people listed as suspects during the hunt for the Granny Killer, hundreds, like the people above, were easily and speedily eliminated. But hundreds, too, were considered by O'Toole and his men to be worthy of serious investigation. After many months of meticulous and protracted enquiries, a list of the 10 suspects most likely was compiled and the vast weight of resources thrown into probing them.

But before that could be done, every one of the 740 had to be checked out: from informants' fractious neighbours to an international con artist, from a psychotic young man who tried to throttle his mother and grandmother and had a morbid fascination in police affairs to a mysterious grey-haired, middle-aged man who kept fading in and out of witness's lists of things and people noticed in crime vicinities. Until a sequence of events led police to put that grey-haired man at the top of their list, the psychotic young man was suspect No.1.

Among the many priorities of the detectives investigating suspects was to locate the youth on the skateboard who sped away from the grounds of the Garrison Retirement Village and startled a group of people tending the bashed Doris Cox. Also the search was on for the blond youth who hit 60-year-old Ray Roper on the back of the head as he walked in Raglan Street one night in April, just a fortnight before Lady Ashton was slain in the same street. This assailant, like the youth on the skateboard, was never found.

One suspect who *was* found, to the chagrin of the police whose job it was to drive him to task force headquarters, was a bagman who lived in a large storm water drainpipe at a council compound in Frenchs Forest. The fellow had been seen with a number of knives and sticks and was wanted for questioning over the Olive Cleveland murder at nearby Belrose. When police picked him up rifling through garbage bins at the rear of a Frenchs Forest fast food shop it became immediately and suffocatingly obvious that he had not bathed for months. Windows down, the police drove him to Chatswood where he was interrogated and released, to the immense relief of the detectives who had been cooped up with him in the tiny, airless interview room.

In Mosman one day at the height of the hysteria an elderly lady noticed a well-presented and handsome middle-aged woman, her brown hair tied back in a bow, following her as she left the Mosman Medicare office. Frightened, she hailed a taxi to take her home. A month or so later the well-presented woman approached the elderly lady outside a Mosman delicatessen and struck up a conversation, during which she asked a number of personal questions which the old lady refused to answer. Ten days later, the well-presented woman telephoned the old lady and offered to do her shopping for her. The aged woman lied and said she lived with her son who took care of all of her errands. She told police she had never ever given her persecutor her name or telephone number. The task force considered the middle-aged woman a prime suspect and investigated her background. They learned that she had a record for assaulting a female and resisting arrest. When called to stand trial on those charges, she had harassed witnesses and accused them of devil worship. When convicted, she phoned the arresting police officer and claimed that he, the Crown and her own defence counsellor had formed a conspiracy against her. The woman kept ringing the constable, sometimes six or seven times a shift. Contacted by task force members, he described her as mentally unstable, persistent and vengeful. When detectives called on her she was able to convince them she was innocent of the serial killings. As they left her apartment, she quipped, "Happy hunting!"

Another hot suspect was a Canadian conman who claimed vast family wealth, an Olympic gold medal for ice skating and invented for himself fanciful double-barrelled names, adding a "III" at the end when he was really out to impress. A homosexual in his early 20s, his victims included many wealthy, sometimes prominent, Mosman men whom he would seduce in bars. The Canadian sported dyed yellow, brown or black hair and kept a briefcase filled with bottles of skin-cleansing lotions and cologne. He was usually weighed down with many cheap gold bracelets and necklaces and wore lizard-skin cowboy boots. His scam was to move into his lovers' houses, steal their money and sell their clothes and jewellery and then vanish, seemingly safe in the knowledge that his hosts would be most unlikely to report him to police for fear of having their own double life exposed.

Unhappily for the Canadian, some victims did feel sufficiently outraged to risk their reputations and report him to police. Investigators on the task force heard of this fellow and were able to positively place the con man in the vicinity on the days of the Mitchelhill and Ashton murders. In fact, 30 minutes before Lady Ashton was attacked the Canadian was identified in a Military Road ice cream shop not 200 metres from her Raglan Street home unit block. An Identikit Penri was released on May 12 by investigators who urgently wanted to question the man about the murders. Two days later the spooked conman fled the country for Los Angeles via Honolulu. He vacated his apartment without notice, leaving almost all of his belongings behind.

The task force contacted the Federal Bureau of Investigation in the United States and soon after Canadian police arrested the wanted man on false pretence charges in Vancouver and extradited him to Ontario where homicide detectives, acting on a brief from the Australian task force, interviewed him at length on video. The video was despatched to Australia, converted to the Australian system by police contacts at Channel Nine and viewed with interest by the investigators. The man's responses to the Canadian police questioning were guarded and evasive. "He's looking good," exulted the task force members. So good, that Miles O'Toole packed his bags to fly to Canada to interview the man himself. Then, on November 2, just before his seat was booked for Ontario where the Canadian was languishing in gaol, Madge Pahud was murdered in Lane Cove.

Sexual offenders and people with a history of assaults were obvious suspects, and so, much less obviously, were local schoolchildren and servicemen attached to the various military and naval bases in Mosman. The decision to canvass schools and bases was in part due to the advice of the eminent forensic psychiatrist Dr Rod Milton, who had assisted police back in June with a profile of the possible offender after the Mitchelhill and Ashton murders. Now, in late November, the killer had struck three times more and it was time for an update.

In his revised report to police, Milton reiterated his earlier opinion that the killer could be a schoolboy or a serviceman with a hatred of elderly women; that the murderer was probably not a woman because of the strength and ferocity of the attacks, and not a severely mentally sick person because of the high degree of organisation, persistence and determination exhibited by the offender. And that the offender would kill again.

Milton prefaced his summary to police by saying that while his conclusions were, at best, educated guesses, "and you will no doubt remain open to the prospect of the offences having been committed by someone outside the confines of my predictions... I suggest that the offender is male, of reasonably normal manner and appearance, aged in his late teens or early 20s, perhaps a student or serviceman. I think it likely he lives in the Mosman area and lives with family members. I doubt that lack of money is a serious issue with him. I do not think he has a serious drug problem or that drugs form the motivation for robberies.

"I think he probably has serious difficulties in his relationship with his father, who himself would be likely to have emotional problems concerning aggression and hostility although these would apparently be under control. The difficulty in the offender's relationship with his father had probably resulted in marked conflicts in his feelings about women, especially those in a mothering or a vulnerable role.

"He might well have just done the Higher School Certificate and the subjects of which he would be capable (assuming normal intellect but preoccupation with his internal emotional conflicts interfering with concentration) could largely have been completed by the time he killed Mrs Pahud.

"He might have acquired a driver's licence between killing Lady Ashton and murdering Mrs Pahud.

"He remains in intense emotional conflict and obviously cannot tell anyone about it. He fears detection but welcomes control of his own destructive urges, and for this reason might give himself up or make tentative attempts to do so.

"Further attacks are likely unless or until he kills the person in his family who is the principal focus of his aggression, or until he is arrested.

"I suspect his interests lie in the field of computing and war games. I earlier thought he would be involved in martial arts; but the post mortem findings supplied to me recently do not support that view so well now. He might also have hobbies involving building models of a very detailed kind.

"Not only is it important to explore the avenues offered by existing information, but we should anticipate direct contact from the offender. Police officers likely to take the call will need to be aware of the possibility of him calling, and of the need to handle him with great care.

"You might consider making further checks of the high schools in the area to see if school teachers have had time to reflect on your earlier contact and to review any opinions expressed earlier. The membership of local RSL groups should be cross-checked against school enrolments and specific comments sought from teachers on the sons of servicemen or ex-servicemen.

"The offender's family might respond to a careful announcement to the media, which would include an indication of the risks to which they are currently exposed. I do not think this should mention the risk of the offender suiciding if not caught."

Dr Milton thinks back today on how he was able to piece together his profile of the Granny Killer. "The two things that struck me was the orderliness of the crime scenes — shoes, sticks and so on stacked neatly by the body — and the incredible massive violence and speed with which the murders were committed. These factors stayed in my mind as I prepared my reports for the police.

"I kept looking at the photographs of the victims, trying to make some sense of it. In my book, there is no such thing as a senseless murder. There is always some kind of reasoning behind a killing. But what was it here? Violence and order? That's what the army is all about. And it is not uncommon to find people with an interest in extreme violence in the armed forces. So my recommendation was that the police interview servicemen.

"As for the killer being a schoolboy, there is a school near the Mitchelhill, Ashton and Falconer murder scenes and the Cox assault location. The attacks were in the late afternoon just after school was over for the day. As well, the high risk involved in murdering in busy places in broad daylight made me think the offender could be an adolescent, even though I often did have doubts and pondered, 'Now, *could* he be someone older?' But risk-taking is adolescent behaviour. And the enormous violence and anger exhibited in the blitzkrieg attacks also pointed me towards a young person being the killer. As it turned out, the murderer was not young, but when I interviewed the offender later in gaol, I noticed at once that he had many adolescent qualities."

The killings betrayed misplaced anger, says the psychiatrist. That is, anger felt towards one person but taken out on another. "I kept asking myself, 'Now why is he killing old people?' And the answer I came up with was that he hates his grandmother, mother, mother-in-law, or wife so he is going around killing substitutes. That was certainly the case."

Even before he murdered Muriel Falconer, Dr Milton was convinced that the killer would attack a relative or close friend. "Mike Hagan and I contemplated running an advertisement in the paper warning that the offender might strike close to home. The reasoning was if someone close to the killer suspected anything about their loved one, the ad might move them to come forward and tell police what they knew." In spite of a front page *Daily Telegraph* story to this effect, nobody close to the killer came forward. And Dr Milton's prediction that a close acquaintance of the killer might pay for their friendship with her life came tragically true.

A man who must be known in these pages as "Mr A", an explosively aggressive and enormously angry Mosman resident in his early 20s, was the living, breathing embodiment of Dr Milton's hypothetical violent young menace to society who was driven by a hatred of his mother and grandmother. Attempts to strangle his mother and his grandmother, along with many other dangerous and anti-social tendencies, made Mr A for almost a year the strongest suspect in the task force's rogue's gallery of likely Granny Killers.

Mr A was a paranoid psychotic with a lengthy psychiatric history who at the time of the murders was undergoing medical treatment and anti-depressant medication. Nominated as a suspect by a psychiatric nurse after the Ashton slaying, he gave police an alibi that could not be confirmed. When questioned later about the Doris Cox assault, he said he could not remember where he was on October 18, but it was ascertained by police that he was in the vicinity of the Garrison Retirement Village at the time. After Olive Cleveland was murdered, photographs of suspects were shown to residents at Wesley Gardens and Mr A was pinpointed as being in the vicinity. When interviewed after the Falconer killing in November, Mr A again gave an alibi, and again it was proved to be false. It was learned that he kept newspaper clippings of all the killings.

This suspect had an abnormal interest in police activities. He routinely listened in to police transmissions on his radio scanner and strutted around Mosman with a police baton attached to his belt. The baton was tested by the task force for bloodstains but proved clear. He was suspected of making anonymous telephone calls to the police about the serial murders.

He was placed under heavy surveillance. Dog squad members were alarmed to see Mr A on numerous occasions chatting to elderly female strangers in the shopping centres and assisting them across Military Road. However he was never observed following them home.

Surveillance chief Doodles O'Toole calls Mr A "the madman of Mosman". "This bloke was on our radio wavelength so whenever police were called to a traffic accident, a fire, any kind of tragedy, there he'd be, just standing and watching. He was a complete schizophrenic. One minute he'd be talking rationally to someone, next he'd fly into a deep rage. He hated his family and anyone else who upset him. And he had a fetish for police activities. He knew we suspected he was the Granny Killer and he enjoyed that and would go round the suburb talking about how the police were trying to pin the murders on him."

At the behest of Mr A's mother, the present-day mayor of Mosman Dom Lopez once employed Mr A to help count money and do odd jobs in his cigarette vending machine business. The young man repaid Lopez by secretly cutting an ignition key to his boss's car and joy-riding around Mosman in the vehicle at night. Every chance he'd get he'd tell people he was on patrol for the mayor. When Lopez discovered his employee's after-hours activities he sacked him.

"I never believed Mr A was the killer," says Lopez. "He's too stupid to be a murderer. He just enjoyed the notoriety of being a suspect and loved it when the police questioned him. Mr A is bad news, but he's not capable of mass murder."

Mr A was subjected to concentrated surveillance and the dog squad maintained this pressure on the suspect right until the very end. At last, when the real culprit was caught and stood trial, there in the public gallery of the courtroom as the sentence was handed down was Mr A.

Then there was the grey-haired, middle-aged man. This fellow had been mentioned, usually as an afterthought, by quite a few of the witnesses to a significant number of the crimes. At one stage Detective Sen Const Paul Tuxford approached Miles O'Toole and said, "I've got your murderer. I don't know who he is, but I've got him." Tuxford then brought to light the numerous sightings of the grey-haired man. Among those sightings, logged away in the MIIRS computer, were:

• Margaret Todhunter identified a 50-year-old broad-shouldered, thick-chested, large-stomached man with well-kept grey hair as her attacker in Hale Road, Mosman, back on January 11 — and police had an artist's impression of the man based on her description.

• A fellow with similar features was seen acting suspiciously and following an elderly woman outside the Buena Vista Hotel, Mosman on July 6.

• Then a well-built, white-haired man was reported for punching 82-year-old Euphemia Carnie at Lindfield's North Haven Retirement Village on August 25.

• A 30-35-year-old grey-haired man, agitated and wearing jeans and white joggers, was seen making an unsuccessful snatch for an elderly woman's bag at the corner of Military Road and Rangers Road, Mosman.

• Two hours before Madge Pahud was killed on November 2, a grey-haired, solidly-built 50 year old was observed standing aimlessly in the car park of the Pottery Nursing Home in nearby Longueville Road. Then at 2pm, one hour before the murder, it was an elderly, healthy-looking man of medium build who had helped Dorothy Beencke, Madge Pahud's friend and neighbour, carry her groceries down the very lane in which the Pahud attack took place. Just 15 minutes after Madge Pahud's slaying a 40-year-old grey-haired man of Australian appearance and medium build was spotted acting suspiciously in Longueville Road, close to the murder lane.

• Two hours after Olive Cleveland was killed next day at Wesley Gardens, a 50-year-old grey-haired man with a sun-tanned face and driving an early-1980 model Ford or Holden asked a delivery van driver for directions in the nursing home car park. When the driver told the grey-haired man to follow him, he did not.

• On the morning of November 23, a Muston Street resident noticed a well-dressed, middle-aged, grey-haired man in the street, the same street where Muriel Falconer would be murdered that afternoon. A few hours later, a man searching for a light distributor in Muston Street observed a grey-haired, 40-year-old, solidly-built man "with a bit of a gut" in four separate locations in the vicinity of Muston Street.

But that was all police had. There were millions of middle-aged, grey-haired, thickset men out there. Most Australian males over the age of 50 could answer that description. Without a name or any other meaningful identification — no nursing staff member who could connect the pie salesman to assaults of elderly women had come forward and reported him to police at this stage — this grey-haired fellow, even if it *was* the same person at every murder or assault site, might just as well have been the Invisible Man.

"Yeah, we discussed the grey-haired man a fair bit," says task force deputy commander Ron Smith. "We thought it was out of character for an older bloke to be doing the killings. Then we got to thinking how *easy* it would be for a nondescript-looking fellow to get away with these daytime attacks in busy locations. Somebody you wouldn't notice — somebody like a conservatively-dressed, grey-haired man who blended into the crowd — would stand a much better chance of getting away with murder in broad daylight than would, say, an erratic druggie or an armed robber or a punk in outrageous clothes or an obviously bad-looking bloke who stood out like the proverbial. The grey-haired man was right up there in our top 10 suspects, but there wasn't a damn thing we could do about it."

CHAPTER 12

The Net Descends

John Glover had been defying the law of averages for 10 months. It was inconceivable, but in committing five murders and numerous assaults, all in busy areas and in broad daylight, he had left behind just one significant clue to his identity: the shoeprints in Muriel Falconer's hallway. And they would only be of use in placing him at the scene of that particular crime *after* he was caught. Impossible to believe, but there had not been a single concrete identification of Glover and he had left nothing incriminating — save the prints — at any murder location.

Glover enjoyed phenomenal luck almost all the way, but there is no doubt that the washing clean of clues of the death scenes and the fact that no one bothered to report the nursing home and retirement village assaults to police were factors that prolonged his rampage.

For all the hard slog of their investigation — the thousands of interviews, the computer systems, the surveillance and grilling of suspects, the forensic work — as the new decade began police were no closer to arresting the serial murderer than they had been back in March, 1989, when his reign of terror began. As police admitted throughout the steamy, wet Sydney summer of 1990, the Granny Killer could be anybody. But now, at last, John Glover's good fortune began to turn bad.

"You seem to be losing your body heat," said the pleasant, grey-haired man who could so easily have been a doctor to the 82-year-old woman sitting up in bed in Room No.1 in the palliative care, or terminal, ward of Greenwich Hospital in River Road, Greenwich. The woman was fanning herself with her lunch bib. It was noon, January 11. The bed-ridden cancer patient had seen this fellow in his brown slacks, blue spray jacket with what looked like a hospital identification badge pinned on it and carrying a clipboard, pass in and out of her room two or three times, and now he was standing close, on the left-hand side of her bed. "Just a little," the woman agreed with his prognosis. It was a terribly hot day.

At that, John Glover reached his beefy hand down the front of the patient's pink nightie and held her right breast before moving his hand around and rubbing her back. He duplicated his assault on her left breast and back. Next, he softly massaged the woman's stomach, all the while soothing, "Yes, you *are* losing your body heat." He finally withdrew his arm and disappeared into the corridor without another word.

Nurse Jodie Smith saw a stranger with a clipboard acting suspiciously in the corridor while on her way to make a routine check on Room No.1. When she arrived the patient was highly agitated. "A man just came in and put his hand down the front of my nightie and up again," she cried to the nurse. She then stammered something about "body heat". The nurse told the old woman she should have rung immediately for assistance. "But I thought he was a doctor," protested the woman.

Jodie Smith reported the incident to Sister Pauline Davis who had herself noticed the stocky man with the clipboard lurking in the hospital minutes earlier. She had seen him standing on a verandah near the elderly woman's room, moving his head from side to side. After hearing the nurse's report Sister Davis set off after the man. She found him speaking on a public telephone at the end of a hallway. As she approached, Glover hung up the phone. She was to the point. "Are you lost? Are you looking for someone?" she demanded.

"The catering supervisor," said Glover. "Her name escapes me."

"Were you just in the ward? Have you been into Room No.1?"

"No," protested Glover, "I've just come in. But there was another man wandering around. I sent him upstairs."

Sister Davis hurried off to see if the elderly woman could identify her attacker. Glover paid a quick call on the kitchen staff before making off to his blue station wagon parked in River Road. A close call, he thought, as he drove away, but none of the other hospital or nursing home staff had ever dobbed him in, he gloated, so there was

Gay and John Glover on their wedding day, June 1, 1968.

Above: The home unit block where Gwen Mitchelhill was murdered.
Below: Doris Cox was bashed at the Garrison Retirement Village.

Victims, clockwise from top left: Gwen Mitchelhill, Lady Ashton, Doris Cox, Madge Pahud, Olive Cleveland, Muriel Falconer.

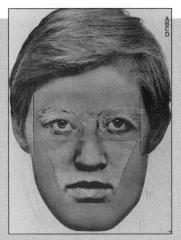

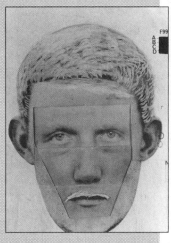

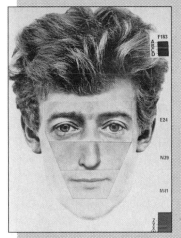

A number of Penri sketches, Identikit composites and artists' impressions of the possible serial killer were published as the manhunt ran its course.

Right: This impression of the attacker of Margaret Todhunter bears a strong likeness to John Glover.

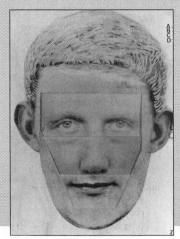

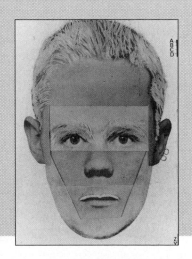

ARTIST'S IMPRESSION OF OFFENDER RE AGGRAVATED ASSAULT
ON 84 yr old FEMALE   HALE St. CREMOURNE JAN 1989

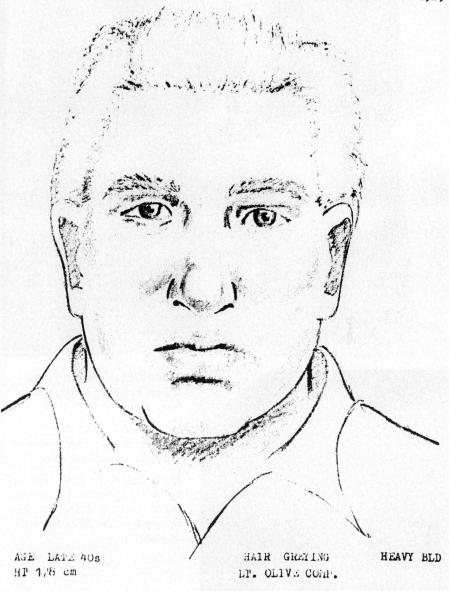

AGE LATE 40s   HAIR GREYING   HEAVY BLD
HT 176 cm   LT. OLIVE COMP.

Above: Glover tracked victim Muriel Falconer through her front garden.

Left: Glover's false step; his faint shoeprint on the carpet at the Falconer murder scene.

Right: Both sides of the note left by Glover upon his first suicide bid in January, 1990. Note the reference to "No More Grannys" on page one.

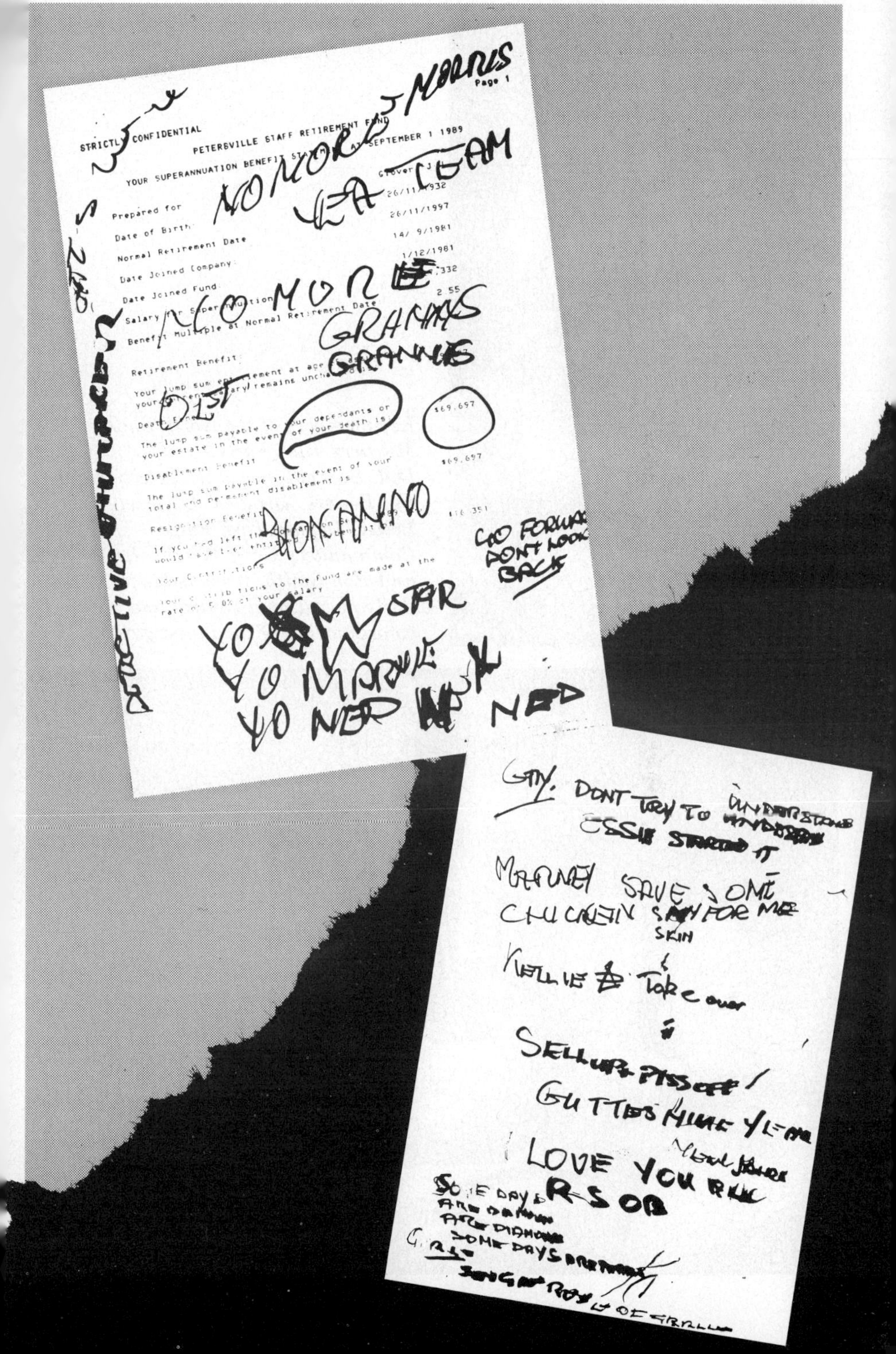

Key members of the North Shore
Murders Task Force.
Left: Surveillance chief Detective Sen
Sgt Dennis "Doodles" O'Toole.
Below: Deputy Task Force
Commanders Geoff Wright (left)
and Ron Smith, responsible for
daily operational control and
co-ordination of all investigations.

Right: Detective Sgt Dennis "Miles" O'Toole, who headed the homicide investigation and was there when the Granny Killer was finally arrested.

Below: Task Force Commander of Operations Mike Hagan who ran the soul-destroying year-long hunt for the serial killer. Miles O'Toole described Hagan as "a man you'd walk on hot coals for".

In February 1990 surveillance cameras set up throughout busy Mosman areas kept an electronic eye on the by-now red-hot suspect John Glover as he went about his shopping.

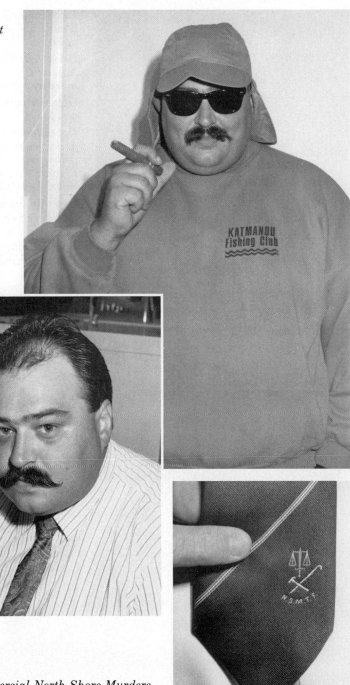

*Right and below:
Detective Sen Const
Paul Jacob who
donned this
disguise to drive
Glover out of
hospital and to the
Sydney Police
Centre. The ruse
fooled the media
who had beseiged
the hospital for a
glimpse of the
killer.*

*Right: The controversial North Shore Murders
Task Force tie, representing the triumph of
justice over the Granny Killer.*

Left: The killer's vehicle, photographed by surveillance police.

Below left: The house in Pindari Avenue where Joan Sinclair was murdered and Glover captured.

Opposite right: The murder weapon.

Opposite far right: Glover's pants, socks and shoes, found by police in a room adjoining the Pindari Avenue house bathroom where he tried to commit suicide.

Opposite below: The bathroom, minutes after the semi-comatose Glover was discovered by police. Note the killer's watch, pill containers and whisky bottle on the vanity.

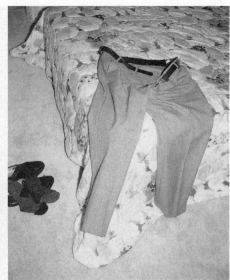

SEARCH AREA

Above: Parkland in Mosman where police searched for victims' belongings.

Left: Ashton Park, where Glover hurled purses stolen from Lady Ashton.

This page: Following his committal, Glover accompanied task force members, including homicide detectives Murray Byrnes (in short-sleeved shirt) and Paul Mayger to the sites where he had disposed of his victim's belongings.

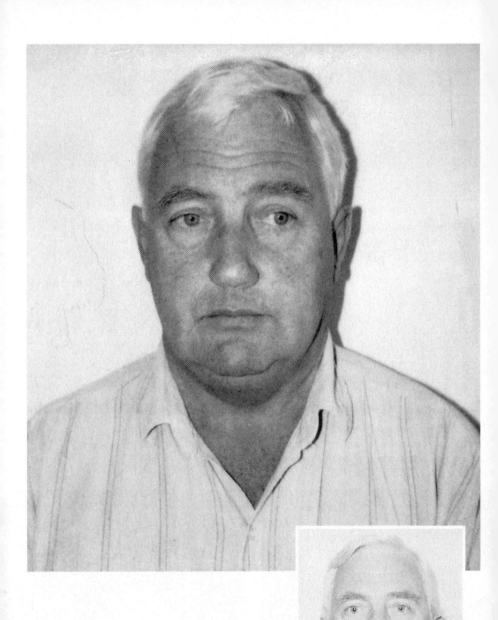

The police Polaroid taken of Glover following his first suicide bid. The photo played a role in bringing the Granny Killer to justice. Inset: The most recent photo of Glover, taken in Long Bay Gaol, April 1992.

no reason to believe Sister Davis would report him to the police either. He was wrong.

Sister Davis telephoned Chatswood police station and asked to speak to somebody about an indecent assault. At 5.20 that afternoon Detective Const Pam Whittaker arrived at Greenwich Hospital. There kitchen staff were able to identify the stocky, grey-haired attacker of the elderly woman as a jolly Four 'N Twenty pie salesman whose name was John Glover.

At 5pm next day, the telephone rang at No.18 Wyong Road. Glover answered. "May I speak with John Glover, please?" said the voice at the other end of the line.

"Speaking."

"I'm Constable Whittaker from Chatswood police station. I am making enquiries about an alleged assault which occurred about 12 midday yesterday at Greenwich Hospital. Can you tell me anything about this?"

Blood rushed to Glover's face and his knees buckled, but his voice was calm, "I was at the hospital about that time for work, but I don't know anything about an assault." Oh, Christ!

"I would like to speak with you further about this allegation. Are you able to come to the police station?"

"No," said Glover, then thought better of it and agreed to meet Constable Whittaker at Chatswood police station next day, Saturday, at 5pm. "Christ!" thought John Glover, "Oh, Christ!"

* * *

The following afternoon the 25-year-old policewoman sat in an office at Chatswood police station wondering where on earth this bloke was. Glover was an hour late for their appointment. She dialled his number. A woman answered the phone. "No," said Gay Glover, "John's not here. My husband tried to commit suicide an hour ago and has been taken to Royal North Shore Hospital."

Sometime between 4pm and 5pm that Saturday, distraught that he was about to be exposed, Glover had swallowed a quantity of Benzodiazepines and Normethadone and washed the pills down with a bottle of scotch whisky. As his mind heaved and roiled just before blacking out, he took a Petersville Staff Retirement Fund form from a table at his bedside and scrawled, in lurching capital letters, a suicide note to his wife and daughters. Gay Glover soon afterwards found him unconscious and rang for an ambulance. She was at her husband's side, panic-stricken and uncomprehending as to why her husband of 23 years would want to kill himself, when he was wheeled into the casualty department. It was not long before doctors were able to assure her that Glover would survive. She then gave Dr Dominic Rowe the note she had found at the scene of the suicide attempt. Before filing the note away in the patient's medical records, the doctor photostated the document and gave the copy to Gay Glover.

When Constable Whittaker arrived at Royal North Shore Hospital with her colleague Constable Alison Cremen later that evening, she spoke to Dr Rowe who assured them too that the patient would live and gave Whittaker another photostat copy of the suicide note.

In the following days the young policewoman had time to study the note. She found it a strange document. The semi-comatose Glover had scrawled in thick pen over the top of the neatly-typed financial details on both sides of the superannuation fund form a number of nonsensical phrases, observations and exhortations. She puzzled over "Yo Star, Yo Marnie, Yo Ned", "No more Morris", "Yea team", "Buon Anno", "Gay, don't try to understand, Essie started it", "Sell up and piss off", "Marney, save some chicken skin for me", "Love you all RSOB" and there, about halfway down one page, the words "No more grannies". Constable Whittaker, unable to make neither head nor tail of any of this, filed the note away.

Interestingly, the original suicide note disappeared and has never been found. While interviewing Glover, doctors had remarked to the patient that the note was in his file. Shortly after this, when the hospital staff looked in the patient's medical record folder they saw that the note was missing. Those records were within reach of Glover while he was being interviewed by a psychiatrist.

On Thursday, January 18, Constable Whittaker interviewed Glover in Ward 4E at Royal North Shore Hospital. The man in the hospital bed looked robust and confident as Whittaker advised she was enquiring into the sexual assault at Greenwich Hospital and she was going to ask him some questions and that any answer he gave could later be used in evidence. "What was your reason for being at the hospital?" she began.

"I am a sales representative for Four 'N Twenty Pies and I was there to see the catering officer."

"Were you carrying anything when you were in the hospital?"
Glover was affronted. "Just a board with my price list on it. I have been told by my solicitor not to answer any of your questions, so I'm not answering any more," he snapped.

The constable was not deterred. She questioned Glover about the words and phrases on the suicide note, but he was vague. When asked about the reference to "No more grannies" Glover coolly explained that he was referring to his daughters' grandmothers, his mother and his mother-in-law, who had both recently passed away.

Whittaker asked permission to take two Polaroid photographs of Glover "for the purpose of continuing my enquiries". Glover let her photograph him but refused to sign the policewoman's notes detailing their discussion or record that he had given permission for the shots to be taken. Later that afternoon Constable Whittaker drove to Greenwich Hospital and showed the Polaroids to Sister Davis who confirmed that the man staring blankly out of the photo was the man she had confronted scurrying from Room No.1. Glover's victim, the elderly cancer patient, agreed that the chap in the picture was "most like" her attacker but could not be certain and anyway made it clear she was in no condition to give evidence in court. It was elementary that the suspect, the victim and hospital staff would all have to be questioned further before charges could be laid against Glover. It was at this point that Constable Whittaker interrupted her investigation to attend a detectives' course at Goulburn Police Academy. She passed the responsibility for the investigation on to her young colleague Constable Alison Cremen.

More than a fortnight went by, during which time the task forcers, headquartered only across the road from Constable Whittaker's base at Chatswood police station, continued their frantic hunt for the murderer of five women.

Then, in Goulburn, on February 5, the penny dropped for Constable Whittaker. The attack on an elderly woman... the suicide note with its reference to "No more grannies". Could John Glover be the north shore serial killer? The policewoman put through an urgent call to Constable Cremen at Chatswood. "Take the suicide note and the Polaroid picture of Glover to the task force right now," she said. Minutes later there was a knock on Miles O'Toole's office door. That knock sounded the turning point of the investigation.

Today Mike Hagan looks back ruefully on the constables' inexplicable delay in taking the suicide note and the photo to the task force. He describes their oversight as "unfortunate", but believes that, as it turned out, the mistake made not one iota's difference other than that if the task force had known earlier they would have been able to do a lot more basic groundwork on Glover while he was in hospital and later at home recuperating from the suicide attempt. Hagan says the two young policewomen simply did not link the assault on the woman in Greenwich Hospital with the serial killings. "They thought they were doing the right thing," he says. "Their investigations were quite proper and adequate in terms of an individual assault upon an old lady but, yes, it certainly would have been more beneficial if they'd relayed that information to the task force immediately."

The task force investigators were stunned when they compared the Polaroid photograph of John Glover with the police sketch of the man who had bashed 85-year-old Margaret Todhunter back in January, 1989, in Hale Road, Mosman. The photo bore an astonishing resemblance to the sketch. Here, staring out of the photograph, was the grey-haired, middle-aged, thickset man who had been sighted again and again by witnesses in the vicinity of the murder and assault locations. A flow chart listing all the times a grey-haired man had been noticed at the crime scenes was pumped out of the computer. John Wayne Glover was now the North Shore Murders Task Force's leading suspect. Other non-eliminated suspects would still be investigated, but Glover was their No.1 man.

The decision was taken then not to proceed with an investigation into the alleged Greenwich Hospital assault, but to put him under heavy surveillance and hopefully arrest him as the serial killer as soon as he showed his hand again. The task force was to come under virulent media criticism that this decision to turn Glover loose enabled him to kill one last time, but Mike Hagan today insists that the investigators had no choice because they had no firm evidence connecting Glover to the murders at that stage. Their only chance of nailing him as the Granny Killer was to shadow him and observe his movements, recording meticulously his actions in the vicinity of elderly women. Then, should a strong pattern of stalking emerge, confront him with his behaviour. Police were mindful that Glover was not obliged under law to co-operate. At best, they would need plenty of luck. Adding to the pressure was the ever-present possibility that he may harm another defenceless victim. Under no circumstances could police risk this happening. On one occasion Glover was observed wandering along Milner Crescent and Shirley Road, Wollstonecraft, eyeing elderly women. Those actions alarmed John May of Surveillance who radioed Miles O'Toole. Within 10 minutes O'Toole was in the vicinity, however Glover returned to his vehicle without incident and drove home. This was a valuable lesson for the task force. Next time Glover went wandering in suburbia detectives were within striking distance in case Glover approached a possible victim.

Task force detectives embarked on a full-scale canvass of north shore nursing homes and retirement villages. They were astonished to learn how many assaults had been committed and not been reported and how many times the grey-haired man in the Polaroid or someone resembling him closely had been either the attacker or been seen in the vicinity at the time. Glover was recognised at Kamilaroi Retirement Centre, Lane Cove, Wybenia Nursing Home, Neutral Bay, Caroline Chisholm Nursing Home, Lane Cove, Wesley Gardens Retirement Village, Belrose, Mosman Nursing Home, Mosman, Greenwich Hospital, The Garrison Retirement Village, Mosman, and many more.

The task force checked Glover's criminal record and learned of his long list of crimes. Of particular interest to them were his indecent assaults on the two women in Melbourne in 1962 and his peeping tom conviction in 1965. They covertly probed his family life, his banking history and his medical files. His dry cleaner was interviewed. A fax was sent to Interpol in Britain seeking details of his life before he arrived in Australia in 1957. The task force was on a roll.

Investigating his family, they discovered that the Essie who "started it" was the late Veronica Rolls, Glover's mother-in-law, toward whom Glover harboured a deep and well-known hatred. It came to the investigators' attention at this time that Glover also resented his mother, now dead too, whom he believed had rejected him when he was a boy and gone on to lead a promiscuous lifestyle.

The detectives had secret talks with senior management at Four 'N Twenty Pies. They learned that Glover was an employee of eight years, a salesman whose territory was the metropolitan area but who concentrated on the north shore. This was the first time a suspect had been linked with all of the murder suburbs: Glover lived at Mosman and his work took him often to Lane Cove and Belrose. The task force learned then, too, of Glover's bitter feud with his supervisor Morris Grant. The words "No more Morris" were scrawled on the suicide note.

Glover remained in hospital for a week then went home to Wyong Road to recuperate. No charges having been laid, he was confident that he had been eliminated as the attacker of the old woman in Greenwich Hospital. He returned to work mid-February, oblivious to the fact that the task force had him under close visual surveillance by police on foot and in unmarked cars. The detectives had been ordered not to let him out of their sight and to act as soon as an attack was imminent. There were always enough men on hand to make an arrest, but they had to stay well out of sight yet still be close enough to prevent another murder. It was like walking on eggshells.

Because of their quarry's erratic movements he was no easy man to tail. Typically in between business calls he would prowl the streets of the north shore garden suburbs — Mosman, Neutral Bay, Wollstonecraft, Lane Cove, Belrose, Greenwich — in his blue station wagon, sometimes travelling at only two, three or five kilometres an hour. He would stop outside a block of units or nursing home and sit and watch, then prowl again. Often he would park the car, get out and lurk around unit blocks, peering into doorways and windows. Some days he was logged by surveillance police as stopping more than 25 times to conduct his sinister reconnaissance. Never once, however, did he make a wrong move, never did he illegally enter premises, never did he approach a soul.

Surveillance chief John May co-ordinated observation of Glover. "To look at the bloke, you'd never suspect him of the crimes," he says today. "Apart from his prowling, he was just another John Citizen. He went to work, obeyed the traffic rules, spent time with his family, worked in the garden." But it was this very normalcy that made his behaviour at other times more frightening. John May recalls Glover crawling at only a few kilometres an hour 10 times around the same block. He remembers, too, how the suspect would sit and stare at old women. "One day he got out of his car and strolled past a block of home units. He saw an old lady walking down the street carrying groceries. We were on red alert but couldn't approach him because he'd done nothing wrong. But he just sat on a fence and stared at her for five or 10 minutes until she was out of sight. Then he returned to his car and drove away. Another time there was an elderly woman gardening. He sat nearby, watching her as she worked. At times like these I thought to myself, 'Yes, this bloke *could* be the Granny Killer'."

Glover did claim one victim during this period — but only indirectly. Surveillance operative Detective Const Michelle Parker was tailing Glover in her car when another vehicle powered around a corner on the wrong side of the road and collided head-on with the unmarked police car. Detective Parker's leg was crushed. She spent the next 12 months in Royal North Shore Hospital where her leg was pinned and metal plates inserted. She still receives monthly treatment for the injury.

The police would follow Glover to the RSL and often May, posing as a member, would strike up a conversation with him, observing his reaction closely to try to gauge whether Glover realised he was under surveillance. "I'd say, 'G'day. How are you going?' and he'd reply, 'Oh, OK, yeah, had a terrific day. Working hard?' and I'd say, 'Oh, just doing a bit here and there'. He'd come back, 'Well good, see you later, see you tomorrow'. He was never really interested in saying much more. He just wanted to get stuck into the pokies and go home. He really put a lot of money through those machines."

Glover's prowling made visual surveillance dangerous. If he suspected he was being followed and observed, there was no way he would make a false move. Mike Hagan called a meeting to discuss solutions and Ron Smith came up with the idea to put Glover under a combination of visual and electronic surveillance. At that time the Police Communications Branch was trialling a new system called Quiktrak whereby a device is secretly fitted to the suspect's vehicle and when the vehicle is in motion the device transmits a signal to a computer screen at the police station. The screen comprises a street map of the area in which the car is being driven and the moving car is represented by a red light that can be tracked moving along the streets of the map. Detectives can then relay the whereabouts of the suspect to visual surveillance police in cars or on foot so they can stalk their quarry from close range yet never be seen. Never, said O'Toole, would Quiktrak have a better application than the surveillance of John Glover.

The job of planting the device on Glover's company car fell to John May and his surveillance men. Police obtained lawful permission from Glover's employer to take the company vehicle. May organised for a key to be cut that would fit Glover's car's doorlock and transmission, so police could covertly drive it away to Mosman police station where the Quiktrak device would be fitted. But there was the tricky problem of hijacking the blue station wagon without raising the suspicions of its owner. Police watched Glover's movements and awaited their opportunity to make off with his car. It was no good breaking into his garage at night when he was asleep and taking the car; he would almost certainly be woken by the sound of the familiar engine. They would have to strike when he was out and about.

One night Glover went to the doctor and while he was in the surgery the surveillance police moved in. They opened the car door, started the ignition and were about to speed off when the stocky, grey-haired figure they had come to know so well emerged early from the surgery and made straight for his car. In a split second the police switched off the ignition, secured the car and disappeared into the darkness. Glover climbed in and drove home, suspecting nothing. The police in the shadows watched him depart, their hearts pounding. There were other occasions in the next few days when they were almost away with the car but each time Glover returned prematurely and the police had to bail out fast.

On March 13, Gay and John Glover went supermarket shopping in Mosman. Glover parked the blue company station wagon in an underground carpark and the pair set off for the shopping centre. Police hiding in the carpark saw them depart, Glover with his arm protectively, lovingly, around his wife's shoulders.

John May snapped the key into the doorlock, opened the door, started the car and motored sedately out of the underground carpark, bound for Mosman police station.

In a garage at the rear of the station the Electronics Unit, the "Sparks", worked feverishly to install the shoe-box-sized device underneath Glover's car. The scheme was to plant the transmitter then return the car to the carpark before its owner even knew it was gone. Precious minutes ticked by, but the job was a tricky one and had to be done right. Meanwhile the dog squad maintained surveillance on the Glovers as they continued their shopping. Their movements were relayed by radio to May who was cooling his heels across the road at the Buena Vista Hotel. Suddenly the word crackled through that Glover was returning to the carpark. There was no chance of installing the device and getting the station wagon back before he arrived.

"What the bloody hell!" exploded John Glover when he saw his car was missing. "Bastards have pinched the car! These are the kind of bastards that've come to live in Mosman!" Cursing and swearing, he rushed to the other levels of the carpark to make sure the car hadn't been left there. When he saw it hadn't, the Glovers, laden with shopping bags, hailed a cab and returned to Wyong Road. Then, still scarlet-faced and fuming, he stormed off in his wife's Datsun to Mosman police station to report the theft.

Miles O'Toole, sitting in the squad room, watched intently as the furious and abusive Glover gave details to the uniformed constable on duty about his stolen car. As he ranted and raved about the bastards who had dared to steal *his* company vehicle, Glover had no way of knowing that the car in question was not six metres away from where he stood. Nor, for that matter, did the constable or any of the other general duties officers at Mosman. The entire device-planting operation was covert. Task force detectives had distracted the Mosman police as May roared down the passageway beside the station and into the garage and were keeping them busy with jokes and other banter as the Sparks fitted the Quiktrak transmitter.

Finally Glover left and was seen to drive away up Military Road. Minutes later, the device was in place. The plan was to leave the blue station wagon somewhere in Mosman as if it had been stolen for a joyride then dumped. May leapt in the driver's seat and, adrenalin high, went to reverse back up the passageway — and slammed straight into the garage door. The whole building shuddered at the collision. The uniformed constables inside tried to run to the window to see what the hell had happened, but found their way blocked by the task force detectives. They knew then that something heavy was on and didn't push the issue.

Outside John May inspected the damage. A dent in the bumper. "Oh, well," he thought, "the thieves could have done it."

May then drove the car towards Taronga Park Zoo to test that the Quiktrak transmitter gave off successful signals in the hilly terrain in that part of the suburb. As he drove, not a kilometre away John Glover in his own car was trolling the streets of Mosman on the lookout for his car and the thieving low-lifes who had pinched it. May's dog squad kept the surveillance man informed of Glover's movements. To cross paths would be disaster. When satisfied that Quiktrak was working perfectly, May left Glover's car by the wharf at the Harbour entrance to the zoo.

A few hours later, police notified John Glover that they had found his car and would he mind making his way down to the zoo to pick it up. Police watched from a safe distance as the grey-haired man walked slowly around the vehicle, inspecting it for damage. When he noticed the damaged bumper he stopped and shook his head. He then drove home. But for the next four afternoons police observed him driving slowly in the bushland roads near where the station wagon had been recovered. He was not about to forgive nor forget the hoons who had stolen his car. If he found them, they'd be sorry.

Also on March 13, the Quiktrak computer and screen were installed at the Chatswood headquarters of the Task Force and as soon as Glover retrieved his car monitoring was commenced.

Police would be in front of the screen as dawn broke. There before them on the computer screen would be the street grid of Beauty Point. All eyes would be fixed on Wyong Road, on a little square on the high side of the street a couple of hundred metres along from the MacPherson Street intersection. In the three-storey house, John Glover would be showered, dressed and breakfasted by six. He would be in his car by 6.15 or thereabouts. Ignition on and off to work. As the pistons fired and the motor roared, the Quiktrak device came to life, sending its message to the investigators at Chatswood. It was always a chilling moment at Task Force headquarters when the little red light flashed on for the first time that day and the man they knew now in their hearts was the Granny Killer drove off into the early morning.

Visual surveillance teams in unmarked cars, their movements

directed on police radio by the technical surveillance men charting Glover's car on the screen, kept a close but discreet distance from their quarry. Quiktrak, however, became useless when Glover parked his car and set off on foot. It was then that the visual surveillance team was put right on its mettle.

"Quiktrak was a great help, but it still didn't relieve the pressure on the dog squad," says Ron Smith, who was operating from a room adjoining the Quiktrak set-up. "As soon as Glover's car came to a halt the light on the computer screen would blink. Then we had no way of knowing whether Glover had stopped at a set of traffic lights or if he was chasing some granny. We'd get straight on the radio and say, 'Target has stopped at so-and-so intersection just south of such-and-such shopping centre'. Our code names for Glover were 'Target' and 'North'. When the visual surveillance guys picked him up they'd radio back, 'Roger, roger, we've got eyeball. He's out of the vehicle. He's walking down River Road, he's just gone into a shop on the corner of Brown Street or he's making a business call at so-and-so nursing home or he's sitting on a fence watching an elderly woman digging in her garden...'"

While the visual and technical surveillance teams observed Glover's every move, sweating on him to strike again, and other detectives probed his history, yet more investigators were detailed to gather evidence on past crimes he may have been responsible for. One such was Kim McGee, a detective for nine of her 30 years. Her area of expertise was serial sex offences. Tall, thin and attractive with a pleasant manner, she had been attached to the Regional Crime Squad North for four years and was a valued member of the North Shore Murders Task Force.

Since Glover had been tagged as the assailant at Greenwich Hospital and the man most likely to be the Granny Killer, her role had been to take a folder of photographs around to nursing homes in the Mosman, Lane Cove and North Sydney areas. There were 12 photographs in the folder: 11 were shots of middle-aged men who had been snapped at a shopping mall, the 12th was John Glover. Glover had been picked out on several occasions by nursing home staff. McGee who, to protect the integrity of the Granny Killer inquiry, would say to staff only that she was investigating sexual assaults — never that she was enquiring into the serial killings — had particularly good luck at the Caroline Chisholm Nursing Home at Lane Cove where patients and workers were able to positively identify the pie sales-man as the man who had sexually assaulted a number of residents there. The case against John Glover, sexual assailant, was right in place, but still there was nothing to connect him to a single murder.

On March 15, a humid Thursday, just past 10 in the morning, Kim McGee turned up with her folder in the reception area of the James Milson Nursing Home in High Street, North Sydney. While waiting for the matron to appear, the detective exchanged small talk for a few minutes with the office secretary, a tall, middle-aged women, intel-ligent, well-groomed and wearing glasses.

"How long have you been here?" asked the policewoman.

"Oh, about eight years, from memory," smiled the secretary.

When Detective McGee commented that this was a very nice nursing home, the secretary agreed, "Yes, it's lovely. They look after the old people very well here."

Finally the matron arrived and Kim McGee explained that she was making enquiries about sexual assaults in nursing homes and would the matron mind telling her if any of the men in her photo folder was a pie salesman who had ever caused any trouble at James Milson.

"Oh, look," said the matron, "I'm not sure. I haven't been here that long. You'd be better off asking my secretary." She motioned to the woman with whom the detective had just been chatting. "Gay's been here a long time."

The secretary, close enough to overhear their conversation, looked shaken. She asked, "Oh, is it Four 'N Twenty Pies?"

"Yes," Kim McGee said, "as a matter of fact it is."

The secretary was visibly shocked. "His name wouldn't be John Glover, by any chance?"

"Yes, it is."

Said the secretary, "That's my husband."

The experienced policewoman shook and her palms grew clammy. Gay Glover now became very distressed and agitated. She demanded to know why the police were still asking questions about her John, even after the last time when they called him into the police station and he'd become so depressed at the prospect of getting into trouble for something he hadn't done he'd tried to take his own life. She then asked what was going on with the police inquiry into the Greenwich Hospital assault. Gay Glover then calmed down, fixed Kim McGee in an icy glare across the desk and said, "This hasn't got anything to do with the Mosman murders, has it?"

The detective said it hadn't, that she was only investigating sexual assaults in nursing homes. It came into her head then that this lively, clever woman must have been deeply troubled by the reference to "No more grannies" in the suicide note, while not daring to believe for a moment that her husband of 23 years could be the serial killer.

Kim McGee then asked, "Are you going to tell your husband that I have been here today?"

"Oh no," said Gay Glover, "I couldn't tell him that. He tried to commit suicide the last time. I'm under so much stress. It would just be too much of a worry."

The detective rose to leave. "Well, OK." She left the secretary her name and phone number, then said, "I'll get back to you if I find out what is happening with the Greenwich assault inquiry." She walked through the reception area to the door.

She remained composed until she was outside in the fresh air. Then Kim McGee ran, ran at 100 miles an hour, to her car. "It was the most incredible feeling," she says today. "The adrenalin hit me and I just let go."

Back at task force headquarters she told Mike Hagan and Miles O'Toole what had happened. Their first worry was that her conversation with his wife would let on to Glover that he was suspected of being the Granny Killer and knowing this restrain himself from making further attacks. But Detective McGee convinced her superiors that she had stressed to Gay Glover that she was only enquiring into sexual assaults and that the woman had believed her. However, just to be safe, an order was given that any member of the public enquiring about Kim McGee must only be told that she was attached to the Sexual Assault Unit.

Next morning at 8am the policewoman's phone rang. It was Gay Glover, who told her that she had in fact alerted her husband to the fact that police suspected him of other assaults in nursing homes. She said Glover had scoffed and said, "Oh, look, don't worry about it. If they really suspected me of anything they would have come to talk to me by now," and then went off to work as usual, without a care in the world. Gay Glover was, however, putting this matter of police harassment in the hands of her solicitor Don Wakeling. Her husband, she swore, was innocent of the Greenwich Hospital assault, nor had he committed any other offences. But for all Gay Glover's bravado, her voice gave her away. An experienced cop such as Kim McGee could tell that she was a woman under enormous stress.

CHAPTER 13

Flashpoint

John Glover opened his eyes to the shrieks of demons. All night as he turned and twisted alone in his bed they had been doing their work and doing it well. Now in his first few waking seconds he knew already what he must do. Today he would kill Joan Sinclair and then he would kill himself.

The pie salesman had met the stylish 60-year-old divorcee 18 months before at Mosman RSL. She, he big-noted to detectives later, had taken an instant shine to him, grabbing him lustily by the tie and suggesting he accompany her to her handsome Beauty Point home "to inspect her butterfly collection". An affair, said the pie salesman, had ensued. The 60-year-old divorcee's sons tell a different story. They swear their mother and Glover were only ever friends who would lunch occasionally and enjoy together the amenities at the RSL. They say that in the weeks before her death she was growing tired of her friend, and had come to believe that his sly bonhomie masked an intention to somehow get his hands on her money. She was looking to phase him out of her life.

Glover tumbled out of bed just after 7am — late for him, but today was no ordinary working day — and glanced blearily through the window, down across the precise order of his front garden and on over the red-tile rooftops of his suburb to the pale pink waters of Quakers Hat Bay. High in the sky a crescent moon resisted a spectacular autumn dawn.

As was his custom every morning, he made his way quietly to the kitchen, careful not to wake Gay in her bedroom — he had not slept with his wife for seven years — or Kellie and Marney in theirs. There in his pyjamas he breakfasted on toast and tea. Finished, he stacked his plate and cup neatly on the sink. After showering and combing his hair he returned to his bedroom and dressed. Today it would be black shoes, grey trousers and a white business shirt with black stripes. He selected a tie but did not put it on.

Before he left the house he made two hasty and whispered telephone calls. One was to Four 'N Twenty Pies, where he informed a superior that he would not be working today because he was meeting his lawyer to seek redress against the scurrilous and outlandish sexual assault allegation against him. The other was to Joan Sinclair. Would she like to go to lunch? Terrific. He'd drop in sometime in the late morning to pick her up.

Glover went to the garden shed in his backyard. The claw hammer was on the bench near the container of hydrochloric acid. He picked up the hammer and placed it in his briefcase. Then, for the last time as a free man, John Glover, grey-haired, well-dressed, a picture of middle-class respectability, strode down the brick path through his well-tended flower beds to the garage where his company car waited. He put his briefcase and tie on the back seat of the car alongside his Four 'N Twenty spray jacket then eased his bulk into the driver's seat and turned on the ignition.

At Chatswood command centre the red light on the Quiktrak computer screen flashed on. "He's away!" said the task force detectives. They watched as the beacon on the screen slowly moved along the grid that represented Wyong Road and turned left into MacPherson Street. It was 9.10am, March 19, 1990.

As Glover accelerated into the morning, the dog squad who had been positioned a safe distance down the street radioed Chatswood to confirm that the target was on the road.

For the next hour or so, like a king surveying his domain, Glover drove slowly around the streets of Mosman and Balmoral. John May and his visual surveillance police, tracking his every move, held their breath when once he stopped to watch an elderly women in her garden. But after a short time he moved on.

When the bottle shop at the Buena Vista Hotel in Middle Head Road opened at 10am Glover went in and bought a bottle of Vat 69 scotch whisky. He put the whisky in his briefcase beside the hammer and drove north up Military Road to Spit Junction and along Spit Road. Half a kilometre south of the Spit Bridge he turned left at Central Avenue and headed in the direction of Beauty Point.

Miles O'Toole was at task force headquarters pounding away on his police issue typewriter. He was finishing a resume of his discussion the previous day with psychiatrists who had interviewed Glover in hospital after his suicide attempt. O'Toole was typing how Glover had claimed to the psychiatrists that he tried to take his own life because of family problems then had changed his story and said he had become depressed because he was being victimised at work. This, and not the sexual assault charge, was what had triggered the suicide bid. The psychiatrists had concluded, typed O'Toole, that Glover had deep sexual inhibitions and that these, coupled with his intense resentment of his mother and mother-in-law, gave him a propensity for violence.

O'Toole was typing "...Glover also allegedly keeps a cut-down baseball bat or..." when he was rudely interrupted. "Miles, to the operations room, quick!" John May was on the line from a surveillance vehicle. Glover had just entered a house at No.14 Pindari Avenue, Beauty Point.

Earlier O'Toole had learned from an executive at Four 'N Twenty Pies, a man who was aware of the police interest in their employee, that Glover had phoned in to say he would be visiting his lawyer that day to discuss the sexual assault charge. Says Miles O'Toole, "This information, along with Glover's purchase of the whisky, indicated to us that Glover planned to have a working lunch with his solicitor in this Beauty Point home. We checked the records and learned that the home was owned by a Joan Sinclair who, as far as we knew, could have been a solicitor or a friend hosting the meeting between the solicitor and his client. We'd followed Glover for weeks and he'd done nothing wrong. We had no reason to believe he was about to do what he did that day. No reason in the world."

When Glover pulled up outside the house in Pindari Avenue at 10.26, John May's dog squad took up vantage points along the street. This was an obviously wealthy area and No.14 was a typical residence, a large, modern, rambling home hidden behind high garden walls and thick foliage.

Glover sat quietly in his car for 10 minutes, looking out the window and occasionally appearing to read from papers on the front seat beside him. He paid no attention when a tough-looking bloke slouched along the footpath and passed close by the vehicle. That bloke was John May.

A few minutes later Glover reached over into the back seat for his briefcase. He then put on his tie and combed his hair fussily and at length in the rear-vision mirror. Getting out of the car, briefcase in hand, he walked the 30 metres to the front gate of No.14, reached through a hole in the gate, deftly unlatched a security bolt and disappeared into the garden. He locked the gate from the inside. A knock on the door, the sound of the door opening, muffled voices — a man's and a woman's. The sound of the door closing.

Inside, Glover wasted no time. The two friends made small talk as Joan Sinclair bustled about getting dressed and applying makeup. They'd have to get going, she said, because she had to be back from lunch by three to pick up her grandchildren at the local school. Yes, fine. Glover then pretended to make a phone call as Joan Sinclair moved about the house. He held the phone in one hand and with the other opened his briefcase and withdrew the hammer, his body shielding it from Joan Sinclair's view. She called to him from another room. Before we go, she said, could you take a look at a leak in the ceiling down here at the bottom of the stairs. Yes, of course, not a worry. The hammer still concealed at his side, he joined her at the bottom of the small flight. The leak seen to, Joan Sinclair led the way back to the top of the stairs. Glover, following behind, raised the hammer high...

By his familiarity with the bolt on the front gate it was obvious to the men outside in the street watching from their cars that John Glover had been here before. Convinced now that their target was at the house on business, there was clearly nothing more for John May and his team to do but sit tight until he emerged. So the dog squad sat and waited, and waited.

The day stretched on, with the surveillance police radioing updates back to Mike Hagan and Miles O'Toole and the other task force members. O'Toole's second in command Paul Mayger and Detective Sen Const Paul Jacob drove to Pindari Avenue around midday and holed up in a car in an adjacent street for several hours before returning to Mosman police station to await further instructions. At around 3pm, and still no sign of Glover, there were mutterings about what a bloody long meeting he was having. Disquiet slowly set in. Hagan and O'Toole were tempted to storm the premises but quickly thought better of it. If police burst in on a genuine business meeting or even an intimate scene between the home owner and her guest without a legitimate reason there would be hell to pay. For a start they would be up for unlawful entry, but also, and more importantly, the entire surveillance operation would be blown wide open. "With nothing to connect Glover to a single murder we *had* to have a legitimate reason to speak to him," says Hagan. "If he knew he was a suspect he may never have put a foot out of line again and the Granny Killings could well have remained unsolved."

At 3.20 two young boys — Joan Sinclair's grandchildren whom she was minding while their parents were interstate — arrived at the front gate of No.14 accompanied by a teacher from the local school. The teacher had brought the boys home when Joan Sinclair failed to pick them up at the end of classes. However, with the gate locked from the inside, the three were unable to gain entry. The teacher then deposited the children with a neighbour. When the neighbour tried to enter with the boys she too found the gate impassable so dropped a note — "Monday, 4pm: The boys are next door with us — see you soon" — on the other side of the high wall. The three returned to the neighbour's house. Police watching the scene then heard a dog yelping loudly from somewhere inside the premises.

When John May reported all this back to Chatswood, the task force leaders grew seriously concerned. It was decided that Miles O'Toole and Murray Byrnes should drive straight over to Mosman police station and link up there with Paul Jacob and Paul Mayger so the four homicide detectives would be only minutes away in case of trouble at Beauty Point.

As dusk fell, it was obvious that something was wrong. The house had to be investigated, but without compromising the surveillance operation. The decision was taken to despatch two general duties uniformed constables from Mosman to the premises on a false pretext. Constables Dana Wakeling and Leon Bean would knock on the door and tell the occupants that they'd had a complaint from a neighbour about the barking dog and they'd just come to check that everything was OK. The detectives would be hot on their heels if anything was wrong.

At 6pm the constables pulled up outside Joan Sinclair's house. Unable to gain entry through the front gate, they were forced to go into a neighbour's and climb a fence to get into the garden of No.14.

It was growing dark in the yard. There were no lights on inside the house. The pair peered through french doors at the back of the building, straining their eyes, trying to see a sign of activity in the gloom. What they saw was a hammer lying on the floor of a landing in the rear sunroom.

The constables telephoned O'Toole with the news from the neighbour's house. He ordered them to secure the property and not to let anybody into the house. His pulse racing, the detective hung up and leapt to his feet. He swung around to face his three homicide colleagues who had listened to his conversation with Wakeling and Bean white-faced, eyes expectant, from across the squad room. "I think we've got something here," he said urgently. As the detectives strapped on service .38s, O'Toole contacted Mike Hagan at headquarters who notified the rest of the team. The task force prepared for action.

"Let's go!" O'Toole's voice rang out as he and his men dashed from the police station. Five minutes later a squad car screeched to a halt in the street outside the house in Pindari Avenue and Miles O'Toole, Paul Mayger, Paul Jacob and Murray Byrnes stormed into the yard.

Immediately after speaking to O'Toole, Wakeling and Bean had tried the back door to the house and when it opened they had started inside. There near the back door, by the hammer which they now saw was covered in blood, lay Joan Sinclair's body. She was naked from the waist down. A pair of pantyhose had been tied tightly around her neck. Her head had been covered with a towel which was now wet with blood. Bloodstains patterned the walls and carpet around the body. The horrified young constables stumbled from the house and were waiting at the front gate with the surveillance police when O'Toole, Mayger, Jacob and Byrnes arrived.

Dana Wakeling was beside herself. "We've seen the hammer. There's a body in there. She's dead. There's a body in there," she kept repeating. O'Toole, who in his haste had left his gun behind at Mosman police station, took the young policewoman's .38 service pistol and torches from the uniformed police vehicle. Nobody had seen Glover leave the house. He had to be still inside. Telling John May to keep everything covered from outside in case the suspect made a break for freedom, O'Toole and his three colleagues charged through the garden and regrouped at the rear of the house.

"At that stage as we gathered at the back door," says Miles O'Toole, "the adrenalin was really pumping. The house was pitch dark and we knew Glover was in there somewhere, possibly lurking and armed in the darkness, ready to go out in a blaze of glory and take a few coppers with him."

For 30 seconds the four detectives stood there at the back door, "reassuring each other that we could handle this, geeing each other up", says O'Toole. "Then we entered stealthily, with our guns drawn and our torches on, but held away from the body in case Glover started shooting at the light."

The torches lit up the dark, death-still house as the detectives scurried from room to room, throwing bright white circles of light like those cast by spotlights at the theatre. But this was no pantomime or musical. O'Toole's blood turned to ice as he took in the obscenities illuminated by his flashlight's glare. The bloody hammer. The red-drenched carpet. The semi-naked body. The pantyhose. A pair of white women's shoes placed neatly side by side. The seeping towel. Obscenities no less shocking for their familiarity. It was him. John Glover *was* the Granny Killer.

O'Toole, Jacob and Mayger crouched over the body. Jacob tried for a pulse but found none. He then felt Joan Sinclair's arm. It was cold. She'd been dead for probably six hours or more.

The moment that Miles O'Toole realised Joan Sinclair had become the serial killer's sixth victim was the lowest moment in his 25 years in the police force. "Something hit me then that had never hit me before. I can't describe the feeling. It was as though I was almost ashamed to be human. The senselessness of her death was like a literal weight on my shoulders. I felt enormous sadness and everything seemed to drain out of me.

"But then, standing there in the pitch black, I told myself to snap out of it. I realised that in our situation those feelings were an indulgence I couldn't afford. All that mattered to me, to all of us, was catching John Glover — oh, yes, and getting out of that house alive."

Palms sweating, hearts belting, O'Toole and Mayger conferred in hushed voices. "Come on, mate, let's get this over with," said O'Toole. "You and Jako take the left hallway. Murray and I will take the right." They all wished each other good luck then crouched-crept on in the blackness towards the front of the house. The house was a labyrinth of halls and passageways. The detectives knew that every corner they turned could have concealed John Glover, snowy-haired, paunchy, but vicious and with the strength of the demented, waiting there in the shadows with a gun to blow their heads off or, perhaps, a claw hammer to embed in their skulls.

O'Toole and Byrnes entered a room that looked like a study. On a desk there was an open briefcase, Glover's. O'Toole heard Mayger and Jacob in an adjoining room and called softly, "Is everything sweet there, are you two right?"

"Yes mate, fine," came the whispered reply from Mayger who continued on, his gun, loaded with six bullets, held waist-high as he'd learned in training. In the darkness, Mayger could just make out what looked like a set of french-louvred batwing doors leading to a bathroom. Gingerly, he nudged one of the doors open and shone the torch inside. Caught in the circle of light was a pair of human feet sticking up out of a bath.

Paul Jacob's voice boomed through the house, galvanising O'Toole and Byrnes. "We've got him! He's here! He's here!" O'Toole saw a light snap on in the next room and he and Byrnes tore toward it.

The four stood together before the batwing doors. Mayger and Jacob again pushed one door open with their torches. The four detectives could see one end of a bath. The bath was filled with murky water. The feet were protruding from the water at the visible end of the bath. The other end of the bath was out of sight. The detectives took stock. The feet were probably Glover's but who was to say that he was not playing possum, feigning unconsciousness or death, and then coming to life and blasting away when the policemen showed themselves in the room? They decided to move on the man. Guns levelled at where they knew the man in the bath's head must be, Jacob, Mayger and O'Toole piled into the bathroom. The first thing they noticed was the shock of grey-white hair.

The naked bulk of John Glover lay in the tepid bathwater. He was semi-conscious. His head was pitched forward and his partially-submerged face was contorted. He was vomiting into the water and groaning weakly. The water was filmed with vomit. An empty bottle of Vat 69 scotch whisky stood in a paper bag on the floor beside him and on the vanity table were a number of empty pill packets and bottles, among them an open container of Sinequan. The medicine

cabinet doors hung open. Glover's watch was on the basin. On his left
wrist were a number of half-hearted scratches. There was a broken
glass at the bottom of the bath.

The detectives remember today exactly what passed through their
minds when they saw their quarry lying there in the bath. They had
been tracking this man for a year. They had seen the horrific results
of his handiwork. All those old ladies murdered so savagely. Paul
Mayger recalls thinking, "You mongrel! You absolute bastard!"

O'Toole, who had also attended the post mortems, was similarly
repulsed. "As much as I loathed Glover for what he had done, I was
obsessed by a feeling that we had to save him so he could stand trial.
If he died all the other murders would remain unsolved even though
we knew he was our man." O'Toole grabbed Glover by the hair and
pulled his mouth and nose clear of the water. The detective then
cleared his mouth and nose of vomit and mucus. Glover then began
to breathe heavily and make incoherent remarks as he lay back in the
bath. "Watch him, make sure he stays alive. We can't afford to lose
him," O'Toole told Mayger while he left the bathroom to telephone
000 for an emergency ambulance. "This is Detective Sgt O'Toole from
Homicide. I want an ambulance immediately to 14 Pindari Avenue,
Beauty Point. This is an emergency. There has been a very serious
drug overdose." Four minutes later, at 6.56, ambulancemen Mark
Goodmanson and Mick Doyle were on the scene.

Next call, on the police radio this time, was to Mike Hagan. O'Toole
told Hagan the news, but cryptically, to thwart any media listening
to the police frequency. "Mike," he said, "we've got another one. We've
got the boy. But we've got another one." So much went unspoken
between the two men, but each was thinking the same thing: "After
a year of frustration, hell, heartbreak and sacrifice, we've finally got
our man. But at what a cost."

"We're on the way, we're there," was all Hagan said.

O'Toole returned to the bathroom where Mayger, Jacob and
Byrnes kept guard on the limp and fleshy form of John Glover.
Looking down at him, wallowing there so ignominiously, the detectives were filled with disgust. His bulk was wedged into the narrow
bath, preventing him from slipping under the water. It was that, and
the fact that he'd vomited up all the pills and most of the alcohol, that
saved his life.

The ambulance officers with help from Paul Mayger and Paul Jacob pulled the deadweight of Glover from the bath. They lumped him on the loungeroom floor where he proceeded to vomit up what was left in his stomach, all over the carpet. The policemen passed ironic looks. "This was the final indignity. Here's a bloke who'd killed the woman of the house and now he was vomiting all over her carpet. I thought that at the time. It was just one of those things that passes through your mind," says O'Toole.

Glover lay there wrapped in a thermal blanket. O'Toole told the ambulancemen, "I don't care if you never do another thing in your bloody career, you've got to save this bloke. You can't let the bastard die." At that they called paramedics Jack Spicer and Peter Gregg who gave the prisoner oxygen and assured the medicos that the man they now knew to be the Granny Killer was going to live to stand trial.

O'Toole went to the front gate to brief John May and the dog squad on what had happened inside. He gave Constable Wakeling back her gun and directed her and Constable Bean to keep everybody who did not belong there out of the property. He ordered that a guard be placed on Glover's car. As he barked out his commands, O'Toole kept telling himself, "OK, keep it going. Forget how you feel about Glover. Forget how you feel about the murdered woman. Just think logically. Cover every base and don't lose a shred of evidence."

Back in the study, police found papers that confirmed that the murdered woman was Joan Sinclair, the owner of the house. In Glover's briefcase they found a clipboard on which was attached price lists for the range of Four 'N Twenty pastries. This was the clipboard identified by some of his victims and staff members in nursing homes.

Just before Glover was placed in the ambulance, Mike Hagan, Ron Smith and Geoff Wright arrived. Hagan and O'Toole shook hands. Said Hagan, "Well done, mate. You've got him. You handle it. What assistance do you want?"

O'Toole then went to set in train the scientific men, the fingerprinters, the Physical Evidence team, the photogrammetry boys. But Hagan had arranged all of that *en route*. As soon as Glover, escorted by Murray Byrnes and Paul Jacob, was taken away to Royal North Shore Hospital, the police specialists moved to preserve the house and retain all evidence of the terrible deeds that had taken place there that day.

Detective Sen Const Dave Forbes of the Physical Evidence Section of the task force had been in the middle of dinner when the call came from a mate on the surveillance team. "We've got him. No.14 Pindari Avenue, Beauty Point. Bring the video gear." Forbes drove straight to Chatswood headquarters. In their rush to get to the murder scene, the task force members had slammed the door to the command centre office closed and left the key on the inside of the door. Forbes was locked out of his own office with the video gear inside. The resourceful detective smashed a window, climbed into the room, grabbed the camera and was at Beauty Point 15 minutes later.

A viewing of the video Forbes shot that night can only impart a hint of the sad and dreadful carnage. The hammer, the body on the floor, the towels, the bloodstains, Joan Sinclair's white shoes, Glover's underpants near the hammer, his bloodied shirt draped over a balustrade on the stairway. Carefully draped over Joan Sinclair's bed were Glover's trousers. His shoes, side by side, were on the floor beside the bed. Not far away in the dressing room was the victim's handbag, lying open. The camera panned over the bathroom. The broken glass in the by-then-empty bath, the broken scotch bottle on the floor, pills and their bottles and packets strewn all over the vanity. Vomit on the vanity. Glover's car, too, was also photographed before it was driven back to the police garage at Chatswood.

Once filmed, Forbes's Physical Evidence colleagues Dave Hughes and Phil Flogel collected all the exhibits from the house and Glover's car — the hammer, the clothing, the pills, the whisky bottle and broken glass, blood swabs, particles of vomit, his Four 'N Twenty spray jacket and price list, everything — and rushed them back to headquarters for scientific examination and classification.

Hagan despatched another group of investigators, including Kim McGee, to the hospital to check on Glover's condition then notify his family of the day's events. That done, they were to go to Glover's home at Wyong Road with a search warrant. Their mission there, to search the premises and take possession of clothing, shoes, anything of relevance to the investigation.

As the Physical Evidence men photographed and dusted and measured and scraped and collected, O'Toole and Mayger remained on the scene. Later they would have to break the news of their mother's death to Joan Sinclair's sons; the victim's daughter had learned earlier when she arrived to collect her two boys from the neighbour.

At 2am one uniformed policeman asked the two detectives, "Have you blokes eaten?" They hadn't. "Well there's something for you here," said the constable, and produced a family-size container of cold McDonald's hamburgers that had been bought for the investigators much earlier in the day. The homicide men took the container out into the backyard where they sat chomping as an autumn dew descended on the garden.

"Can you believe this?" said Miles O'Toole to his colleague and friend. "Can you bloody-well believe this?"

CHAPTER 14

When Nightmares Come True

When Kim McGee arrived at the hospital shortly after 7pm she consulted Murray Byrnes and Paul Jacob and the detectives directed nursing staff to place a call to Gay Glover at home. "Mrs Glover, your husband is here in the Royal North Shore Hospital. Please come down."

When Gay Glover arrived, accompanied by her eldest daughter Kellie, around 7.30pm and asked to see her husband, they were ushered into a small counselling room off a hospital corridor. Gay Glover recognised Kim McGee at once and knew something was terribly wrong. With the policewoman was Detective Sen Const Vivienne Crawford.

Detective McGee explained gently that John Glover had again attempted suicide and he was unconscious but stable and was going to live. She said he was found in a house at Beauty Point, paused, then added softly, "But unfortunately he was found in this house with a murdered woman."

Gay Glover remained composed and collected at this news. Detective McGee believes she went straight into shock. Neither mother nor daughter said much, just sat and listened in that grim little room. There were no tears, but as the reality of the situation took hold the women's faces grew taut with stress and their hands and shoulders trembled. At one point Gay Glover asked was her husband responsible for the death of the woman. Said Detective McGee, "Well, you know, we are not 100 percent sure, but it appears so." The wife maintained her dignity, just sat there looking stunned. Says Kim McGee today, "Gay and Kellie just didn't know where to go or what to do or what to think."

There had been no mention of the Granny Killings at that stage, but, looking back, the detective feels that perhaps everything — Glover's sexual assault charge, his first and now his second suicide bid, the words on the suicide note, the dead woman — was beginning to fall into place for Gay Glover and the thing that she had dreaded in her heart of hearts when she first read "No more grannies" on that note was not just a nightmare, it was the stark, staring, unbearable truth. She had shared her life with a serial killer.

The police sought permission to conduct a thorough search of her house. It was granted. Together the group, Gay and Kellie Glover and detectives McGee, Crawford, Paul Tuxford and Glen Kendall, returned to No.18 Wyong Road and trudged up the path to the front door. Inside, the police made straight for Glover's wardrobe.

"There they were," recalls Kim McGee, "the brown brogues. It was wonderful. I looked at the sole of the right one and knew pretty-well for certain this was the shoe worn by the killer of Muriel Falconer. This was the shoe that had made the print on her bloody carpet. The wear mark was etched on my brain." Also in the cupboard were items of clothing — such as the brown leather jacket with patches on the elbows — familiar from witnesses' descriptions of garments worn by the grey-haired man who kept turning up at the crime scenes.

A curious item was found by the telephone. There, used as a message pad and covered in a red scrawl of phone numbers and names, was the photostat copy of Glover's suicide note. The copy that Dr Dominic Rowe had given to Gay Glover at Royal North Shore Hospital back in January.

Next day, Kim McGee and Vivienne Crawford returned to Wyong Road. Gay Glover was there with her daughters and her doctor. It was clear that she was under sedation. The detectives told the shattered woman what she by now already knew. That police believed her husband was the north shore serial killer.

CHAPTER 15

Dead To Rights

After Murray Byrnes and Paul Jacob accompanied the retching and semi-comatose John Glover to Royal North Shore Hospital, Miles O'Toole remained behind at Pindari Avenue sifting through the carnage and assisting investigators from the Physical Evidence Section and the Government Medical Officer Dr Christopher Lawrence. Later, shaken and exhausted, he returned to the Regional Crime Squad office at Chatswood where he worked through the night.

When Glover arrived at Royal North Shore casualty earlier that evening, the doctors and nurses had set about their normal procedure for reviving a victim of drug overdose. Then, when they learned he might be the Granny Killer, they took to their work with a vengeance. Without deviating from their professionalism at all, some hospital staff that night felt sufficiently angry to forget their bedside manner as they gave John Glover what is perhaps best described as "no-frills" treatment.

When they had finished and he was out of danger, Glover was left alone in a private, one-bed room under the guard of Byrnes and Jacob. Byrnes remembers Glover at one stage opening his eyes, secretively, in the hope that his captors wouldn't notice. As the reality of his predicament dawned upon him through the pain and confusion, Glover looked sad and lapsed back into sleep, or pretended to.

Just after 4am the doctors advised Jacob and Byrnes that Glover was now fit to answer questions. The pair telephoned the news to Miles O'Toole and Paul Mayger. At 4.50am on March 20 the two Homicide men drove the five kilometres down the Pacific Highway from Chatswood to Royal North Shore Hospital where they greeted their colleagues at Glover's bedside.

When O'Toole entered his room, Glover was propped up in bed on a pile of pillows. He looked to be in good spirits as he called to a nurse for a glass of water, but when he saw the detectives he slumped down into the bed, pulled an oxygen mask up over his face and closed his eyes. O'Toole was not to be put off. He came to the bedside and introduced himself and asked if Glover could hear him. Glover nodded, then demanded his solicitor be present.

O'Toole and Mayger then left the hospital and returned to Chatswood headquarters where a high-level conference was in progress. Mike Hagan was briefing the North Shore Murders Task Force top brass about the murder of Joan Sinclair and the subsequent capture of John Glover. Present were Executive Chief Superintendent Joe Parrington, Assistant Commissioner Charlie Parsons, Chief Superintendent Norm Maroney, Superintendent Brian Hetherington and Superintendent Jim Rope, who were the district commanders in two of the north shore regions where the murders were committed. On a telephone hook-up were the then-Police Commissioner John Avery and the then-Deputy Commissioner and State Commander Tony Lauer.

Mike Hagan led the police hierarchy through the events of the past weeks and established procedure for the weeks to come. Glover would have to be interviewed, then hopefully he would be taken on a runaround of the crime sites and to the locations where he had disposed of his victims' belongings. At this meeting it was decided to impose a total media blackout. The investigators were certain that Glover was the serial murderer, but there was still much to do before he could be charged and what had to be done could be done much more effectively away from the media spotlight. For a start, Glover had to be given the chance to hear the allegations against him. It was imperative that his name and crimes be kept from the public until his committal hearing which, all being well, would be held the following week.

Midway through the conference, O'Toole was called to the telephone. It was Murray Byrnes. "Miles, Glover has asked to see you. You'd better get yourself down here. He just said to me, 'Tell O'Toole he's got his man.'"

Says O'Toole, "I informed the meeting very, very briefly about what Murray had just told me and took off back to the hospital with Paul Mayger. Only a few hours before when I discovered Joan Sinclair's body was the lowest point in my career, but I'd have to say that Murray's phone call was the highest. I wanted to jump in the air and scream and shout."

Murray Byrnes and Paul Jacob were detailed to remain with Glover. He had already made two attempts on his life and it was feared, even in his weak condition, that he might try again. At 7.10am Glover was sitting up in bed drinking a cup of tea and chatting with hospital staff. Byrnes fronted him.

"How are you feeling, John?"

"Throat's a bit sore, but alright," came the reply.

"Do you know who I am?" asked Byrnes.

"Police."

"Yeah, I'm Detective Byrnes and this is Detective Jacob, Murray and Paul."

Asked Glover, "Do you know what's happened to my wife?"

"She was here last night with your daughter. I think she's at home. Sgt O'Toole said he'd ring her."

"Which daughter?" Glover wanted to know.

"I don't know... tall, dark hair."

Glover nodded, thought for a moment, then asked, "What happens about gaol? I'm never going to see the sea again for 25 years."

Byrnes held out. "I understand that you've already told Detective O'Toole that you don't want to speak to anybody without a solicitor present?"

Glover replied, "My solicitor doesn't know what I've been doing, only the Greenwich thing, I told him I didn't do it."

"You know, John," said Byrnes, "you're not obliged to speak to me about any of these matters as it could be used in evidence."

"Yes, I know."

Byrnes, unable to believe his luck that Glover clearly wanted to unburden himself, then asked, "Why did you pick on elderly women?"

Glover answered, "You probably noticed the photos in the paper (the photographs of his victims), they all have an uncanny resemblance to my mother-in-law."

"Where's your mother-in-law live?" pursued Byrnes.

"She's dead."

"Did she use to live with you?"

"Yes."

"Did you have some sort of problem with her? Did she create problems with the family?"

"Oh, yeah," said Glover. "In my first suicide (attempt), I wrote a note mentioning Essie. She began it all."

"What do you mean?" asked Byrnes, realising he may have stumbled upon the motivation for Glover's murder spree.

"Essie... I just wished she'd hurry up and die, even my wife said that."

"How did you think that Essie influenced your behaviour?"

"I don't know," mused Glover. "One side of me was alright, the other is dark, evil. I can't control it. If I plead guilty, what happens?"

"I can't predetermine what a court is going to do," said Byrnes.

"What happens about gaol?" Glover persisted. "They'll get me inside a week. Neddy Smith and Tom Domican (two well-known inmates of Long Bay Gaol) have a contract out on me, $150,000!"

Byrnes said flatly, "If you're concerned about your welfare we can arrange to have you placed in protective custody."

"What about my family?" Glover now demanded, a panicky edge to his voice. "There's no way they can stay in Mosman, they know too many people."

"We'll just have to address that problem should it arise," replied Byrnes.

"It won't be long till it's out. The whole of Mosman will say, 'Oh no, not John Glover!'"

Said Byrnes, "Your main concern is for yourself and family, shouldn't be worried about anybody else."

"I've done the deed, I shouldn't be worried about my safety," said Glover, "I should be strung up."

Glover then asked whether the police would contact a former neighbour who was now the chaplain at a prominent eastern suburbs private school and who had read a moving eulogy at the funeral of one of Glover's friends. "I thought I could talk to him or he could talk to Gay at home. She's gonna need it."

Byrnes changed the subject. "John, where did you get the hammer from?"

"From home."

How did you take it there (to Joan Sinclair's home)?"

"Had it in my briefcase."

"Is that what you used in the other murders?" pressed Byrnes. "What about the Pahud murder at Lane Cove? Did you use it on her?"

"Yes."

"What about the blood on the hammer?"

"I took it home and washed it with acid and left it in the yard."

"Where did you get the acid from?"

"I used it to clean bricks at home." Glover then added that everything was a bit hazy and he could not remember if he'd carried the hammer in the briefcase at all of the murders.

"What about the Cleveland murder at Belrose? How did you come to be there?"

"I called on the chef in the kitchen."

"Do you remember if you hit Cleveland with the hammer?"

"It's all a bit hazy."

"What about the ladies' underwear? John, why did you remove that?"

"I didn't touch them sexually. My problem was as soon as it's over I just jump in the car and carry on as normal. Invariably I'd go down the club."

"What about the blood on your clothing?"

"I wasn't aware of any blood on my clothing."

"What about Joan Sinclair, how did you come to meet her?"

"She wasn't a casual friend. It's what you call a bit of hanky panky."

"What, she was your girlfriend?"

"Yeah," said Glover, "but Gay didn't know. Her sons will be after me now."

Byrnes again changed tack. "How are you feeling?"

"Good, before I had that anti-police thought. I've lost that now. I can talk all day."

"John, the main thing is to worry about yourself and your family."

Glover's fears for Gay and the girls resurfaced. "Will there be any repercussions against my family?" he wanted to know.

"As I said, John, that's something we'll have to address when the situation arises. Your main concern is to get some counselling," said Detective Byrnes.

Glover was despondent. "With psychiatric help or not, I'll never see the sea again. You don't get bonds for multiple murders. I used to go to Long Bay Gaol selling confectionery for Nestles about 12 years ago."

Murray Byrnes still remembers his shock when Glover made his admissions. In spite of the detectives cautioning him that he was under no obligation to speak to them, he would not be silenced. "I really think at that stage he wanted to be caught. I'm no psychiatrist but I believe he wanted an end to the whole thing. I was stunned when he kept on talking, and I was buggered after the events of the day before and had gone almost two days without sleep, but I just hung in there trying to remember details of all the murders so I could keep hitting him with questions. I had no questions prepared. All the time Paul Jacob was taking it down. A doctor came in right in the middle to examine him, and we had to call a halt, but Glover began again when the doctor left the room.

"Then and later when he was interviewed about his crimes at length, the only time he showed any humanity was when he was talking about his family. The rest of the time he was cold and calculating. He'd relate all the dreadful details of his murders, then in between interviews he'd tell us jokes. I thought that was completely and utterly offside, but that's the sort of bloke he is. He'd tell us little jokes and try to make us laugh along with him. I thought, 'My God, what sort of a man is this?'"

Soon after O'Toole and Mayger arrived at the hospital. Nerves still jangling after the incredible events of the previous day, O'Toole pummelled Glover with questions as Mayger recorded the conversation in his police pad. "I am Detective Sgt O'Toole and this is Detective Mayger from the Homicide Squad. Are you John Wayne Glover?"

"Yes," came the weak reply. Glover's skin, usually ruddy, was parchment pale. His hair, usually so neat, was an unruly shock of white.

"We are making enquiries into the death of Joan Sinclair at her home yesterday. We found you in the house at the same time. I am going to ask you some questions about this matter, however you are not obliged to answer unless you wish as anything you do say may later be given in evidence. Do you understand that?"

"Yes," replied Glover, "but I won't answer unless my solicitor is present."

"Whether or not you answer is up to you. There are still a number of questions I wish to put to you," O'Toole persisted.

"Okay," said Glover.

"What can you tell me about Joan's death?"

From the prisoner, "Half of me wants to do it and half of me doesn't."

"What do you mean by that?"

"I can't help myself. Half of me wants to do these things and half of me doesn't."

"What things?"

"Like Joan."

"What happened to Joan?"

Glover made no reply.

"Did it happen as soon as you got there or sometime later?"

"Not when I got there, later."

"A hammer was found near Joan's body. What can you tell me about that?"

"I want to tell you all about that, but I want to tell you with my solicitor."

"What is the name of your solicitor?"

"Don Wakeling. My wife knows how to get him."

"I will contact your wife and make arrangements to interview you in the presence of your solicitor," said O'Toole. Then he added, "There are other matters I wish to speak to you about, including the murders of several elderly women."

"Yes, I know that," said Glover with resignation. "I'll tell you about them when my solicitor is here."

O'Toole said: "You are under arrest and you will be charged with the murder of Joan Sinclair later today. Do you understand that?"

"Yes," said Glover.

O'Toole telephoned Gay Glover and asked her to contact Glover's solicitor Don Wakeling. As they spoke, Kim McGee, Vivienne Crawford and their fellow detectives were at work all around her, searching the Wyong Road premises. Gay Glover said to O'Toole, "It's more than the assault, isn't it."

"Yes it is," said O'Toole. "I wish to speak to John about the murder of six elderly women on the north shore."

There was silence on the other end of the line.

"Are you OK?" asked O'Toole.

"I knew it was something other than the assaults," said Gay Glover.

O'Toole remembers the phone call. "In hindsight, I don't know whether telling her over the phone was the right thing to do or not, but I felt I couldn't tell her any lies. She had a right to know. All the way through she co-operated with us. She and Kellie and Marney are wonderful people and they certainly didn't deserve any of what happened to them. We did our very best to shield them from all the drama and controversy in the days ahead."

It was crucial that Glover confess fully to all his crimes. The shoeprint taken at Muriel Falconer's home remained the sole concrete piece of evidence against him. They had him dead to rights as the murderer of Joan Sinclair and Muriel Falconer, they knew that, but it would be a giant headache for the investigators if he chose to deny killing Gwen Mitchelhill, Lady Ashton, Madge Pahud and Olive Cleveland or assaulting the other women because no evidence existed linking him to these offences. He simply *had* to make a complete confession.

At 12.42pm O'Toole again questioned Glover at his bedside in the casualty department. Once more Mayger kept a record but this time, because this was an official record of interview, the detective typed out O'Toole's questions and Glover's answers. Also present were Glover's solicitor Don Wakeling and psychiatrist Professor Christopher Tennant from the hospital.

No pleasantries, O'Toole went straight to work. "Would you care to tell me," he began, "what knowledge you have of the death of Joan Sinclair at her home yesterday?"

"As to how or why or who? Which one do you want?" asked Glover.

"Are you able to tell me the person responsible for the death of Mrs Sinclair?"

"I was... or am," replied Glover.

"Did you know the woman Joan Sinclair prior to yesterday?"

"Yes."

How well did you know her?"

"Intimately."

"How long had you known her?"

"Eighteen months, approximately."

"When did you last see Mrs Sinclair?"

"Yesterday."

"Would you care to relate to me the circumstances as to how you came to see Mrs Sinclair yesterday?"

"I rang Joan to see if she would like to go to lunch and she said, 'Yes, come over.'"

"What time did you arrive?"

"About 11.30am to 12 o'clock."

"That was at her home address?"

"Yeah."

"What did you do upon arrival at her home address?"

"I went through her front gate to her front door, entered the house," recalled Glover. "I had to get rid of two dogs she was looking after. I had to put them out of the house. She got changed to go out and I made a pretence of making a phone call and she was getting ready, flitting here and there, when I was still pretending to make this phone call, which was next to my briefcase. I took the hammer from my briefcase. She called me down a small flight of stairs to look at a rain leak and then she proceeded back up the stairs and I was right behind her and I stayed behind her and then I struck her."

"Where did you strike her?"

"About the head."

"How many times did you strike her?"

"Three times."

"With what did you strike her?"

"With the hammer."

"What happened then?"

"She fell to the ground. I then went to her bedroom, came back with a pair of pantyhose and tied them around her neck."

"Why did you do that?"

"I really don't know. I know I did it but I don't know why."

"What happened then?"

"I went to my briefcase, took out a bottle of whisky. I went to the bathroom... oh, before that I got undressed. I started to run a bath, went to the bedroom and got undressed, went to the bathroom, took pills from the cupboard, sat in the bath, took all the pills and drank the scotch."

"And what happened then?"

"Went into oblivion, I suppose."

"What type of pills did you take?"

"I only remember one type of brand. I was on that particular type of pill for a depressant."

"Why did you take the pills and the scotch?"

"To try and kill myself."

"Why did you try and kill yourself?"

"I wish I knew."

"Why did you strike Mrs Sinclair with the hammer?"

"To kill her."

"Why did you want to kill Mrs Sinclair?"

"I don't know."

"Where did you get the hammer?"

"From home. I bought the scotch on the way."

"After you struck Mrs Sinclair, what did you do with the hammer?"

"Left it on the carpet."

"When police arrived at Mrs Sinclair's home and found her body on top of the stairs, her clothing had been removed from the lower part of her body and a towel had been placed over her head. What can you tell me about that?" asked O'Toole.

"I did take her undergarments off but for no reason, certainly for no sexual reason. I used the towel just to cover her head up," Glover replied.

"Mrs Sinclair's shoes and panties were found placed side by side in an adjacent room. What can you tell me about that?"

"It's not a room, it's like an inside patio. I can only assume that I put them there."

"Would you care to tell me why you would assume that?"

"Because there was only myself and Joan in the place."

"Do you actually recall placing those shoes and panties in that position?"

"No."

"Do you recall seeing Mrs Sinclair's handbag whilst you were in the house?"

"Yes, it was in the bedroom. I saw it when I went to get the pantyhose."

"Did you touch that handbag in any way?"

"Yes, I opened it."

"Why did you open it?"

"To see how much money she had."

"Did you remove anything from her handbag?"

"Nothing at all."

"Would you care to tell me why you brought the hammer from home."

"It's part of a tool kit I've always got at home, for towing caravans."

"Why did you take the hammer to Mrs Sinclair's home?"

"To kill her."

"Why did you buy the bottle of scotch on the way to Mrs Sinclair's home?"

"To drink it."

"How did you get to Mrs Sinclair's home?"

"I drove there in my car."

"Is there anything further you wish to tell me about this matter?"

"That's it, cut and dried."

The interview ran to six typed pages and as well as telling how he had murdered Joan Sinclair, Glover admitted killing Gwen Mitchelhill, Lady Ashton, Madge Pahud, Olive Cleveland and Muriel Falconer. His accounts of his first five murders were, however, perfunctory and comprised only the barest details of each attack. Glover refused to be drawn into elaborating on each killing, claiming he had received legal advice not to do so. At the end of the interview he was served a meal. Then a bedside court was convened by Chamber Magistrate John Levett and Glover was formally charged with the murder of Joan Sinclair.

Miles O'Toole then approached Glover. "John, I have spoken to your solicitor and your doctor and I propose to interview you further regarding the matters we have just discussed and additional matters. On your discharge from hospital you will be taken to the Sydney Police Centre prior to your appearance at court and during that time we will speak to you at length about those matters. Do you understand that?"

"Yes," replied Glover. "Will it be the same as today?"

"It will be in the form of a record of interview in each case, yes."
Glover sighed. "The sooner I get this off my chest, the better," he
said.

* * *

That night, back at Chatswood headquarters, the North Shore
Murders Task Force got roaring, gloriously drunk. Mike Hagan
organised cartons of beer and wine and food and, for later, cars to
deliver the inebriated investigators safely home to their beds. The
normally reserved Miles O'Toole, who at one stage was sighted
standing on a table and bellowing out, "A you're Adorable, B you're
Bee-utiful..." has but a hazy recall of the party. "I've certainly been
drunk in my time, but never as drunk as I was that night. Only then
did it all sink in. There would be no more elderly ladies lying dead, no
more examinations at the morgue. We could go back to our families
and loved ones again." After a year when murder piled upon murder,
horror upon horror, frustration upon frustration, sleepless night
upon sleepless night, at last there was a chance for the investigators
to let their hair down a little, to savour the relief, the release, from
pressure, to try to deaden with alcohol the memories they knew they
could never forget.

* * *

The days following the Sinclair murder were frustrating ones for
the press. All police would divulge to reporters was that an elderly
woman had been murdered in her home at Beauty Point, Mosman,
and that a man found on the premises had been taken into custody
and charged with the killing. But in spite of the lack of official
confirmation, the word somehow spread throughout the north shore,
the state, the nation, that the Granny Killer's reign of terror was over.
Just as, a decade before, people seemed somehow to know all about
the the events surrounding the death of baby Azaria Chamberlain at
Ayers Rock even before they had heard the circumstances detailed on
the news or read about it in newspapers, now Australians seemed to
be connected to some jungle telegraph that beat out the news that the
man under guard at Royal North Shore Hospital was the serial killer
of six elderly women and the vicious assailant of others.

TV radio and press reporters were under intense pressure. Determined to be the first with the news if the man in Royal North Shore
turned out to be the Granny Killer, media representatives had staked

out the hospital since Glover's arrival by ambulance two days before and had been filing updates to their editors and beaming regular reports to viewers. These articles and reports were long on speculation but clearly short on facts. Most reporters enjoyed a good working relationship with the detectives who came bustling in and out of the hospital but no policeman would confirm or deny that the man in custody was the Granny Killer. Since the recent disastrous, wrongful and very public arrest of the former detective superintendent Harry Blackburn on sexual assault charges, the lawmen were not prepared to depart from strict, formal procedure and give any journalist a break, friend or no friend. There could be no film footage of or uninformed media speculation about John Glover. His identity, and the extent of his crimes, had to remain a secret for the time being.

On the afternoon of March 22, one TV crime reporter was staking out the driveway of Royal North Shore Hospital, preparing for that evening's story on the condition of the man whom all Australia by now hoped against hope was the notorious Granny Killer. The reporter's news instincts stirred when he saw a brightly-coloured Mazda commercial delivery van flash out of the hospital delivery dock, through the front gate of the hospital, and turn down the Pacific Highway towards Sydney. "No, surely, they wouldn't be sneaking the prisoner out of here in a delivery van," he thought, and continued his vigil in the driveway. The identity of the driver of the van should have registered with the crime reporter. He knew him well.

Detective Sen Const Paul Jacob was a huge moustachioed man usually with a beaming smile on his face, a young version of the portly actor William Conrad — hence Jacob's nickname "Jake And The Fatman", which is the title of the TV series in which Conrad stars. Although disguised in sunglasses and a sinister hat and looking for all the world like a Palestinian terrorist, Paul Jacob of the task force Homicide Squad was the driver of that van. Miles O'Toole, Payl Mayger and Murray Byrnes were sitting out of sight on the back seat and stretched out at their feet on the floor of the van was John Glover.

The media given the slip, the detectives and their precious cargo tore down the Pacific Highway in the delivery van. Glover, handcuffed and lying flat on the floor of the vehicle, began to gripe bitterly about the cloak and dagger operation, unable to believe the lengths the detectives were going to to conceal him from the media. O'Toole knew how to keep him quiet. O'Toole replied, "Go right ahead, then, John, but if you don't keep your head down your photograph could be taken and it'll be plastered all over the front pages of the newspapers and on television." Glover grumbled, "You're fuckin' kidding," and stayed right where he was, instantly reverting to his normal jocular self.

As the van crossed the Sydney Harbour Bridge, O'Toole, remembering Glover's wistful comment to Murray Byrnes about never seeing the sea again, looked down at Glover on the floor and said, "John, if you're quick, hop up and take a good look at the Harbour." Glover declined the opportunity.

The van, now escorted by unmarked surveillance police cars, sped to the Sydney Police Centre in Goulburn Street, Surry Hills. There the detectives bundled Glover out of the back and locked him up in cell 17, a juvenile offender's cell, where he was kept under constant visual supervision. Throughout Glover's time there a guard sat outside the cell, constantly looking in. The guard was rotated regularly. Police there were advised that the prisoner's wife and solicitor were to be the only visitors and that these two were to make no physical contact with the man in the cell. Glover was allowed to change his clothing if he wished, but if he had no extra garments of his own he was to be issued with gaol clothing from the Police Centre stores room.

Chief Inspector Holland, Commander of the Sydney Police Station, issued written instructions to his men: "Whilst this person is showering, shaving etc, I direct that two police accompany him and keep him under constant supervision in the exercise yard/shower area." The following words were heavily underlined: "It should be clearly understood that this person has been charged with a very serious offence and has twice attempted to end his own life."

Lest police still not fully realise that there was a crucial need for their new charge to remain fit and well while under their supervision, Holland added at the end of his edict: "These instructions... should be strictly adhered to as the consequences of any unfortunate incident involving the prisoner will be very grave."

At 3.30pm Glover was escorted to the interview room on the third floor of the Sydney Police Centre. Waiting for him there were Miles O'Toole, Paul Mayger, Murray Byrnes, Paul Jacob and Glover's solicitor Don Wakeling. O'Toole told Glover he was about to ask him further questions about the attacks on the elderly women. He informed him that both his questions and Glover's answers would be recorded by Detective Mayger on the typewriter and that the typescript would be an official record of interview.

* * *

Over the following days, Glover was questioned at length by O'Toole about the deaths of Gwen Mitchelhill, Lady Ashton, Madge Pahud, Olive Cleveland, Muriel Falconer and Joan Sinclair, the assaults on Doris Cox, Margaret Todhunter, Euphemia Carnie and Phyllis McNeill and acts of indecency committed to four elderly residents of nursing homes. During the session Glover identified the Stanley Hercules wooden-handled claw hammer found at the Pindari Avenue death scene as the one he had used to slay four of his six murder victims.

Glover's crimes were rendered no less horrifying by his flat, emotionless responses; no less tragic by his total lack of remorse when recounting the details of his dark adventures.

Glover maintained his blank composure throughout the lengthy interview sessions that followed. His voice was soft, his responses precise, his manner personable. The only time he would betray any emotion was when his family was mentioned. Then, he seemed desperate for police assurance that Gay, Kellie and Marney would not be besmirched by his crimes and was anxious that they be protected from the media spotlight.

Miles O'Toole suspected that Glover was not above playing mind games. He was, for instance, intrigued when the prisoner admitted bashing his victims on the head with a hammer, but would deny punching them and breaking their ribs, deny beating them with their own walking sticks. It was as if such common assault was beneath the dignity of a man of his station.

Gradually O'Toole came to know Glover as a vain, ego-driven man, complex and of above-average intelligence, and always keen to one-up his interrogators. He was eager to prove himself smarter than the police, the doctors and psychiatrists he came into contact with each day. Once, when he and O'Toole were discussing the murder of Joan Sinclair and how O'Toole and Mayger had dragged him from the bath, Glover said he wanted to thank O'Toole for saving his life — but then added imperiously, "Next time though, try to be a bit less clumsy, will you... when you pulled me out you cracked my head on the back of the bath and it's still tender today." O'Toole, whose dark hair became flecked with grey during his hunt for the man who now sat before him, today has no trouble admitting that his jousts with Glover disturbed and physically drained him. Even now, two years later, he dreams of the man.

Glover seemed more at ease, less threatened, when talking to the genial O'Toole, than with, say, the brusque, matter-of-fact Paul Mayger who had trouble concealing his abhorrence of the killer. At one stage when he was telling how he had murdered Muriel Falconer, Glover seemed irritated that he had actually been forced to hit the 93-year-old woman a second and a third time with the hammer to finally silence her. His attitude was, "Well, she *would* keep struggling and crying out, what else *could* I do?" At this stage Mayger, recording Glover's words on the typewriter, could hardly suppress his disgust, and it showed. "Oh, shit!" he thought and shook his head. Glover noticed the effect his callousness was having on the detective and O'Toole noticed that Glover noticed. "Come on, mate," O'Toole said to Mayger, "Let's just keep it going. We'll get this thing out of the way." During a later conversation, Glover would again repel the investigators when he joked how Lady Ashton had "put up a good fight for a small woman". At the end of one session Glover looked at O'Toole, his expression one more of sorrow than anger, and said, "You despise me, don't you."

* * *

The following exchanges have been excerpted from the records of interview recording the confessions of John Glover. The question and answer sessions were conducted between March 22 and 27, 1990, in the interview room at Sydney Police Centre — a small, featureless room, bare except for five chairs, a table and a typewriter.

Detective O'Toole began the first interview at 3.55pm on March 22. "We are making enquiries into the death of Gwendoline Louise Mitchelhill outside her home unit block at 699 Military Road, Mosman, on March 1, 1989... Would you recount to me, to the best of your recollection, your movements on March 1, 1989."

Glover responded: "I went to work, reported for work, and finished my day's work and then I went to the RSL in Mosman. I got there about four to 4.40pm, or it could have been earlier. I left the RSL, went to my car. I saw this lady walking towards me. I got out of the car, placed a hammer down my belt, followed the woman. She turned into the flats and when she went into the entrance to the foyer, I then struck her from behind. She fell to the ground. I opened her handbag and removed a wallet, put that in my pocket, returned to the car."

"What happened then?"

"I drove to a road near my place, I can't recall the name, it leads down to Jolls Boatshed. I took the money out of the wallet and then I got out of the car and threw the wallet into a bush. Then I drove home."

"Are you able to indicate or direct us to that location at a later time and show us where you threw the wallet?"

"Yes."

"Are you able to tell me how much money you took from the wallet?"

"There was a $100 bill in the wallet. That's all I took."

"What did you do when you arrived home?"

"Parked the car, went into the house and stayed there."

"From the time you followed Mrs Mitchelhill in Military Road into the entry foyer area, did you see any other person in that area?"

"No."

"Did you see any other person alight from the lifts within the home unit building?"

"No."

"You stated that you followed Mrs Mitchelhill and then 'struck her from behind'. Would you care to tell me what you mean by that?"

"I hit her across the head with a hammer."

"Are you able to tell me how many times you hit Mrs Mitchelhill across the head with the hammer?"

"Well, certainly once and maybe twice. I'm not sure."

"We have received medical evidence that indicates that apart from lacerations to the head of Mrs Mitchelhill, she received injuries to the right side of her face and a number of rib fractures to the right side of her body and those injuries are consistent with being punched by a closed fist. Is there anything you can tell me about that?"

"Not a thing, I made no further contact with her after hitting her across the head."

"Did you know the identity of Mrs Mitchelhill when you saw her walking down Military Road that day?"

"No, I didn't. I didn't have a clue who she was."

"Would you care to tell me why you struck Mrs Mitchelhill with the hammer?"

"I don't know."

* * *

At 6 o'clock that evening O'Toole pressed on with the murder of Lady Ashton. "We are making enquiries surrounding the death of Winfreda Isabelle Ashton in the ground floor area of her home unit block at 186 Raglan Street, Mosman, on May 9, 1989. Do you agree me that (on March 20, 1990, at Royal North Shore Hospital) you informed me that you were responsible for her death?"

"Yes," replied Glover.

"To the best of your recollection, would you recount your movements for me on May 9, 1989?"

"Well, I went to work during the day and on the way to the RSL after work I was driving in Raglan Street and I saw a lady walking down Raglan Street towards me from Military Road. I parked the car, took a pair of gloves and I followed the lady on foot into a block of flats. The lady went through a door into a bin room. I grabbed her from behind. I threw her to the floor. I banged her head on the floor of the bin room and she became still. I removed her shoes and pantyhose and tied them tightly around her neck. I then went through her belongings and took, I think, a wallet and some purses. I left the scene, got into the car, drove to Ashton Park where I removed all monies, threw the wallet and purses into the bush and then drove either to the RSL club or straight home, I'm not sure which."

"When you grabbed Lady Ashton from behind, could you describe for me how you grabbed her?"

"I put my hands around her, one hand on her mouth to stop her screaming and the other hand on the back of her head, pushing it forward... sorry, pulling her backwards. We both fell to the ground."

"What happened then?"

"I'm not sure, I might have landed on top of her."

"Did you punch or strike her in any way whilst she was on the ground?"

"No, once she hit her head on the ground she became still."

"Did she scream or make any other noise at this time."

"No."

"Were you wearing gloves?"

"Yes."

"Why?"

"To avoid identification."

"Would you care to tell me why you tied her pantyhose around her neck?"

"To strangle her."

"In addition to the head injuries and strangulation caused to Lady Ashton, she received seven fractured ribs on the right side of her body. Is there anything you can tell me about those injuries?"

"I didn't strike her in the body. I don't know how those injuries occurred. I did fall on top of her."

"From medical evidence it would appear that Lady Ashton may have been struck by her own walking stick, across her right breast. Is there anything you can tell me about that?"

"Well, I didn't strike her. She may have fallen on her own walking stick."

"How many times did you bang Lady Ashton's head on the ground?"

"From memory, twice. I had my hand over her nose with some force and I bashed the back of her head onto the ground."

"Did you know the identity of Lady Ashton?"

"No."

"Would you care to tell me why you assaulted and strangled Lady Ashton?"

"I don't know."

"What did you do with the gloves you were wearing that day?"

"I burned them in the incinerator at home."

"Why did you burn them?"

"To eliminate evidence."

* * *

The interrogation of John Glover began again next morning, March 23, at 11.15. O'Toole commenced by telling Glover that he was making enquiries into the murder of Margaret Frances Pahud who was found in a laneway near her home unit block off Longueville Road, Lane Cove, on the afternoon of November 2, 1989. He then asked Glover to recount his movements that day.

The prisoner replied: "I was completing a day's work and I finished at Lane Cove. I parked the car in Longueville Road. I saw this lady walking towards me. I took the hammer from under the seat, followed her down the lane and struck her about the head."

"How many times did you strike her on the head with the hammer?"

"From memory, twice, I think."

"Why did you strike her on the head with the hammer?"

"To kill her, I suppose."

"After you struck the woman on the head, what happened then?"

"Well, I hit her from behind and she fell down. I put the hammer back in my belt and I removed her handbag or picked up her handbag and I went back up the lane to the car and drove to the road that goes down by the Lane Cove Country Club. River Road, I think. I parked the car near the entrance to the club, emptied the contents of the handbag and took what money there was in the bag and put the bag in the stormwater drain and then I drove to the Mosman RSL Club."

"Are you able to tell me how much money you took from that handbag?"

"It was in excess of $300."

"What did you do with that money?"

"I went to the club and spent it. I probably spent it over a period of time."

"Did you know the identity of the woman you saw in the street that day?"

"No."

"Would you care to tell me why you followed the woman down the laneway and struck her with the hammer?"

"To kill her."

"If you didn't know the woman, why did you want to kill her?"

"I don't know."

* * *

Two days later in the interview room of Sydney Police Centre, at 11.25am, the men regrouped. This morning the subject was the assault on Doris Cox in the grounds of the Garrison Retirement Village on October 18, 1989. O'Toole reminded Glover that he had already confessed to the attack and asked him to tell what had happened that day.

Said Glover, "Yes, I parked opposite the Garrison in Spit Road. I pulled up to the post office right opposite, I think to make a phone call. I saw a lady walking on the footpath adjacent to the Garrison. I went across the road and befriended her and walked her down the stairs in the grounds of the Garrison. I talked to her for a little while and then pushed her to the ground and I opened her handbag. There was nothing in it and I left, took off."

"Would you care to tell me how you attacked the lady?"

"From behind, pushed her to the wall and she fell down on the steps."

"How did you push her to the wall?"

"I grabbed her from behind, on the head, with both hands. The front of her head, her face, went into the wall."

"How many times did you push her face into the wall?"

"Just once I think, pretty hard."

"We have received medical advice that Mrs Cox received severe injuries to both the front and rear of her head. Is there anything you can tell me about that?"

"The front, yes. But the rear, I didn't hit her with any instrument or anything. I don't know about that."

"Why did you grab Mrs Cox and push her head into the wall?"

"To keep her quiet. To silence her, I expect."

"Why did you want to keep her quiet or silence her?"

"To stop her calling out and attracting attention."

"After you had pushed Mrs Cox's head into the wall, what did she do?"

"She fell down and just lay there."

"Why did you initially approach and speak to Mrs Cox?"

"I don't know, you just seem to see these ladies and it seems to trigger something. I've just got to be violent to them."

"What did you intend to do with Mrs Cox?"

"Certainly to harm her, possibly to kill her."

"You said you befriended Mrs Cox. Would you care to elaborate to me what you meant by 'befriended'?"

"I can't remember word for word. I just engaged her in general conversation."

"Why did you go through the contents of Mrs Cox's handbag?"

"To make robbery seem like the motive."

* * *

After sandwiches and coffee, the interrogation continued. Glover was asked to try to remember the events of November 3, when Olive Cleveland was killed in the grounds of Wesley Gardens Nursing Home, Belrose — the day after the murder of Madge Pahud.

"Well," Glover told the men, "a normal working day and I had called at the Wesley Gardens village to follow up a call to see the chef. I can't remember whether he was in or not. I had seen him a couple of times but I think he had gone that particular day. I proceeded back towards my car which was parked in the grounds. On the way to my car I saw this lady sitting on a bench. I sat alongside her, engaged her in conversation. She got up to go to a door leading into the homes. I followed behind her and before she had a chance to go into the doorway I pushed her around the corner, grabbed her from behind and pushed her heavily to the ground. She lay quite still. I thought I'd killed her. I removed her shoes, took off her pantyhose, and tied them tightly around her neck. I then rifled her handbag and removed all monies. Then I went back to the car and drove off."

"I have been informed that Mrs Cleveland received severe head injuries as a result of this attack upon her," said O'Toole. "What can you tell me about that?"

"That would have resulted from banging her head on the pavement."

"Could you describe to me how you grabbed her from behind?"

"I grabbed her on the back of the neck with some considerable force and then banged her head down onto the concrete landing or walkway."

"How many times did you bang Mrs Cleveland's head on the pavement or walkway?"

"I think twice."

"Would you care to tell me why you first engaged Mrs Cleveland in conversation?"

"To gain her confidence."

"Would you care to tell me why you grabbed Mrs Cleveland and banged her head on the concrete pathway?"

"To kill her."

"Would you care to tell me why you wanted to kill her?"

"I don't know."

"You stated that after you thought you had killed her you 'took off her pantyhose and tied them tightly around her neck'. Why did you did that?"

"To make sure she was dead."

"You stated that you then 'rifled her handbag and removed all monies'. Would you care to tell me why you did that?"

"To point to robbery as a motive."

"Did you take any monies from the handbag?"

"Yes, it wasn't much. I think about $60... I put it in my pocket and spent it over a period of time."

"When did you decide to kill Mrs Cleveland?"

"Well, when I started to lead or usher her around the corner."

"Would you care to tell me why you did not use a weapon in this attack?"

"Well, I hadn't gone back to the car so I didn't have anything with me."

"What was in the car that you could have used as a weapon?"

"The hammer."

* * *

Miles O'Toole's third interview on this gruelling day concerned the murder of Muriel Falconer, the nonagenarian from Muston Street, Mosman, on November 23. The questions began at 3.20pm.

"I finished my day's work," began Glover. I went up to the Buena Vista Hotel to check on specials in the bottle shop. I saw the lady and when I saw her she was walking very slowly away from the shops in Middle Head Road, on the opposite side of the street to the hotel. I went back to the car, which I had parked on the other side of the hotel opposite the police station, picked up a pair of gloves and a hammer, went back to the area where I sighted the lady. She was still walking along the street. She turned into Muston Street, crossed the road and I saw her go through her front gate. I followed her through the gate to her front door. She put her parcels down, opened the front door, she picked up her parcels, went through the front door. I followed her in, grabbed her around the mouth. She started to call out and I struck her with the hammer."

"What happened after you struck her with the hammer?"

"She fell down and I pulled up her clothing and she started to call out and I hit her again with the hammer and I removed her pantyhose, tied them around her neck and pulled her clothing further up over her head. She was still making noises. Again I hit her with the hammer and then I got up and closed the front door. Then I went through her purse which was on the floor, which was empty. Then I went through into a parlour or room on the right hand side of the wall to a chest of drawers. I went through the top drawers and I found money which I removed and put in my pocket. I went back into the hallway. I removed the gloves, put them in a plastic bag, one of her shopping bags, and left. I went back to the car and then home."

"Are you able to tell me how many times you struck Mrs Falconer with the hammer?"

"I think three."

"Would you care to tell me why you struck Mrs Falconer with the hammer?"

"To kill her."

"What part of the body did you strike Mrs Falconer with the hammer?"

"The head."

"Why did you remove Mrs Falconer's pantyhose?"

"To strangle her."

"Were you aware of the identity of Mrs Falconer when you first saw her walking in Middle Head Road?"

"No."

"Would you care to tell me why you followed Mrs Falconer to her home that day?"

"To kill her."

"Why did you want to kill Mrs Falconer?"

"I don't know."

* * *

The following day, Glover told the detectives of his attacks on Margaret Todhunter, Euphemia Carnie and Phyllis McNeill. He could not, however, remember making three of the other indecent assaults he had been charged with. He simply could not recall attacking those women, he said.

In his soft, emotionless voice, the prisoner, now looking drawn and old beyond his years, recounted how he had king-hit 84-year-old

Margaret Todhunter in Hale Road, Mosman; how she hadn't screamed in terror but instead had abused him and called him a "rotten bugger" as he fled to his car with her handbag. This assault, he told O'Toole, taking place as it did on January 11, 1989, 10 days before Essie Rolls's death, was "the start of it all".

Euphemia Carnie was punched to the ground outside the North Haven Retirement Village, Lindfield, at about 1pm on August 25, 1989. Said Glover: "Well, it was during the course of a normal working day. I was working the area. I pulled up outside the place to canvass the home... I saw this lady outside the drive. I knocked her to the ground. I punched her and she fell to the ground. I picked up her bag and ran back to the car."

"Are you prepared to tell me why you struck Mrs Carnie," asked O'Toole.

"It's the same reaction I get when I see these old ladies. I've just got to harm them in some way."

"Can you tell me what clothing you were wearing at the time?"

"I'm sorry to be so stereotyped. I've got two outfits that I wear for work and it would be either blue or brown."

Glover added that he knew neither Margaret Todhunter nor Euphemia Carnie before assaulting them. Phyllis McNeill, the blind woman he had indecently assaulted at the Wybenia Nursing Home, Neutral Bay, on September 6, 1989, was also a stranger to him. She was just there, defenceless and alone in her room, and he was compelled to assault her.

"Can you tell me why you went into Mrs McNeill's room?"

"I'm there, I do it," answered Glover. "I don't know why."

* * *

Murray Byrnes took over the interrogation on Tuesday, March 27. He questioned John Glover on the events that followed the indecent assault on the 82-year-old woman at Greenwich Hospital on January 11, 1990. The prisoner agreed that after the assault he had been contacted by detectives who requested that he appear for questioning at Chatswood police station on Saturday, January 19. He agreed, too, that on the day of the appointment he had attempted to commit suicide by drinking a large amount of alcohol and swallowing a quantity of drugs.

Byrnes then produced a photostat copy of the suicide note Glover had written while under the effects of the alcohol and drugs. The note was scrawled in large, heavy capital letters all over both sides of a form headed "Strictly Confidential — Petersville Staff Retirement Fund". Byrnes said, "Can you tell me anything about these two pages?"

"The first page that you mention," Glover began, "just gives details of my superannuation fund that I obtained in September last year. The other page would be the back of the same staff retirement page. About halfway through taking some of the tablets and grog, I took this piece of paper from the bedside table drawer to use as a goodbye note. That's my writing on both pages."

"I'll refer you to what I will call page one. At the top of that page there appear to be the words 'No more Morris'. What do you mean by that?"

"No more Morris Grant, my boss."

"Underneath that the words 'Yea team' appear. What do you mean by that?"

"I was referring to my family."

"Under that again there appear to be the words 'No more grannys'. Can you tell me what you mean by that?"

"I was obviously referring to the problems I was having."

"Under that the words 'Det' and 'Grannies'. Can you tell me what you mean by that?"

"I think I wrote 'Grannies' 'cause you couldn't read the word 'Grannys' above it. The 'Det'... I think I was going to write 'Detective Whittaker' but there was no room. That's what is written down the side of the page."

"I believe that Detective Whittaker was the person who contacted you in relation to this assault. Is that correct?"

"Yes."

"Underneath the word "Grannies" there are two circles. Can you tell me what they depict?"

"Yes, it's a lump sum payable to dependants on the event of my death."

"Under that appears the words 'Buon anno'. What did you mean by that?"

"It's Italian for 'Happy new year'."

"Underneath and to the right of that appears to be the words 'Go forward, don't look back'. Is that correct?"

"Yes."

"Under that again appear the words 'Yo Star; Yo Marnie, Yo Ned' and 'Ned' appears again. Can you tell me what you mean by that?"

"Just terms of endearment I use for my wife and children."

"At the top of the second page the words 'Gay, don't try to understand; Essie started it' appear. Can you tell me what you mean by this?"

"The first bit is self-explanatory. It's a message to Gay. By referring to 'Essie' I'm referring to my mother-in-law."

"Under those words there appear the words 'Marney save some chicken skin for me'. What do you mean by that?"

"My daughter Marney and I are both good pickers and we both vie for the chicken skin before Gay cuts it up for our dinner."

"Under those words, 'Kellie take over' appears. What can you tell me about that?"

"She's the oldest daughter. She'd be replacing me."

"Under that appear the words 'Sell up and piss off' immediately followed by something 'year'. Can you tell me what that refers to?"

"The first part is obvious. The words under that is German for 'Good new year'. I'll spell it for you: G-U-T-T-E-S N-I-U-E J-H-A-R-E."

"Under that the words 'Love you all RSOB' appear. Can you explain what you mean by that?"

"RSOB stands for 'Rip, shit or bust'."

"Can you tell me what the words are directly under that?"

"Yes," said John Glover, "'Some days are diamonds, some days are stones, girls sing, Rose of Tralee'."

CHAPTER 16

Exposed

Australians were expecting the north shore serial killer to be Satan incarnate, with demonic looks to match his foul crimes. What they got was a pleasant-looking, roly-poly old bloke named John Wayne Glover who could have resembled their favourite uncle, a Father Christmas without the beard. The artists' impressions, composed when Glover was charged with murder and assault in Glebe Local Court on March 28 and published in the next morning's newspapers, were most people's first look at Glover. Those who remarked on the very ordinariness of his appearance suddenly understood how this man had passed unnoticed as he carried out his killing spree in the well-to-do and conservative garden suburbs of Sydney.

The mayor of Mosman at the time, Barry O'Keefe, remembers the sensation that ripped through the suburb when the identity of the Granny Killer was officially released. He recalls being accosted by person after person, all wanting to talk about John Glover. "People kept stopping me to talk about him. There was just this enormous outpouring of surprise and relief. 'Could you believe it!' they'd say, 'Isn't it fantastic they've got him! Thank God! Now whoever would have thought a Mosman person would be capable of that!' I have to confess I was as shocked as anyone. We were all expecting the killer to be a young man, not a middle-aged fellow, and not John Glover, whom so many of us knew.

"When the shock of the killer's identity subsided, there was a genuine concern for Glover's family. 'That poor woman. I wonder whether the children will change their name. Those two nice girls.' People's hearts went out to Gay, Kellie and Marney. There was no gawking and prying like we got when Dr Victor Chang was shot in 1991 and people put flowers on the kerbside. No, with Glover it was a low-key, typically Mosman response to his family's plight. The whole community closed ranks behind their own, much like the people did in Nyngan when floods almost destroyed the town. The Granny Killings showed that quite ordinary people are capable of both terrible things and very good things."

At Loreto Convent, Kirribilli, where Marney Glover was in year 11, the students were called to assembly. They were told to support their schoolmate and rally behind her in this trying time. The principal, Sister Margaret, told the children that anybody overheard gossiping about the Glover family should be reported to her at once. One acquaintance of the popular, gifted Marney says today how everybody at Loreto marvelled at the dignified and courageous way in which she coped with the situation — "Marney handled it really well, as if it had never happened". The friend understood, however, that the elder sister Kellie, who had left the school by the time her father was named as the Granny Killer, was devastated by the revelation. In the months to come both Glover girls and their mother boarded at the convent to escape media attention.

Glover was escorted into Glebe court for his committal shortly before 10am, guarded by a contingent of police and accompanied by his solicitor Don Wakeling. When Glover's name was called and he made to leave the cell adjoining the court room to take his place before Magistrate Kevin Waller, he stopped, looked up and chuckled, "I don't suppose I could say, 'No appearance, Your Worship.'"

He was led to the dock where he sat stock-still and expressionless, his bulky frame squeezed into a bucket-bottomed plastic chair. Mike Hagan, Miles O'Toole, Paul Mayger, Paul Jacob, Murray Byrnes and other members of the task force sat in the police enclosure primed to see the legal system deliver stage one of the *coup de grace* to John Glover. Not once did the accused acknowledge his nemises. Nor did he react when the media army and a crowd of curious citizens stormed into the court at 10.10am and craned from their seats to catch a glimpse of him.

Although sitting slumped with his feet spreadeagled, Glover looked robust for a man who nine days before had been hauled close to death from the bath in the house in Pindari Avenue. His once-again ruddy face accentuated his startling, thick crop of grey-white hair which was tending now to curl at the back. He wore baggy blue jeans, no belt, a light blue denim shirt open at the front that revealed his strong bull neck, and white sandshoes, no laces. Glover's steel-blue eyes bore into a spot on the floor in front of him as police prosecutor Sgt Robert Redfern detailed the 14 charges against him to Magistrate Waller.

Redfern in a monotone listed the charges in chronological order and advised the magistrate that Glover had admitted the crimes in signed records of interview:

• Assault and robbery of Margaret Todhunter, Mosman, January 11, 1989, involving theft of $209.

• Murder of Gwendoline Mitchelhill, Mosman, March 1, 1989.

• Murder of Lady Winfreda Ashton, Mosman, May 9, 1989.

• Assault and indecent assault of an elderly woman (name suppressed), Belrose, June 28, 1989.

• Indecent assault and robbery of an elderly woman (name suppressed), Lane Cove, July 24, 1989.

• On the same day, indecent assault of another elderly woman (name suppressed), Lane Cove.

• Assault and robbery of Euphemia Carnie, Lindfield, August 8, 1989.

• Assault of Phyliss McNeill, Neutral Bay, October 6, 1989.

• Attempted murder of Doris Cox, Mosman, October 18, 1989.

• Murder of Margaret Pahud, Lane Cove, November 2, 1989.

• Murder of Olive Cleveland, Belrose, November 3, 1989.

• Murder of Muriel Falconer, Mosman, November 23, 1989.

• Assault and performance of an act of indecency on an elderly woman (name suppressed), at Greenwich, January 11, 1990.

• Murder of Joan Sinclair, Beauty Point, March 19, 1990.

Sgt Redfern briefly outlined the circumstances of each crime then informed Magistrate Waller that the accused had a long record of convictions for theft and assault dating back to 1947.

Don Wakeling, for Glover, advised the court that his client entered no plea and requested that the magistrate suppress Glover's address to protect his family. Waller granted the request. He also acceded to a plea from Wakeling that Glover be held in protective custody at Long Bay Gaol's psychiatric wing until he made his next appearance in court on May 9.

On April 5, a drizzling autumn day, a squad of unmarked police vehicles drove out of the gates of Long Bay Gaol hospital. In the lead car were Miles O'Toole and John Glover. The defendant had agreed to indicate to investigators the places where he had discarded his victims' property. First stop was Ashton Park, Mosman, where he led police to the bushland near the gun emplacement where he had thrown Lady Ashton's belongings. Next it was to bushland off Julian Street, Mosman, where Miles O'Toole sheltered his prisoner with an umbrella while he pointed out where he had dumped Gwen Mitchelhill's property after he had killed her. Glover then directed his escort to Soldiers Memorial Park in Tryon Road, Lindfield. Into undergrowth there he had hurled a plastic bag containing the groceries and purse of Euphemia Carnie, the woman he had punched at the North Haven Retirement Village, Lindfield. Her property was all police turned up that day. Lady Ashton's purse had already been found, and Gwen Mitchelhill's goods were never recovered. Dave Forbes of the Physical Evidence recalls, "He seemed pretty co-operative. Seemed just like an ordinary bloke to me, really."

On that runaround, recalls Miles O'Toole, the car carrying the detectives and Glover pulled up at traffic lights in Anzac Parade and an attractive young woman crossed in front of the car. Says O'Toole, "One of the police commented that she was very good-looking. 'Yeah,' said Glover, 'I wouldn't mind getting my hands on her!' O'Toole looked at Glover then and saw he was not admiring the young woman at all, but an elderly woman pushing a shopping trolley on the other side of the road.

Glover was not in court on May 9 to hear his case adjourned until June 13. He was, however, close by, waiting in the Glebe Local Court cells.

When he made his second appearance in the dock at Glebe court, on June 13, Glover again entered no plea to any of the charges. He listened impassively as Magistrate Derrick Hand intoned that a committal hearing would begin on October 8.

It was evident to all in court that day that life in the prison hospital was agreeing with John Glover. In his neat blue jeans and beige jumper, he looked healthy, slimmer and fit. He would later give reporters an insight into life in the psychiatric wing, cheerfully boasting of his popularity with fellow inmates and telling how he played chess, did the crosswords, joined in birthday celebrations for other prisoners and indulged in such practical jokes as short-sheeting beds and hiding cockroaches in his fellow inmates' salad sandwiches.

October 8 found John Glover once more in Glebe Local Court. During his committal hearing the court was presented with a weighty four-volume brief by Crown Prosecutor Wendy Robinson, QC. The brief, which had been painstakingly put together by Paul Jacob, contained the terrible litany of Glover's crimes: the recorded and signed interviews with the defendant; police, doctors', ambulancemen's and witnesses' statements; photographs, many almost unbearable to view, of the murder scenes and of the murder victims; the suicide note; testimony of Glover's victims who survived. Robinson also submitted two shoeprints left on the bloodied carpet in the hallway of Muriel Falconer's home, shoeprints which matched one of Glover's brown brogues.

Wendy Robinson, like almost everybody else, found it hard at first to believe that the cheery, benign-looking fellow in the dock could be a serial killer. "He looked so sedate and grandfatherly," she says. "It took me a while to come to grips with the fact that this man was one of the worst killers in Australian history. He had murdered six women. However, when I became fully acquainted with the case, the first thing I said to police was, 'Where are the others?' It seemed overwhelmingly unlikely to me that he had not murdered more women than he was charged with killing."

At the end of the committal proceedings, Magistrate Hand asked the defendant if there was anything he wanted to say before being committed for trial at the Supreme Court. Glover rose and said, so quietly that many of those present missed his words completely, "Well, your worship, I wish to say that I reserve my defence."

CHAPTER 17

Probing The Demons

In mid-1991, forensic psychiatrist Rod Milton, who had prepared a possible personality profile of the Granny Killer in 1989 when hysteria was at its height, was contacted by the Department of Public Prosecutions and asked to interview John Glover and assess whether he merited any defence on the grounds of diminished responsibility. On October 4, after many weeks analysing the four-volume task force brief of the investigation and the findings of other psychiatrists who had interviewed Glover, he drove to Long Bay Gaol remand centre where he questioned the prisoner at length about his life and motivation for the murders. Rod Milton's findings would seal John Glover's fate when he presented them to the jury at Glover's trial for murder the following month.

In his report, Milton described Glover as an extremely dignified, white-haired man of good height, a little stooped. He noticed many small veins on his face, consistent with heavy drinking over many years. Throughout their three and a half hour interview, Milton found Glover's manner, in the main, convincing. He also had trouble reconciling the person before him with someone who had killed elderly women repeatedly and in a most violent fashion and molested or injured many others. Though Glover claimed to be extremely remorseful, Milton found this unconvincing. He got the impression that the prisoner did not experience guilt or remorse as other people do.

Milton reported that Glover was accurately oriented in time and place and was reasonably capable of simple subtractions. However he could not memorise a complex sentence even after a few tries. He could interpret proverbs but not especially well. His general knowledge appeared "satisfactory". Overall, Glover's intellect could be rated "average or slightly better, possibly affected by his intake of alcohol over the years". The psychiatrist felt Glover was capable of presenting himself as more intelligent than he really was.

There was no doubt, felt Milton, that Glover was aware of the charges he faced, knew of his right to challenge the jury, and was aware of the functions of various officers of the Supreme Court. He seemed capable of instructing his barrister and of following the course of the trial. He knew it was wrong to kill and he knew what he was doing at the time of the killings.

Milton went on to lead Glover through each of his crimes and noted his responses. Glover's recollection of the Mitchelhill killing included the following: "She was walking down the street. This is where it becomes frustrating to me because as John Glover, sales manager of Four 'N Twenty Pies, there seems to be another personality or whatever comes out of me, sees this person and wants to harm her. This personality, alter-ego, whatever, like Mr Good Guy and Mr Bad Guy, picks up a hammer from under the seat of the car, kept there for work purposes, and follows her into her flat entrance. It comes to me that I recall it in detail because I was there, but not as the perpetrator of the act, but as another part of me committing this act."

Glover maintained it was hard to explain how he felt at the moment when he hit Gwen Mitchelhill with his hammer. "It's as if I'm watching someone committing this act. I'm saying that I really don't know the feelings of the person that's doing this dreadful thing."

Dr Milton reported that Glover told him that each night he tried to work it all out, but never with any success. "The longer it goes the more it starts to disappear in the mists of time," said Glover. "I've tried to reason with it, I know what happened, I saw it happen, it was very quick. This other part of me finishes what it's doing. I'm back in the car, and I'm John Glover, sales manager, going back home."

Glover told Milton that he was aware of the details of his aggressive acts but felt no accompanying emotion. "There's no way as a family man I could do such a thing," the prisoner added.

He seemed unwilling to comment when Milton again questioned him on his feelings as he committed murder. "Instead," reported Milton, "he talked about not having much education and said this made it hard for him to describe his feelings." Said Glover: "How could

another personality emerge? Was it latent, was it built-up frustra-
tions from the years before?"

When Milton asked him if killing gave him satisfaction and helped
him discharge aggression, Glover responded, "You mean was there
any gratification? I knew there was something wrong happening, but
I wasn't in control. I was observing. I was fully cognisant of what was
happening... I can't even think of it after it was all over. Bear in mind
that this thing only took seconds." Glover could not remember getting
into his car after a slaying and thinking, "That was good."

When questioned by Dr Milton about his relationship with Joan
Sinclair, Glover told him they first met at Mosman RSL. "We were
just bloody good friends. A bit of sex play and some initial attempts
at sex, but just gave up. The friendship remained. She liked to drink,
she liked to have lunch, she liked to go to the club and play the
machines."

Glover told the psychiatrist that killing Joan Sinclair and his own
suicide attempt were connected. He said the suicide attempt was to
eliminate his alter-ego. "To finally get rid of this other guy." Glover
added, "This is when there seemed to be a takeover by the second
personality — to apparently methodically go about going to her home
with the intention of committing suicide and whatever the triggering
device was, to want to kill again."

Milton noted that after he had said this Glover put his head on his
hand and "gave the impression of experiencing emotion. I noticed a
tear in each eye. After a few minutes I asked him if he would like to
talk further and he said, 'I just get this rush of remorse. I start to feel
for the relatives of the victims, for my own family, apart from it being
a horrendous affair. I wish I could have stopped it from going on.'"

Dr Milton probed Glover's background. The prisoner told of his
early days in Wolverhampton. Of how his parents had separated
when he was around nine years of age and he had been shunted to and
fro between his unambitious father and extremely ambitious mother.
His mother Freda he described as "outgoing" and "a hard worker who
placed her family first". A forthright and assertive woman who
would, her son remembered, "say her piece if she felt like it". Dr
Milton reported that although Glover claimed his mother was capable of affection, displays of this were few and far between.

Glover described how his mother had remarried when he was 12 and that he "just got on" with his step-father. He and his younger brother were joined soon afterwards by a step-sister and a step-brother, but the step-brother was the son of another man not his step-father. His mother was, by that time, "a bit fast and loose, or becoming that way". She would marry four times before dying in 1988 in Australia from breast cancer.

Glover told the psychiatrist that he did not enjoy being pushed from one parent to another as a child. "It's amazing to me how parents can treat their kids — like a bit of bloody merchandise." However, when he was 14 his mother had welcomed him home "with open arms" because he had "the potential to earn a quid". For his part, Glover said to Dr Milton, "It suited me to be with my mother, a better lifestyle, more money at Mum's end than Dad's."

Glover told Dr Milton his schooling was "a joke". Disrupted by his moving around, his formal education had ended when he turned 14. And that was a pity because he believed himself to be "very intelligent and quick on the uptake, with a flair for music and languages". He blamed his non-completion of an electrician's apprenticeship on his being upset by his parents' marital strife.

Dr Milton heard how Glover had accepted his childhood lot. "It was a matter of acceptability — you didn't argue with things in those days, you accepted them as they were." He had girlfriends with whom he was successful sexually and as for emotional problems in his younger years he had experienced "only the normal falling in and out of love as a teenager". He had no pets except a rabbit which was killed by the family cat.

He fobbed off his five convictions for stealing between the ages of 14 and 22 with: "It was a bohemian attitude. If I didn't have something that someone else had, I just took it, as opposed to stealing for gain."

Glover denied getting into fights as a youth, except for "a pretty mild affair at one of the dances I went to — I can't remember the details". This statement moved Dr Milton to note, "As the interview progressed I was to find that this kind of answer characterised most statements made by Mr Glover if the answer was likely to be derogatory to him. Thus, although he gave a superficial impression of being open and feeling deeply about things, when it came to the point he was careful not to reveal much about himself, particularly any negative information."

He told the psychiatrist how he had enjoyed his army life, especially the order and stability, the security and the camaraderie, the neatness and tidiness. He boasted how he had climbed the ranks quickly and come out as a radar operator/bombadier, "the equivalent of a corporal". He had been good with weapons and once "drilled 600 men on the square". His army experience had followed him through life. "Even now I'm first up, shaved and showered in the morning."

When he left the army aged 20 he found the freedom of civilian life difficult to handle. Although working as a bus conductor and delivery van driver he considered himself a misfit, and found life in England unsatisfactory, going "from job to job, parent to parent, girlfriend to girlfriend". The ad calling for tram drivers and conductors to work in Melbourne was the stimulus he needed to emigrate.

In Australia Glover had many girlfriends and was "always successful sexually", but in 1962 he committed an indecent assault on a woman. Of that and his crimes in the future, he told Milton, "The same unknown urge seems to have arisen again in later years." The psychiatrist said that at this point in their interview Glover looked puzzled and said he deeply wanted to find out what caused him to do such strange things. "There's no rhyme or reason," he said.

Three years later, in 1962, he got into trouble for peeping and prying — "I was into voyeurism." While he had had normal sexual relations with women previously, "For that short time I preferred to observe. The fact that I was seeing something that shouldn't be seen without their knowledge was important to me." He had peeped at both young and old women.

When Dr Milton asked him what he felt when committing the later offences, the assaults and murders, Glover replied, "It's hard to describe because I've got this duality — it starts to appear then. Normally John Glover, the happy working person, the life and soul of the party, wouldn't hurt a fly; then his alter-ego comes out, wants to hurt people. It wasn't like striking with instruments, it was humiliation."

Glover went on: "By saying things like alter-ego, humiliation, etc, I'm not trying to dodge the responsibility for what I've done — I'm seeking to clarify." Glover said it annoyed him that he could not explain his behaviour. He had spent many hours thinking about it.

He asked the psychiatrist if he could suggest anything that might "make it all clear to me". "What's worrying me is, if you look at the '62 matters, those urges or whatever you call it were there, then we (Milton noted the plural pronoun) went through a period of stability with marriage and family and home, then it recurred in a frightening way."

After his marriage in 1968 Glover felt his life found a new direction. He told Milton how his wife had recognised his potential and intelligence and prompted him to become a liquor salesman. "I became John Glover, sales representative. Instead of driving a delivery truck I was driving a company car. It was a fillip to me — the result was good. I became the collar and tie brigade. I was very successful at it, wines and spirits initially, later a wider range — wine casks, palletisation, discounting." He added that he was always a gentleman in his business dealings and maintained good relations with the opposition.

Two years after his marriage, Glover told Milton, he and his wife had moved to Sydney and his daughters were born in 1971 and 1973.

The psychiatrist brought Glover forward in time to the serial killings. He reported, "I questioned him in detail about the Mitchelhill and Ashton killings, but did not ask him much more about further killings apart from that of Mrs Sinclair, for his answers in each case were essentially similar — he recalled the basic details, and always maintained that another entity, not really himself, took over...

"When telling me about his business career, his life as a child and his service in the army, Mr Glover spoke confidently, with dignity and an assured manner. He was less assured, even becoming some-what unsettled, when I began to question him about the offences. He broke out in a sweat and was not keen to answer.

"In response to a question about stealing from his victims, he replied, 'I took property from all of them' but said the stealing 'certainly wasn't for monetary gain — a throw-off as a motive'. He said it was the other part of him, the alter-ego or another personality, which emerged at these times, causing him to do dreadful things, and this part of the personality worked out the idea of taking money in order to suggest this as a motive — a distraction to police."

Glover then spoke further about his "good" self. "John Glover,

Good Guy, wouldn't have one of these thoughts in his life — they've manifested themselves in this other — you can't say person, I'm really at a loss for words — alter-ego."

When Dr Milton brought up the washing of the death hammer in acid, Glover explained this was an attempt to erase evidence. The psychiatrist then pointed out to Glover that his earlier accounts suggested that the other, bad, personality stopped being active when he got back into the car, at which time he became "John Glover, sales manager" and asked which personality had washed the hammer clean of blood. Glover's uncomfortable response was that the bad personality must have returned briefly when he arrived home to wash the hammer, but really "I can barely recall doing anything with it".

Questioned as to why he had carefully and neatly arranged Lady Ashton's and Gwen Mitchelhill's shoes and walking sticks beside their bodies, Glover sighed and said, "I've thought about this quite a lot, once again I've not tried to evade any issues, but I can't find any issues, it doesn't mean anything to me."

As for the five-month gap between the murder of Lady Ashton on May 9, 1989, and the attempted murder of Doris Cox on October 18, Glover said, "Obviously the memories of it and the guilt and responsibility of it, but it seemed as if this other personality was carrying it — it wasn't me. Sort of let the responsibility be concerned, be worried. I went about my life and work quite normally."

Dr Milton interpreted this statement as indicating that it was not up to the good John Glover to worry about the offences. Since they were committed by the bad John Glover it was up to that entity to worry about them. "The murders were on the conscience of the bad John Glover and not on the conscience of the good John Glover."

Glover claimed in the interview that he had become totally impotent two years before the killings began. He said his impotence had not worried his wife who accepted it as "one of the inevitable changes of age". Glover did not believe his alcohol intake was to blame. "My grandfather and Charlie Chaplin were both pisspots but they were both horny at 93."

The prisoner expounded on the guilt and horror he felt over his actions during his reign of terror. "I wanted to tell myself what the hell was going on. I couldn't." When asked by Dr Milton whether he had ever wanted to confess to somebody and so unload his guilt, he said, "If I'd had something to tell them, I'd say yes... How can you tell somebody that there's a part of me doing wrong things."

Dr Milton put it to Glover that, as a responsible person, the good John Glover, sales manager and family man, should have confessed to the murders while he was in hospital after his first suicide attempt. Glover did not respond. However his suicide attempt after murdering Joan Sinclair had been "to stop this other side of me from doing anything else. If I had to go with it (that is, die too), then so be it."

Glover then told Dr Milton how his mother, his step-father and step-sister had come to live in Australia, in Sydney and then at Gosford, in the late 1960s or early 1970s. Glover had continued to see her and it was a respectful relationship — "Due deference, if you can put it that way" — but he could not deny that he continued to harbour a sense of an unsatisfactory childhood and some negative feelings towards his mother because of that. He had been sad when she died of breast cancer but "accepted that she had to go". He confided to the psychiatrist that he had himself contracted breast cancer four years before in 1988 and had undergone surgery, a mastectomy.

The prisoner left the psychiatrist in no doubt as to his feelings towards his mother-in-law. "I couldn't stand the woman. My wife couldn't stand her either. We lived with them (his in-laws) for a long time." Although his mother-in-law gave his father-in-law "a hell of a time" Glover had not made waves about this: "Once again, the old values came through and I paid due deference to her. I respected her for being my mother-in-law."

* * *

Tall and lean, quiet and bespectacled, Dr Rod Milton is a good listener and observer, as befits his profession as a forensic psychiatrist. He remembers his first impression of John Glover, when they met in a private section of the remand section of Long Bay Gaol on October 4, 1991. "He was a dignified-looking, grey-haired man, urbane and cool. He gave a reasonable account of his background, but when I pressed him for details about relationships in his family and concerning his killings he became evasive. And this was the way the entire interview went: great friendliness, great willingness to help, but then evasion when confronted with questions about things he wanted to keep to himself.

"I guess in his evasion there was a sense of self-preservation, but also of shame or a sense of wanting to preserve his dignity, his self-respect. Even though he knew that I knew he had done these things, he somehow derived emotional benefit from avoiding talking about them."

At no time when the psychiatrist and the ferocious killer were together did Dr Milton fear for his life. "No, I never considered my safety to be at risk. Glover's anger was specific to a certain class of person — elderly women. I didn't fit that class. That he might attack me just didn't occur to me. I have interviewed many dangerous people, and I don't see myself as a participant in the battle between authority and the accused. I'm sort of a professional person a bit to one side, so, no, I didn't feel afraid."

The forensic psychiatrist considered Glover's claim that he had an alter-ego, "the bad John Glover" who committed the crimes, as his most significant statement in the interview. "This was a charade which he needed to maintain. But there were many holes in his scenario. For instance, he said the bad John Glover committed the murders, then would return to his car where he would revert to being the good John Glover. Then who destroyed the gloves at home, who washed the hammer? Did the bad John Glover make sudden reappearances like a jack-in-the-box? That just didn't hold water. His charade was shallow and a pretence easily seen through."

Dr Milton says, "John Glover wanted to convey to me his version of things. I wanted to get from him what I thought was the truth. There was a difference between the two. I don't believe he told me what I wanted to know about his background and I believe he has a need to protect himself from that knowledge. I believe that the reasons he committed the crimes were related to intense conflict within himself. Nobody commits such crimes because they are happy. No murder is committed out of happiness. Murders are the end result of deep unhappiness. The murder fulfils a purpose for the murderer by relieving tension, however the murderer invariably wants to avoid acknowledging those tensions within himself because that then faces him with the deeper underlying reasons which are being repressed."

The psychiatrist found Glover's dignified demeanour as bogus as his claim that there were two John Glovers. "The dignity and urbanity were part of an elaborate posture to maintain self-respect.

You see, people like this are really fairly hollow and without much substance, but they sometimes give the impression of living a life of substance because they are very adept at presenting a certain aspect of themselves to the world. That was how Glover struck me, as a person living a sham life. The family man, the sales manager, the respected citizen and pillar of the community — all these were shams. John Glover's real life was his anger and his sexual interest in elderly ladies.

"Although he hotly denies it, Glover's crimes had a sexual motivation. He did sexually interfere with those old ladies in the nursing homes. That happened often. And the taking off of pantyhose and leaving his murder victims' sexual organs exposed is further evidence of his sexual preoccupation. It is also possible that there was sexual exploration of some of the victims' bodies. His other motivation was anger. The two go together. For instance Glover had a very complex, troubled and unhappy relationship with his mother, and I believe he may have had incestuous feelings toward her. His shame and anger over those feelings may be his motivation for his murdering, defiling and humiliating the elderly women."

Dr Milton believes that, intense as his dislike of his mother-in-law was, she was only ever a convenient focus for a pre-existing anger. "I don't believe his hatred of Essie prompted him to commit these terrible killings. You would have to go back to an earlier time in his life — to his relationship with his mother. Essie was perhaps representational of this time. The only significant woman in Glover's early life was his mother. I believe his difficulties lie with her. He could not deal with what he considered her promiscuity, but he was not about to go into detail about that with me. He's bottling a lot up inside. So far, John Glover has told us only what he wants us to know. He is a man largely unknown, largely alone. I doubt that he will ever fully reveal himself."

* * *

Dr Rod Milton's official report to the Public Prosecutions Office, which follows, was based on his October 4 interview with John Glover, police records of interview and related documents, and information made available to the forensic psychiatrist in 1989 and 1990 while the murders were being committed. It was this report that formed the foundation of the evidence that Dr Milton submitted at

Glover's murder trial and which proved instrumental in convincing the judge and jury that Glover was responsible for his actions and that he was, in fact, fit to stand trial.

"When I endeavoured to understand the motivation behind the killings, I was reminded that most people, when confronted with such outrageous violence resulting in tragedy for so many, are overwhelmed and tend to interpret the violence as the result of mental illness — it is difficult for them to conceive that a sane man could obtain satisfaction from repeatedly killing elderly women and defiling and humiliating them sexually.

"From the outset, when I reviewed material from the crime scenes in mid-1989, I was impressed with the apparent purposeful nature of the killings. Although extraordinarily violent, they were not bizarre if it was assumed that the perpetrator had conflicts over sexuality and his relationships with older women. The murders then became an understandable expression of conflict over and hatred toward elderly women.

"I predicted that the offender would not have a history of frank mental disturbance, which was consistent with Mr Glover's presentation when I saw him recently and with his having had no psychiatric treatment in the past.

"Mr Glover himself spoke of a wish to humiliate his victims: 'then his (Glover's) alter-ego comes out, wants to hurt people. It wasn't hurting like striking with instruments, it was humiliation.'

"He stated that he stole from his victims to divert attention from other aspects of the killings, that is, to supply a false motive. It seemed to me that this was only partly the case, and he probably obtained very real satisfaction from stealing as a further act of aggression against his victims. For example, I think he probably derived considerable pleasure in spending Mrs Pahud's money at a club immediately after killing her.

"I considered various aspects of Mr Glover's background which might have led to his negative attitude to elderly women. While he was informative to a degree regarding his early life, I felt he was guarded about what he revealed of his emotional state as a child and young man. The only time he expressed himself openly in this regard was when he spoke about his enjoyable experiences in the army.

"Despite these limitations it would be reasonable to conclude that he suffered a lot of disruption and unhappiness as a child. His parents separated when he was young, and there was sure to have been unhappiness and conflict between them before they separated. His information about his mother was rather guarded but his account suggested she was repeatedly unfaithful, perhaps obviously promiscuous, and he was aware of this.

"A boy growing up in these circumstances often feels intense anger towards his mother over her infidelity or promiscuity and the associated neglect of her family responsibilities. He told me she was prepared to use people for her own purpose.

"I consider that as a result of early life experiences, in particular his relationship with his mother, John Glover remained at an adolescent level of development — he sought dependence on forceful and older women, while at the same time resenting that dependence and associated incestuous feelings.

"He enjoyed the army immensely. He spoke of the camaraderie experienced with the other men, evidently something he had not experienced with his workmates or in his relationship with his father. He also spoke of his dependence on the army and liking the way the army organised his life for him and how he felt secure there. He spoke of feeling a bit of a misfit after he left the army. All this is consistent with a dependent and immature young man whose emotional state remained largely at an adolescent level of development.

"In this regard, however, I emphasise that he was still essentially normal, that is, there was no mental illness. His conflicts were those experienced by many others. Many men remain in dependent relationships with their older or dominating wives but are normal members of the community.

"Why Mr Glover should have expressed his conflicts by assault and homicide is not able to be explained on the information currently available. I believe there was an element of personal choice in that he decided to express and obtain relief from his inner conflicts at the ultimate expense of others.

"He apparently lived in a stable relationship with a woman he regarded as directing his life. He stated that the marriage was happy but the presence of his parents-in-law in the household caused distress. In his suicide note he attributed the commencement of his serial killings to the effect of his mother-in-law upon him: 'Don't try to understand — Essie started it.'

"I think this is only half the truth. He had shown evidence of serious assaultive behaviour to women earlier. If his mother-in-law had any effect, it would have been only to evoke conflicts and behaviour patterns already in existence.

"Mr Glover maintained that he was not responsible for the killings. He attributed them to an 'alter-ego' which emerged at the time of the killings but which was dormant at other times. He put forward the notion that there were two John Glovers: the first, a devoted family man, respected member of the community, and responsible sales manager; the other, an entity which hated and sought to revile old ladies. Mr Glover professed to be puzzled about himself and to be earnestly seeking to understand himself better and make sense of the whole tragic affair. This was not consistent with the behaviour attributed to him in therapy at the Royal North Shore Hospital. He tried unconvincingly to convey sadness and deep concern for his victims and their families.

"One could accept Mr Glover's thesis at face value, but I think it would be wrong to do so. Mr Glover, like anyone else, has something to gain by presenting himself in a socially acceptable fashion, and something to lose by revealing the full extent of the feelings underlying the killings.

"I had reason to doubt Mr Glover's account during my interview with him. For example, both Mrs Mitchelhill and Lady Ashton had severe thoracic damage which probably occurred as a result of vicious punches or kicks to the chest, but Mr Glover persistently denied acts of this kind. He also denied using a cane to assault Lady Ashton, although the medical evidence was in that direction. When Mr Glover was questioned by Professor Tennant (at Royal North Shore Hospital) about the note left after the first suicide attempt, he said the statement therein, 'No more grannies', referred to his mother and mother-in-law. This was patently untrue. Mr Glover was evasive when I asked him details of the killings, particularly regarding what was going on in his mind at the time.

"I am therefore unable to regard Mr Glover as reliable regarding the account of his emotional state and actions. In this context I note that men who commit sexual homicide — as I believe these killings were — are frequently prudish when speaking of their own sexuality regarding their victims. They need to keep this aspect of themselves totally secret, perhaps because there is continuing emotional satisfaction in mentally re-living the murders and the stimulation associated therewith. Telling others about these inner feelings interferes with this satisfaction.

"Mr Glover explained the killings as being committed by a separate but irresponsible part of himself and denied any satisfaction or pleasure in them. I am unable to accept this interpretation.

"A more likely explanation is that the series of killings occurred because of longstanding sexual and emotional conflict regarding Mr Glover's feelings for women older than himself. It is likely that killing gave him both pleasure and relief, and it is also likely that fantasy over the murders continues to supply him with gratification. For obvious reasons Mr Glover is not prepared to admit this, but says the murders were committed by a hidden part of himself and that he obtained no pleasure or satisfaction from them.

"Mr Glover shows features of the anti-social personality. He is self-centred, has minimal interest in the welfare of others, shows a long history of anti-social acts, and is convincing at projecting a socially acceptable image despite having committed crimes of extraordinary violence. Many such personalities function poorly in society and are repeatedly incarcerated in consequence. Others, however, are better organised and by a variety of measures protect themselves from the results of their anti-social behaviour.

"Killing is an abnormal activity in our society, but not all killing is a result of mental illness. These killings were not the result of any recognisable mental or emotional illness, but reflected Mr Glover's willingness to sacrifice others for his own relief and gratification.

"Mr Glover does not suffer from any mental or emotional disorder.

"The defence of diminished responsibility is not available to Mr Glover... He is fit to stand trial."

CHAPTER 18

Judgement Day

John Glover's plea, when he at last made it on the opening day of his trial in Courtroom No.5 at Central Criminal Court, Darlinghurst, on November 18, 1991, was that he was not guilty, not guilty of murder on the grounds of diminished responsibility. His position was that, yes, he had killed the six women but because of certain factors which he and psychiatrists would elaborate upon during the trial he had not been completely responsible for his actions.

Glover took his place in the dock before Supreme Court Justice James Wood wearing blue jeans and a racy black, white and grey-striped shirt which looked bizarrely out of place among the archaic gowns and wigs of the legal people and the sober suits of the detectives in that imposing rich carved wood-panelled court room. Occasionally the defendant would blink and appear bewildered, looking like a kindly grandfather who had taken a wrong turn while shopping in some suburban mall one Saturday morning and stumbled into this staid and threatening scene by mistake. But there was no mistake, and Miles O'Toole, Geoff Wright, Paul Mayger and Paul Jacob were in the police enclosure looking on throughout the trial as justice was served. Again those present had to strain to hear Glover's words as he whispered his plea of not guilty to all charges. The three charges of assault, robbery and malicious wounding would be dealt with separately at the completion of the murder trial.

As the trial wore on, Glover's records of interview were damning. They stunned and sickened all who heard them. The court learned, as those staccato question and answer sessions were read out, how the compulsion to kill would come upon him, how he would stalk his victims and murder them, usually with a hammer he kept in his car, how he would defile their bodies by stripping them of their pantyhose and tying the underwear around their necks then leaving them with their legs spread apart, how when they were dead he would steal from them, and how he would then revert to being a citizen, husband, father and salesman until taken by his homicidal urge once more. When each recorded confession had been read out Justice Wood asked Glover before the court whether what he had confessed to police in the record of interview was true. Every time, Glover whispered, "Yes."

Throughout, Glover remained ice-cool, seemingly detached from the horrors unleashed on that court. Only three times did his composure break. Once was when Rod Milton testified that he believed Glover harboured incestuous feelings towards his mother and Glover's face had turned scarlet and his hands clenched in rage. Another time was when evidence was given of the suicide note he had written in January, 1990, when he had first tried to take his own life. Glover had wiped tears from his florid cheeks when Murray Byrnes told how Glover had scrawled on the note "Marney, save some chicken skin for me" and how Glover had explained the entry in his record of interview, saying, "My daughter Marney and I are both pickers and we both vie for the chicken skin before Gay cuts it up for our dinner."

John Glover again shed tears when he made his own statement from the dock on November 25. The atmosphere was electric as Glover rose in the dock, faced the jury squarely, and began to read his prepared statement slowly and deliberately: "Your Honour, ladies and gentlemen of the jury. I have been asked to make this statement from the dock as some form of evidence. If I may take your time to fill you in a little on 54 (sic) years of history leading up to the present matters before you.

"I was born in England in 1932. I started my education, if you can call it such, at the age of five years. I went to school until I was 14. Because of divorced parents, during this time, and there happened to be World War II happening at the same time, my education suffered greatly because of custodial swapping around between parents, different towns and different schools.

"Consequently no tertiary education was gone into, no high school was thought of and at 14 I left school. I went to work as an apprentice electrician which I didn't complete but continued through various jobs up until the age of 17 which was compliant to that sort of maintenance work, working with tools and my hands and what-not.

"The switching from one parent to another didn't help at all and at the age of 17 I decided to get out and get into digs of my own, see if I could make a start there. That didn't last too long because I then went back for a short time prior to going into the British army where I did two and a half years service.

"That seemed to have a settling effect on me. I enjoyed the army. I enjoyed the control. The organisation. Knowing what you are doing each day as opposed to what I had been through before. I came out of the army with some rank and no qualification except a driver's licence.

"I'm not being flippant there, it has relevance. I went back home to live with my mother who by now had gone into her second marriage. Her second husband died and I decided to make another break and get into lodgings. I went into various types of jobs, mostly driving because it was the only qualification I had.

"I saw a job opportunity in the newspaper in Australia in Melbourne: tramways operators required. I saw this as a golden opportunity to really make a break from all the mish-mash I'd gone through and make a fresh start. So I arrived in Melbourne in 1956 (sic) and was always gainfully employed.

"I went through the tramways contract which I had to do and (stayed) in various lodgings and through this met a lot of people, made a lot of friends. I applied my driving skills to get into delivery-type work and ran deliveries as a van salesman, always coming up the ladder a wee bit.

"This went on a few years and during that time I got into trouble with the police in Melbourne on two occasions for assaults on women. One was quite young, 35, the other quite old. No death occurred. I was put on probation.

"There was another matter which arose. I was accused of voyeurism which was proved and I admitted anyway. That was six weeks in the Metropolitan Remand Centre in Melbourne.

"I mention these because I think they are relevant to the matters in hand. Explanations I cannot give you..."

Glover choked on these last words and tears coursed down his face. From the police gallery Miles O'Toole looked on coldly at the defendant's display of self-pity. The thought occurred to him that not once during Glover's recounting of his atrocities against those elderly women had this man been moved to tears, not once had he shown an iota of regret or remorse. Now here the bastard was, blubbering about his own problems.

Composed once more, Glover continued. "My relations with women at that time — before, during and after — were quite normal, quite successful. That went by, and I met my wife-to-be.

"I progressed to sales-type work, over the counter in a wine and spirits store.

"I eventually met my wife-to-be who realised some potential in me to get further, which had not been recognised in earlier years. She pushed me along and we decided to get married.

"I continued selling and moved to Sydney, where I started my professional career as a sales rep. I attended sales courses, seminars and training, and caught up very quickly, becoming quite successful as a sales rep and manager.

"I went to live with my wife's mother and father in their house. They were getting on in years and we intended to stay there until we had a place of our own. But looking at their declining years and the potential of the building, we extended to a third storey which accommodated all of us quite adequately. My wife was an only child and she would have inherited the house anyway but that was a far-reaching projection or inevitability.

"We started a family, two girls. Everything was absolutely fine. We lived together amicably, the girls grew up. I was fortunate in having two bright girls and fortunate again in having them go to private school... everything *I* should have had... everything *I* should have had, they were getting..."

Again Glover broke down and sobbed noisily in the dock. Justice Wood ordered a glass of water for the crying man. After a short break, Glover went on, "Things got progressively awkward with the in-laws, which I'm not going to dwell on. I think you all know what I'm talking about.

"My mother eventually arrived in Australia with my married sister and her young children, which was quite a shock to the system after 20-odd years of not seeing them. They stayed in Sydney for a short time and moved to Gosford which was quite close enough and quite far enough away.

"The relationship between us all was respectful. My children went with me and my wife, visited and inter-visited, but it was the case of now two mothers-in-law.

"My mother eventually died of cancer after a previous mastectomy. It developed that I had the same problem and I also had surgery for cancer which was a mastectomy. My mother died of secondaries. I found out later that her sister, and *her* sister, all died of the same thing. Prostatitis ensued with me, impotency followed that.

"Again there was a certain complacency from me on these matters. But with hindsight I wonder was I deeply concerned about these things knowing the previous history of Mum and her sister.

"Work (at that time) as a sales rep took me into institutions, factory canteens, hospitals and nursing homes. I then felt compelled to molest elderly women in nursing homes. There weren't many, but one or two. It's still bad. I have no excuse, no reason. I can't give you what compulsion drove me to do it, but the fact remains it happened.

"It comes now to the matters in hand which you are well aware of. I know they've occurred, I saw them. I don't know why they occurred. They are very clear in my mind, but not clear as to a motive.

"My lifestyle in Mosman was superb. We had lots of friends and no worries about debts, home, or anything like that. The kids were getting through school beautifully. I was well respected in the community. I belonged to good clubs. But these things occurred and I don't want to keep repeating that, but when it happened it was, it was, 'see someone and attack'.

"I felt detached, as if I was witnessing the thing, not actually doing it.

"If that makes sense or not, I don't know... but it's the only way I can explain it."

"Apart from the last victim, Joan Sinclair, I didn't know any of these ladies so there was no predetermined animosity from knowing them. With Joan Sinclair, she was a friend of mine, a very good friend. The fact is that I went there with the means to commit suicide and I also went there with a hammer which is to kill with.

"For me, after 20 months in gaol, locked up night after night, I still can't categorically say why or how or whatever... whether there was a disassociation from the good fellow, both going into the same place, one to get rid of the bad fellow by suicide, and two, which is questionable, to kill and me to commit suicide.

"The reason for the choice of this place to happen was purely a matter of convenience for the suicide — privacy. I thought no-one knew I was there but obviously a lot of people did. I wish to Christ you would have found me before.

"There isn't more I can say except that during the last 20 months I've had ample time for reflection and this may come out during the course of the trial that it has been commented that I have shown no remorse for these matters. That is absolute nonsense. What I've got locked up for, the victims' families, relatives, and mine..." Glover again began to cry and dabbed at his eyes with a tissue. "... I am sorry. I can't say any more..." Glover, his face red and crumpled, slumped in the dock and sobbed.

In the ensuing days the court heard evidence from psychiatrists as to John Glover's state of mind. Dr Rod Milton, the consultant psychiatrist who had been advising police almost from the time the killings began, appeared for the Crown. He said the defendant fitted the pattern of behaviour of a serial killer because he distilled anger and chose to release it as an intense rage directed against women. Milton said that the serial killer whose type Glover matched has a history of resenting an important woman in his life. "He acts out on a look-alike of the mother or wife. He frequents shops and other situations, looks for women and spends his time sizing them up. He hunts the victim and moves at his own pace to rape or kill. Mr Glover's sexual desire remained but his sexual competence was not there."

Milton said that killers of Glover's type kill in a frenzied attack and with blunt force, sometimes taking a weapon to the murder scene.

The psychiatrist then told the court that "This type of offender removes souvenirs. We know Mr Glover removed the victims' purses or money. This type of offender carries out exploration of a sexual nature. He enjoys this because he is still expending energy and the murder is not complete till he carries out his sexual experience or examination. When the circumstances permitted, he displayed his victims with their legs apart and their sexual orientation very clearly in view. It is very likely he carried out some form of sexual exploration."

Milton said he believed that Glover had no recognisable mental or emotional illness and had no defence either of insanity or dimished responsibility. The defendant had a narcissistic personality and anti-social characteristics. One such characteristic was an emotional lack of concern for the feelings of others — "no feeling at all for his victims".

The psychiatrist told the court that ordinary people were shocked "and properly so" when they saw crimes such as those allegedly committed by Glover. "Because we don't share the dissociations in habitual behaviour of the criminal, we don't like to think any individual could behave that way towards another person. We say, 'How could he?' The next step is to say, 'I just could not let myself accept it' and 'Anybody who does something like that has got to have something wrong with him'. Obviously such killings are abnormal. We are so horrified we move away from it. We just refuse to admit he could be normal. When he gets his pleasure and whatever in committing acts of this kind because his behaviour is different, we choose to look at it in a different way. However in Glover's case, the only thing abnormal is the nature of the killings themselves."

He said that pivotal to Glover's problems was his relationship with his mother. The psychiatrist said, "One element was of a sexual arousal by his mother. I am sure that when he referred to her as being 'fast and loose' and described her more or less in various derogatory ways, I think that as an adolescent there was probably some sexual arousal there for him. I think that he also felt guilt at that sexual arousal and felt anger towards his mother arising from that guilt she inflicted on him. He was angry with her, he was stirred up by her, but at the same time was angry with her for stirring him up."

Milton said that a boy, growing up in circumstances such as Glover had, often feels intense anger towards his mother over her infidelity and promiscuity and the associated neglect of her family responsibilities. "I considered that as a result of early life experiences, in particular his relationship with his mother, John Glover remained emotionally at an adolescent level of development. He sought dependence on forceful and older women while at the same time resenting that dependence and associated incestuous feelings."

It was at this point that Paul Jacob elbowed Miles O'Toole hard in the ribs, all but knocking him off his bench. "Have a look at Glover," he whispered urgently. As Milton spoke of Glover's incestuous feelings the accused trembled and grew flushed. He clenched his hands into tight fists and glared at the psychiatrist. It was clear that Milton had struck a raw nerve. Later O'Toole explained to Glover that he had misunderstood Milton. The psychiatrist had not accused him of actually having had sex with his mother, but had implied that he harboured unconscious incestuous thoughts and consequent feelings of guilt. Nevertheless, said Glover, "Milton's got me hung, drawn and quartered. All they have to do now is flay my hide and nail it on the wall."

Two experienced psychiatrists appearing for the defence, however, disagreed with Rod Milton. They believed that Glover indeed had a partial defence of diminished responsibility. Dr John Shand told the court he felt Glover suffered from a personality disorder of a psychopathic type. His opinion was that Glover was a sexual deviant with a long-standing severe personality disorder who had probably committed more offences than he had ever been charged with. His was a personality which was not amenable to treatment and consequently if he were ever released there would be further homicides. Dr John Strum believed Glover had symptoms of a neurotic personality disorder with a tendency towards sexual disorders. They agreed Glover had sufficient abnormality of mind to impair his responsibility for what he had done, which qualified him to claim diminished responsibility for his crimes.

On November 28 the jury, five women and seven men, heard the final addresses of Crown and defence counsel. In Crown Prosecutor Wendy Robinson's 75-minute address, she stressed that Glover was fully responsible for his crimes. "He had organised himself in a premeditated fashion so that he was able to strike again when the opportunity arose," she said.

The prosecutor, who is an expert on the connection between mental health and crime, said that that could certainly be inferred from the evidence concerning the accused's movements, his access to places where he might find suitable victims, and from his repeatedly placing his claw hammer and gloves in his car. The evidence, Wendy Robinson told the jury, was that Glover, who was arrested after murdering for the sixth time, "planned to strike again after each and every one of the first five incidents".

"I would suggest," she said, "the account that has been given in the records of interview would indicate as indeed to the expert witnesses that after each of those instances the accused was fully conscious of what he had done before... The facts of Glover killing the women, with intent to kill or cause grievous bodily harm, have been admitted, and the only issue to be determined is whether he had such abnormality of the mind as to impair his responsibility.

"... It is an issue for members of the community to determine whether you are not prepared to accept that the accused, when he committed these acts, committed murder, or whether he committed manslaughter because he was diminished in his capacity to restrain himself."

She finished her address by telling the jury that Glover had exhibited no real remorse for his crimes, and that his statement to the court had in fact been evidence of that.

Glover's counsel Andrew Leary summed up the case for the defence in 110 minutes. He reminded the jury of the evidence of the psychiatrists Drs Strum and Shand and backed their belief that Glover was not totally responsible for his actions by pointing out instances of the defendant's irrational behaviour, how he continued to murder elderly women in the face of intense publicity and the presence of police in the area. Leary added that Glover had "really no motive" for the murders as he had not known his first five victims.

After deliberating for only two hours and 45 minutes the jury reached their verdict. John Glover was guilty of all six murders.

Justice James Wood ordered Glover to stand and receive his sentence. Glover lifted his head and stood. To Glover's left was the jury on their benches and the detectives in a special police box; to his right, the press, sitting at desks etched deeply with the names of reporters of decades past; at his rear, the two levels of public gallery; ahead of him, sitting high in his ornate, polished wood enclosure, was Justice Wood and his associates. Flanking the dock, which stands isolated in the middle of the courtroom, were two uniformed and armed police. At a desk in front sat Glover's legal representatives.

The judge's voice rang through the hushed room, reverberating off the polished wood surfaces. "The prisoner has been convicted after his trial on six counts of murder occurring between March 1, 1989, and March 19, 1990. Prior to being indicted on those counts he pleaded to three further charges, the first being one of robbery with wounding occurring on January 11, 1989, contrary to S96 of the Crimes Act; the second being one of robbery contrary to S94 of the Crimes Act occurring on August 5, 1989; the third being one of wounding with intent to do grievous bodily harm contrary to S33 of the Crimes Act occurring on October 18, 1989.

"The maximum available penalty in respect of each of the charges of murder is penal servitude for life; while that in respect of the charges of robbery with wounding, and wounding with intent to do grievous bodily harm, is penal servitude for 25 years. The maximum available penalty for the offence of robbery contrary to S94 of the Crimes Act is penal servitude for 14 years.

"The incidents involved all have a common feature in that they comprised attacks on elderly women. It is not necessary to go into them in detail, however it is appropriate to do so briefly..." Justice Wood then related details of the offences in sequence, and made mention of Glover's indecent assaults on women in nursing homes.

When he had finished recounting each crime, Justice Wood went on, "The sole issue in his trial related to that of diminished responsibility. By its verdict the jury clearly preferred the opinion of Dr Milton, who rejected the existence of any abnormality of mind, to that of Doctors Strum and Shand who variously diagnosed a form of abnormality of mind. In the case of Dr Shand, his diagnosis was one of paraphilia with the sub-feature of sexual sadism. In the case of Dr Strum, his diagnosis was one of a mixed neurosis with compulsive and dissociative features.

"All the psychiatrists agreed that the prisoner had some anti-social or narcissistic personality traits, however by their verdict the jury rejected the proposition that either in combination with other conditions or on their own the prisoner suffered to such a degree or in such a way as to possess an abnormality of mind, which substantially diminished his mental responsibility for the offences, thereby attracting the defence of diminished responsibility.

"The prisoner is a man who is now aged 59, having been born on November 26, 1932, in England. He came to this country in 1957. He has a prior record dating back to 1947 when he appeared in a juvenile court. That is a matter which perhaps can be passed over, having regard to its age and outcome.

"However, from 1952 onwards in the United Kingdom there were convictions for stealing clothes or handbags. To those should be added convictions in Victoria for larceny (on two occasions). In New South Wales there was a conviction in 1978 for stealing from a retail store. These were all offences of dishonesty rather than violence.

"More significantly, in 1962 the prisoner was dealt with for two counts of indecent assault on a female, two counts of assault occasioning actual bodily harm, and four counts of larceny. They led him to being placed on probation for three years.

"It emerged in the course of the trial that the assaults on the females related to two separate occasions and they bore some similarity with the offences which have now brought him before the court in this state. On each occasion he attacked a female in the street, knocking her to the ground and removing her underclothing. On each occasion the victim was unknown to him, and fortunately he was interrupted before the matters could develop into any more serious form of injury or sexual invasion of those persons.

"Some three years later, he was convicted of an offence of unlawfully being on premises, and sentenced to three months imprisonment. That related to an offence of voyeurism, a habit or practice to which he apparently turned during those years.

"It follows that he has a significant criminal history dating back over a number of years, which has included offences involving a form of sexual deviation or sexual violence.

"The period since January, 1989, has been one of intense and serious crime involving extreme violence inflicted on elderly women, accompanied by the theft or robbery of their property. On any view, the prisoner has shown himself to be an exceedingly dangerous person and that view was mirrored in the opinions of the psychiatrists who have given evidence in this trial.

"Although Dr Shand's diagnosis of a mental abnormality was not accepted by the jury, it is significant to note that in his view the prisoner was not treatable by any available methods, and it was clear from the evidence of Doctors Strum and Milton that he presents a significant danger to the community. One would not need the psychiatric evidence to come to that conclusion. It is self-evident from the record of extreme violence inflicted on so many defenceless and aged members of this community.

"This is a case where it seems to me that my hands are tied. I have no alternative other than to impose, in respect of each offence of murder, the maximum available. I am satisfied of that, taking into account the considerations expressed by the High Court in Veen No.2 (1988) 164 CLR 465. Clearly I am dealing with a prisoner who is extremely dangerous, and who, if released back into the community, will, when it suits him, again gratify his desires and wishes in the same way which has brought him to commit these offences.

"Regrettably it is clear from his record over that period, from the surveillance evidence, and from Dr Milton's evidence that he is able to control his desires when he wishes. He is able to choose when to attack and when to stay his hand. He is cunning and able to cover his tracks. It is plain that he has chosen his moments carefully. Although the crimes have been opportunistic, he has not gone in where the risks were overwhelming. He has chosen the times and places appropriately, and carefully.

"Where the opportunity and time permitted, it is clear that he spent whatever period was needed to gratify his desires. Where the opportunity was less available and where the risks for detection were higher, the attacks were sudden and he retreated as quickly as he went in.

"This, then, is a man, I am afraid, of extreme cunning, and of extreme dangerousness who is prepared to attack whenever and wherever it suits him, and to stay his hand when it does not.

"The threat he poses to the community denies him any mitigation otherwise available. In order to protect the society, and also to provide the appropriate punishment for the appalling murders of which the prisoner is guilty I have no alternative other than to impose the maximum available sentence which means that the prisoner will be required to spend the remainder of his natural life in gaol."

The judge drilled the defendant with a piercing glare. Glover's expression was blank. "John Wayne Glover, in relation to each count of murder for which you have been found guilty, I sentence you to penal servitude for life. In relation to the count of robbery with wounding in relation to Mrs Todhunter, I sentence you to a fixed term of four years to date from March 20, 1990.

"In relation to the offence of robbery concerning Mrs Carnie, I sentence you to a fixed term of two years to date from March 20, 1990, and in relation to the offence of wounding with intent to do grievous bodily harm I sentence you to a fixed term of three years to date from March 20, 1990.

"Each of the life sentences will date from the same date, that is March 20, 1990.

"I impose fixed terms rather than minimum terms for these three offences, having regard to the life sentences which I have imposed.

"It is inappropriate to express any date as to release upon parole. Having regard to those life sentences, this is not a case where the prisoner may ever be released pursuant to order of this Court.

"I recommend that the prisoner be kept on protection for such time, and in such circumstances, as the Corrective Services Commission considers appropriate to ensure his personal safety."

Throughout the judge's discourse, Glover had shown no emotion. He did not even react when Justice Wood announced that he would spend the rest of his life behind bars, his papers stamped "Never To Be Released". But when the judge had risen and left the court and Glover was left in the dock for a moment to contemplate his fate before being led down the stairs and into the court's holding cell, the realisation that he would never again be free hit John Glover hard. Slumped in his seat in the dock, the convicted killer seemed to shrivel. His shoulders sagged and he clasped his manacled hands in front of him. His head hung low. Blood rushed to his face, turning it bright red, a shocking contrast with his white hair, and his eyes brimmed with tears. His solicitor Don Wakeling whispered something in his ear but Glover paid no heed. For 90 seconds the prisoner sat hunched, then, when it was time for him to be led away, a uniformed policeman grasped him firmly by both elbows, virtually uprooting him from his seat.

At this point, Glover asked his barrister Andrew Leary to tell Miles O'Toole, who was at that moment congratulating Crown Prosecutor Wendy Robinson, that he had appreciated the way he had treated him since his arrest and would be honoured to shake the detective's hand. O'Toole looked across to Glover and their eyes locked. The convicted killer nodded and O'Toole returned the nod. But that was all. Says O'Toole, "I just couldn't do it. I couldn't bring

myself to shake his hand after seeing what that hand had done."
Miles O'Toole spun on his heel and strode out into the warm spring
sunshine.

The police guard hustled John Glover down the stairs of the dock.
An abiding memory for many in No.5 Courtroom that day as the trial
broke up is of John Glover disappearing from view down the steps into
the bowels of the court where he would be locked up in a police vehicle
and sped to Sydney Police Centre for the weekend before being
transported to his lifer's cell at Long Bay Gaol. The Granny Killer and
the demons that drove him were going where they could do no more
harm.

CHAPTER 19

Aftermath

O utside in the clear, bright light of that Friday, November 29, 100 or so people milled around in the driveways and on the lawns of the Supreme Court in Darlinghurst. All of them — police, media, relatives of Glover's victims and ordinary citizens who had turned up to see justice in action — were animated, laughing, infused with a sense of relief. People shook hands and hugged a lot. On busy Oxford Street, noisy and colourful as ever on the other side of the high iron fences of the court complex, life went on as usual.

The major newspapers, TV networks and radio stations were out in force, gathering information and interviews for that night's bulletins or Saturday's edition. The verdict and sentencing of John Glover was lead item and front page news. The media fought and jostled to interview members of the task force. Miles O'Toole's message to all reporters was always the same: "I feel tremendous relief," he said, "for the police involved in the investigation and for the relatives of the victims. They can now get on with their lives."

Mike Hagan, recalling that day of sentencing, says he felt enormous well being and job satisfaction, "not only from the point of view of the task force that the matter was resolved at last, but also for the relatives and friends of the victims. They must have been comforted in their grief to know that justice was done.

"It meant so much to me when relatives of the elderly women Glover had murdered came up and congratulated the police for putting Glover in gaol. The man who had caused so much misery had been located by the process of law, had been dealt with by law and justice was served."

The investigators let their hair down that night. Remembers Hagan: "We went to the Willoughby Hotel and there we congratulated each other, unwound, discussed the entire operation in a

217

leisurely atmosphere. It was an important evening for us. I think it is vital when any investigation is completed that the men and women involved debrief in a relaxed manner. We'd been through so much. The emotional impact of the crimes, the gruelling investigation, the arrest, the trial, the verdict. Our get-together that night was a healthy and a necessary thing to do.

"Yes, of course we talked about Glover. We all had our own theories about him. My own belief is that John Glover is not mad, but he is truly evil. He is a bad man who was motivated by evil to murder old ladies and this gave him great satisfaction. Glover knew what he was doing to his victims, he knew he was destroying not just their lives but the lives of their loved ones as well — yet he kept on killing. He made his own free-choice decision to commit these acts and now he must bear the responsibility of them."

None of Glover's family appeared in court throughout his trial. For a time his wife and daughters boarded at Loreto Convent then went away together for a long, long time. Early in 1992 Gay Glover, Marney Glover and Kellie Glover destroyed everything that reminded them of their husband and father. Today, their past confronted and erased, they are getting on with the rest of their lives.

One who was on the lawn outside the court the day Glover was convicted was Elaine Avis, only daughter of Madge Pahud, Glover's third victim. She had attended the trial most days, the only relative of a victim to do so. She told reporters how she had smiled to herself when the foreman of the jury announced that Glover had been found guilty on all six counts of murder. "The jury made the right decision," she said beaming. "It was the only one they could have made. I came here to court each day probably because I had my needs to see the case through to the end. The police were fantastic all the way. They worked terribly hard."

Not everybody was as fulsome in their praise of the investigators. During and after the trial *The Sydney Morning Herald* was critical of what the paper called "police bungling" in the hunt for Glover. The *Herald* of November 30 in an article headlined "Police Bungling Allowed Granny Killer To Strike One Last Time" zeroed in on the delay by the Chatswood policewomen investigating the sexual assault of the elderly woman at Greenwich Hospital in passing Glover's

"No more grannies" suicide note and the Polaroid of Glover to the task force. Then, the report continued, when the note finally was handed to the task force the "fatal decision" was made not to arrest him for the assault, but to place him under surveillance. An arrest at that time, the report postulated, would have saved the life of Joan Sinclair.

When they read the article, angry task force members pointed out that Glover had not been positively identified as the assailant of the patient at Greenwich and therefore they had no grounds to arrest him. Rather, it was decided, with Glover now prime suspect as the serial murderer, to watch him closely for incriminating signs.

And the newspaper unearthed a woman whose elderly mother had been savagely bashed by a man who resembled Glover at her home in Lindfield in July, 1988. The matter was reported to Chatswood police but the attacker was never located. After the murder of Olive Cleveland, the woman had again contacted police and reminded them of the similarities between the attack on her mother and that on Cleveland and again gave them a description of the grey-haired, middle-aged man who had beaten her mother. She claimed police did not follow up her telephone call. After the *Herald* report was published the day after the end of the trial, police announced that no record existed of the woman's call.

However, from the investigators' point of view, the most infuriating criticism of all was that police should have burst in on Glover at Pindari Avenue on March 19 before he had a chance to murder Joan Sinclair and so saved her life instead of sitting outside in the street for hours. The newspaper story containing this criticism was shown to Mike Hagan the day after the conviction. It deeply distressed the veteran policeman. After all his team had been through — the stress they had all endured, the family sacrifices caused by endless 20-hour days on the job, their ultimate success in apprehending Glover — to be hit with such a claim seemed cruel and unfair.

Hagan, who would later be awarded the prestigious Police Medal for his leadership of the task force, was shattered. "We had had Glover under heavy surveillance for five weeks and we had seen him enter numerous premises and not put a foot out of line. At that stage he was our prime suspect, but we had no reason to arrest him for murder. There was no firm evidence at all. We had nothing concrete on him. All we could do was watch him carefully and as soon as he tried to kill again we would be close enough to act immediately. But we couldn't touch him until he *did something*. We had to catch him in the act. We had no reason not to believe that Glover was at Joan Sinclair's home either for business or pleasure. He had, as it turned out, been a close friend of the woman for 18 months. There was no cause for us to think he would harm her and, anyway, we had no authority to enter the premises. It was neither prudent, proper or ethical to do so. Imagine if we had just barged in on them that day, acting only on a gut feeling, and they'd been sitting down having a cup of tea together; our entire investigation of John Glover would have been blown and he would have gone scot-free to kill again."

Joe Sands, licensee of the Willoughby Hotel, remembers seeing Mike Hagan ashen-faced after the publication of the article containing the bungling allegation. "I went up to Mike and apologised for the article on behalf of all the public out there who were grateful to the task force. I thought it was a low act. I saw these detectives at close hand throughout the whole investigation. I saw their personalities change dramatically because of the pressure they were under. I saw them working so hard to catch that maniac. But, as dedicated as they are, I don't think there would be too many of those police who would want to go through something like this again. If a similar case came up I'm sure they'd all volunteer for traffic duty at Cobar."

Police found themselves under fire once more when the media learned that the task force members had produced a special tie commemorating the epic investigation. On it was an insignia designed around a walking stick, a hammer and the scales of justice. There were howls that the tie was flippant and insensitive. The allegations dismayed Miles O'Toole: "We got plenty of bad publicity out of that but, for heaven's sake, there was no disrespect intended to the victims or their families. We had an excellent rapport with all the relatives, we would never make fun of them. In the end I went on to the Alan Jones Show on Radio 2UE to try to defuse the criticism. I explained to listeners that the tie was just a symbol of the triumph of the law over evil. It's hard to explain to anybody who was not on the task force, but it was just a souvenir of an experience that each of us who went through it will remember until the day we die.

AFTERMATH

"I know that I have never worked so hard and under such pressure. I accumulated five or six months leave in lieu of the overtime I worked during the investigation. I was about to take my first fortnight off in two years when Dr Victor Chang was murdered, in Mosman ironically, and I became involved in that case. I still haven't had a break."

CHAPTER 20

Life In The Garden Gate

Every day, John Glover is the first prisoner awake in the remand centre of Long Bay Gaol. As a "sweeper", he rises from his bunk at 6.30 and goes to the kitchen where he helps make breakfast for his fellow inmates and carries trays to the eating area. Breakfast over, he cleans up the dirty plates and takes them back to the kitchen. He then returns to his cell which he calls his "12 by 8" or in rhyming slang, "the garden gate". He showers and shaves in his basic bathroom which, with typical bombast, he refers to as his "en suite". The cell is spotless and he has hung colourful towels around, "to brighten the place up a bit". "I'm doing pretty well in gaol," Glover says. "I've converted my 12 by 8 to my own personal standards. I know that my life is not my own any more because of the rules and discipline here, but I'm making the best of a bad deal and want to survive."

Although Glover is a lifer, authorities' fears that that life would be considerably shortened if he came in contact with other murderers and violent inmates have led to him doing his time in the remand area. Prisoners are housed in remand before being sentenced and are therefore on their best behaviour and so unlikely to try to make a name for themselves by attacking the infamous Granny Killer.

He remains in his cell, sitting and thinking or dozing, or wanders around in the yard sweeping up or chatting to other prisoners for the rest of the day, the monotony of which is punctuated by lunch and dinner, crosswords and chess. At night if the chance arises he watches ABC TV. He is jealously proud of his job as a sweeper, which includes taking care of prison stores and supplies, and says he takes very seriously the "responsibilities" it carries. The privileged role eases to some extent his frustration and depression at the guards' tendency to frown upon joking and "civilised good humour" among the inmates. Although he is on good terms with his fellow sweeper, a young man named Terry Williamson, known as "The Bulli Rapist", his best friend at Long Bay was a social worker named Dawn, but she has recently left to work elsewhere.

Glover says it is impossible to compare life inside prison with life in the free world. "I wouldn't know where to start. I get on well with everybody here, but when you consider the type of person you come in contact with, well, prison to me is about pure survival." Survival includes learning to speak Spanish and a plan to write a thesis on life behind bars. In time he hopes to be transferred to Cessnock prison which he believes is a "pretty good wicket for prisoners of my calibre".

Although he presently suffers from two hernias and a buzzing in his ears which is worst at night when the gaol is quiet, Glover looks fit and, when allowed to be, is his usual jokey self. In March, 1992, he had the prison barber crop his hair short and he grew a spectacular set of white muttonchop whiskers that cover two thirds of his face. The whiskers, he believes, lend him a distinguished air and also hide the capillary veins that criss-cross his cheeks.

Miles O'Toole has interviewed John Glover in prison scores of times. Two years after he helped end Glover's reign of terror, the detective remains determined to understand this man who haunts his dreams — "Last week I dreamed I was playing golf and I looked across and my partner was John Glover." O'Toole also wants to know why Glover killed and killed again and whether he is responsible for murders that languish in Homicide's unsolved file. The policeman is at once repulsed and fascinated by Glover.

"John Glover is a very strange and complex man," says O'Toole. "But — and there's no other way to say it — we get on very well together. He speaks easily to me. He has a very winning personality and I can see how he would be a successful sales representative. It's easy to be swayed by his charm, but I just keep remembering the despicable crimes the bastard committed.

"He's doing easy time in prison and has adapted well to life behind bars. They didn't put him in maximum security, because he'd stand a chance of being bashed by some of the hard men there. He's in the remand section where everybody has to behave and he's 'cock of the walk' there. He's popular with the other prisoners and with his huge ego he enjoys the notoriety of being the famous Granny Killer.

"I believe that ego is one of the keys to Glover. He has a large chip on his shoulder about his lack of education and it is very important to him to prove he is better than the next man. He is very competitive and likes to play little mind games with police, prison staff and psychiatrists. He is very selective about what he divulges to interviewers. He loves to pull the wool over the eyes of more educated people. For instance, I recall him telling me how his wife, his psychiatrist, his doctor and solicitor all believed him when he told them he wasn't responsible for the assault on the woman at Greenwich Hospital. Then next breath he said to me, 'They all believe me. They all think I'm innocent, but you know that I'm not and I'm telling you that I'm not.' He got a huge buzz out of that.

"He plays cat and mouse. He'd deny the nursing home assaults until we confronted him with the evidence and then he'd confess. We had to worm every one of those confessions out of him. He'd say, 'Well, OK, you've got me dead to rights. I committed *that* assault — but that's the *only* one I committed.' Then we'd say, 'But, John, here's another one." And he'd reply, 'Oh, *alright*, that one too.'

"He still maintains that the bad John Glover committed the crimes independently of the good John Glover," says O'Toole. "But perhaps that's a mind game, too. I certainly don't believe it. For instance he told me he had decided to kill Mrs Beencke in the laneway at Lane Cove. He was alone with her and had every opportunity. But then, he says, he changed his mind and let her go. He killed Mrs Pahud an hour later instead. So if he *decided* not to kill Mrs Beencke, where does this leave his claim that the bad John Glover was out of control and unable to deny his murderous impulses?

"John Glover also swears blind there was never any sexual element in the murders. He told me, 'The impulse to kill just hit me at certain times and I was powerless to resist it. The bad John Glover took over at that time and had to humiliate and defile the old ladies. I was never interested in any of them sexually. And I never had any sexual feelings for my mother either.' But what about his sexual assaults in the nursing homes? And Rod Milton is fairly sure there was a sexual element. Glover hates Milton for what he said about him in court and says his findings were way off track."

And although Glover denies it, O'Toole is certain he wiped the hammer clean of blood after each killing with a handkerchief or cloth before placing it back inside his shirt or trousers or under the front seat of the car. No trace of blood was ever found on any of these items. Why Glover insists on denying that he wiped the murder weapon remains unclear.

O'Toole accepts there is truth in the psychiatric theories that Glover's mother and mother-in-law were the catalysts for his reign of terror. However, he says, the better he knows him, the more he believes that at heart John Glover is an inherently evil man who was just sent over the edge by his experiences with the women in his life. A man who has been evil for most of his life, and who, when the mood took him, simply chose to do evil deeds."

When O'Toole asked Glover whether he knew the extent of the forces of law that were arraigned against him throughout his rampage, the prisoner laughed and said, "Oh, yes, I knew you were all out there somewhere trying to catch me, but it didn't affect what I did or when I'd do it."

Glover says little about his wife to O'Toole, but has repeatedly denied that her life was ever in danger. He claims there is no ill-feeling between them. He also denies she is a domineering woman. O'Toole backs him up. "I have met his wife. I know her. She is definitely not a domineering person. A strong person, yes, but not domineering."

Glover's hatred of Essie Rolls has not diminished. "I despised her, and everybody else hated her as well," he has told the detective. "My mother-in-law's personality overrode us all."

The prisoner maintains to O'Toole that he had no problems as a child and stands up for his mother and father, claiming they gave him a better upbringing than most. Two of his lasting memories, he says, are of being taken on a trip to the English Midlands by his mother, and of being comforted by her during the Blitz in World War II as the bombs exploded nearby. However, for all his protestations that his childhood was normal, he has admitted to the detective that his mother was promiscuous and there were many, many men in her life. He has spoken explicitly about some of her sexual adventures. "It is clear to me that Freda's promiscuity has left a scar on Glover to this day," says O'Toole.

On the other hand, the prisoner swells with pride when boasting about his own sexual prowess. "Ever since childhood I have been successful with the ladies and could have as many women as I wanted as often as I wanted. Another thing I might do in gaol is write the story of the sexual goings on in Mosman. There wouldn't be a day go by that a woman wouldn't give me the come-on at Mosman RSL. But I wouldn't be in it because, apart from my friendship with Joan Sinclair, I was faithful to Gay."

Glover thinks about his wife and daughters constantly. "Glover can and frequently does describe each of his killings in lurid detail, without remorse or emotion," says O'Toole, "but when he talks about his daughters he becomes very emotional indeed. He misses them very much and worries about the affect his crimes have had on them. Sometimes he cries. Once he scared the life out of me when we were discussing some aspect of Kellie or Marney's life. All of a sudden and for no apparent reason he lost control of himself and slammed his open palm down hard on the interview table. I could see all at once the naked rage beneath Glover's benign exterior, and I understood then that those women never stood a chance. I don't mind saying I was terrified at that moment and bloody relieved when warders ran from everywhere."

Such incidents apart, O'Toole believes Glover enjoys their meetings and relishes the chance to play his little games. Glover often manoeuvres himself into a position behind O'Toole and hugely enjoys the detective's discomfort at having a serial killer whose modus operandi was to to attack from the rear at his unprotected back. And when O'Toole departs Glover's cell at the end of their interview and says, "Well, John, look after yourself. I'll see you later," the grey-haired man invariably laughs and says, "Goodbye, Dennis, call in any time you see the light on. If I'm not here, just leave a message."

Epilogue

On June 3, 1957, Elsie Boyes, aged 63, was assaulted and strangled in a toilet block in the Alma Gardens near Chapel Street, Prahran, Victoria. Her handbag was stolen. The killer has never been found.

On October 29, 1961, Emmie May Anderson, aged 78, was stabbed to death in bed in her apartment house in Clarendon Street, East Melbourne. Property was stolen. The killer has never been found.

On March 22, 1963, Irene Kiddle, 63, was stabbed to death in an alleyway near St Kilda Road, St Kilda. A ladder was found propped against a lighted window in a block of flats nearby, leading police to believe the killer peeped at occupants of the flat through the window before murdering Irene Kiddle. The killer has never been found.

On April 9, 1968, Christina Yankos, 63, was strangled in the kitchen of her home in Merton Street, Albert Park, Melbourne. The killer has never been found.

On August 29, 1984, Josephine McDonald, 73, was strangled at her home unit in Bourke Road, Ettalong, on the NSW central coast. She had been sexually assaulted and her pantyhose and panties draped around her neck. The killer has never been found.

On November 21, 1988, the body of Wanda Amundsen, 83, was found in her home at 38 Nelson Street, Umina, on the NSW central coast. She had been hit over the back of the head with a blunt instrument. Pillows and bedclothes had been placed over her face, presumably by the killer, who has never been found.

Throughout 1988, five elderly women were viciously assaulted in the Gosford, Ettalong and Woy Woy areas of the New South Wales central coast. Their attacker has never been found.

Police believe John Glover was almost certainly living or working in the vicinity when these murders and assaults took place. Glover denies responsibility for any of them. Police are continuing their enquiries.

Appendix

On February 28, 1992, the following document was despatched to Mike Hagan at the Chatswood headquarters of the Regional Crime Squad, North:

Recognition Of Police Involved in the North Shore "Granny Murders"

On behalf of the Commissioner, I formally acknowledge the highly commendable contribution of those police involved in the investigation into the "Granny Murders".

Each member in their own way displayed a dedication to duty which should be acknowledged. The Commissioner has referred earlier to the pride in which he held the task force and has been quoted as saying that it was a most professional operation, undertaken in a difficult environment and deserving of commendation. I support the Commissioner's views and commend each member of the task force... I would also request that arrangements be made for appropriate entries to be inserted in the service registers of those involved.

(Signed) Lance Stirton
State Commander

Commended for the outstanding administration of the North Shore Murders Task Force
Assistant Commissioner NW Maroney

Commended for outstanding leadership shown during investigations conducted by the North Shore Murders Task Force
Superintendent M Hagan

Commended for outstanding co-ordination of investigations conducted by the North Shore Murders Task Force
Detective Sen Sgt GL Wright and Detective Sen Sgt R Smith

Commended for the implementation of the MIIRS during investigations conducted by the North Shore Murders Task Force
Detective Sen Sgt R Myers and Detective Sen Const G Green

Commended for diligence to duty on surveillance duties undertaken with the North Shore Murders Task Force
Detective Sgt J May Detective Sen Const S St John Detective Sen Const A Riley Detective Sen Const M Birley Detective Sen Const D Cameron Detective Const 1/c J Farley Detective Const 1/c D Cheney Detective Const P Dunn PC Const 1/c L Rogerson PC Const M Parker

Commended for devotion to duty during investigations conducted by the North Shore Murders Task Force

Detective Sgt BJ O'Neill

Detective Sgt PJ Meehan

Detective Sgt PE Tuxford

Detective Sen Const IB Nicholson

Detective Sen Const GJ Williams

Detective Sen Const DP Patison

Detective Sen Const M Slot

Detective Sen Const KW Larsen

Detective Sen Const MJ Nimmo

Detective Const 1/c DM Hill

Detective Const 1/c RJ Monk

PC Const M Young

Detective Sgt D Brown

Detective Sen Const G Beresford

Detective Sen Const D Minarik

Detective Const 1/c S Dunn

PC Const K Colaco

PC Const M Wilson

Detective Sgt PP Clear

Detective Sgt MG Neild

Detective Sen Const K Dowding

Detective Sen Const GW Kendall

Detective Sen Const JJ King

Detective Sen Const KC McGee

Detective Sen Const VA Crawford

Detective Sen Const AP Waterman

Detective Sen Const MR Lenon

Detective Const 1/c HR Gumley

Detective Const 1/c GR Vicary

PC Const F Lynch

Detective Sen Const W Murray

Detective Sen Const S Emmett

Detective Sen Const J Greville

PC Const K Illingworth

PC Const M Sanson

Commended for diligence to duty in the preservation of physical evidence undertaken with the North Shore Murders Task Force

Detective Sgt J Hughes

Sen Const PM Flogel

Detective Const A Keeling

Detective Sen Const DI Forbes

Sen Const EN Litler

Commended for the supervision of surveillance conducted during investigations undertaken by the North Shore Murders Task Force
Detective Sen Sgt DP O'Toole

Commended for the outstanding leadership of the Homicide Squad associated with the investigations undertaken by the North Shore Murders Task Force
Detective Sgt DJ O'Toole

Commended for the analysis and production of flowcharts which provided valuable information for the North Shore Murders Task Force:
Const M Rochester

Commended for the analysis of information during investigations conducted by the North Shore Murders Task Force
Detective Sgt W Chambers   Sgt PA Gow
Sen Const R Rodgie

Commended for the diligence of intelligence duties undertaken with the North Shore Murders Task Force
Detective Sen Sgt J McNamara

Commended for diligence to duty in the investigation conducted by the North Shore Murders Task Force
Detective Sen Const BP Keeling   Detective Sen Const P Mayger
Detective Sen Const P Jacob   Detective Sen Const ME Byrnes

Commended for devotion to duty associated with investigations into the North Shore Murders Task Force
Detective Const 1/c P Whittaker   Detective Const A Cremen
Insp GR Ferguson   Detective Sen Const V Valente
Detective Sen Const A Langford